CONTENTS

A Note From the Authors 1

Foreword 5

Phase 0: An Introduction To Seo 9

    What Exactly is "SEO"? 9

    Why You Need SEO 12

    A Breakdown of How Search Engines Work 13

    What Makes Websites "Rank"? 16

    The Evolution of SEO 18

    Where SEO is Heading 20

    3 Core Concepts for an Evergreen SEO Strategy 28

    Our Evergreen Approach to SEO 29

Phase 1: The Discovery Process 32

    1.1 - 7 Types of Questions You Need to Ask Before You
Start A Campaign 35

    1.2 - How to Analyze Your Website's Data 40

    1.3 - Taking a Close Look at Your Top Competitors 56

    1.4 - How to Manage Your SEO Campaign 69

Phase 2: The Improving Process 88

    2.3 - In-Depth Keyword Analysis 131

    2.4 - Putting Together a List of "Target Pages" 152

Phase 3: The Building Process 172

    3.1 - Auditing Your Existing Content 173

3.4 - Building a Content Calendar..185

Phase 4: The Promotion Process..**218**

4.1 - Link Building 101 (And Beyond)..219

4.2 - The Current State of Links..222

Phase 5: The Evaluation Process..**242**

5.1 - Creating a Web Analytics Measurement Plan....................................243

5.2 - Evaluating Your Campaign's Key Performance Indicators (KPIs)....247

5.3 - Building Your Own SEO Report (Using My Full Template)............249

5.4 - Why SEO is an Ongoing Process (And What Your
Next Steps Should Be) 265

Appendix: Tools & Resources **268**

Done-For-You: How To Hire WEBRIS to Scale & Automate 270

DIY/Learn: Get Access to Ryan's Advanced
SEO Training Membership..271

The SEO Blueprint

*How to Get More Organic Traffic from
Search Engines Right Now*

By

Ryan Stewart

with contributions from David Krevitt, Julia McCoy

Copyright © 2020 by Ryan Stewart. All rights reserved.

No part of this book may be reproduced in any form or by any electronic or mechanical means including information storage and retrieval systems, without permission in writing from the author. The only exception is by a reviewer, who may quote short excerpts in a review. If you would like to use material from the book (other than for review purposes), prior written permission must be obtained by contacting the publisher at . Thank you for your support of the author's rights.

A Note from the Authors

"There's an easier way"

These words forever changed my life. But before I explain why, I need to give you the context of my life at that point.

It was 2011, I was 24 years old and I was working a corporate consulting job - I hated every second of it.

I hated putting on a suit everyday. I hated sitting in traffic an hour each way. I hated being forced to sit in a poorly lit office with no windows staring at a computer screen for 8 hours (even though I only had 2 hours worth of work).

I don't necessarily believe that "everything happens for a reason", but I do believe if you put a bored (yet motivated) person in front of the internet everyday that change can happen.

Through countless hours on scouring the internet for "ways to make money" I came across an industry in its infancy: internet marketing.

For those of you who have been in the industry for a while, you probably remember these days - it was an online wasteland for get rich quick schemes sold through banner ads and email lists.

Back then companies didn't see a ton of value in internet marketing. They didn't see the internet as a viable source of customer acquisition.

However, I could see the potential, especially on a new app called Instagram. I watched as all of my close friends ditched Facebook for Instagram within a matter of months. People were spending a ton of time on the platform, I knew there was an opportunity to make money there.

So I dove all in. I started connecting with large accounts and offered to broker advertising deals with businesses looking for more exposure. It was a tough sell (for both parties) - as businesses just didn't see the value in paying to be featured on a random account (yes, things have changed a lot since then).

One day I was taking a sales call from a local coffee shop, unsuccessfully trying to convince the business owner on the other line of the potential of advertising on Instagram.

That's when I got a tap on my shoulder and heard the words that altered the course of my professional life:

"There's an easier way".

I looked at the gentleman, confused as all hell. He continued:

"Social media is great, but people are mostly looking at pictures of cats there. Google is where it's at. People are looking to buy what you're selling - there's a way you can make a website rank in the top position for whatever people are searching for. It's called Search Engine Optimization".

He proceeded to break down the process and show me some of his websites. My life, literally, changed forever in that moment.

I became obsessed. I learned how to build and optimize my own websites. Within 2 years I was working with SEO clients, making money from my own lead generation websites and was able to quit that job I hated so much.

Over the last 10 years, I've built and sold a number of businesses that ran on SEO (including a 7 figure SEO agency). SEO has paid for this amazing life that I'm so fortunate to live down here in Miami, FL.

Now, before this turns into a get-rich-quick scheme book, there's something I need to clarify. SEO in 2011 is not the same as SEO in 2020 and beyond.

It's a lot harder now, it requires way more effort, but the results are still the same. Because it's so much harder, there's a lot of folks saying "SEO is dead". It's not, far from it. The landscape has changed, but as long as people are using Google to find stuff, SEO will always be the most powerful marketing tactic there is.

If you can get a website to rank in position 1 in Google you will make money. It's really that simple.

This book was written to help you rank in position 1 *right now* and in the future. We take an evergreen approach to SEO that's safe and flat out gets results. Whether you're running an SEO agency of working in house, this book was written for you.

Finally, *I want to thank you for purchasing this book.* I never would've thought I'd be writing a book and I sure as hell never thought I'd be writing a book someone would want to read. I mean, let's be honest - SEO is a pretty boring topic. The fact that you're willing to spend money and time on this book is what makes this industry so dynamic and amazing.

This book took a tremendous amount of effort, mainly from my team (thank you all!). They picked up the slack at the agency while I was heads down writing this thing. I don't forsee us making a lot of money from this book

- this was just something I felt the market needed and something I wanted to get out of my head and onto paper.

If you like what you read here, there's a number of ways we can work together:

1. Work with me (Ryan Stewart) directly as a marketing consultant. I can provide your team guidance and training on how to strategize and execute advanced marketing campaigns.

2. Work with our agency (WEBRIS) to manage your SEO, end to end.

3. Work with our agency (Coding is For Losers) to build you custom SEO tools in the Google Suite.

4. Sign up for our advanced SEO training membership (The Blueprint Training) where you will have lifetime access to step by step videos, case studies, deliverable templates and SOPs for running the highest quality SEO campaigns possible.

I give away a lot of value for free on our blog, webris.org/blog, and on my YouTube channel, Ryan Stewart. I'd love it if you stayed in touch with me there, and of course, fire away any questions you might have.

-- Ryan Stewart
@ryanwashere (Twitter)
@ryan.was.here (Instagram)

Foreword

By Julia McCoy

I've known and followed Ryan for years, and my agency has even had the honor of working for him and WEBRIS.

A couple of years ago, when Ryan first contacted my agency Express Writers to write SEO content for his clients at WEBRIS, I couldn't have been more elated.

I'd heard of him, watched his YouTube videos, and was in awe of how *thorough* Ryan was when it came to zero B.S., real-world search engine optimization techniques for website owners that worked tremendously well. I'd sat and watched his YouTube tutorials, transfixed in nerdy education-land, for minutes on end. That didn't usually happen when I watched marketers on YouTube. I could sit at his feet, so to speak, and friggin' *learn*--and that just wasn't true for me when listening to a wide array of active SEO marketers on the scene at the time.

So, it was like a celebrity had knocked on my agency's door when Ryan first sent us a message. We started writing for him, and Ryan and my team worked together for months before his merger with From the Future, who came with their own internal resources for content writing.

Ryan and I stayed in touch after we'd concluded working together, and when he sent me a random Facebook message *Hey Julia - hope all is well. I've been working on a book for years...* I couldn't have been more excited.

I'm delighted to be here and a part of The SEO Blueprint, writing the foreword and contributing a couple chapters. Books and long-form content are my *thing*. You already knew that about me, though, if you follow anything I do. Whether you're one of my 6,000-reader tribe over at the Write Blog, an agency client or teammate at Express Writers, a graduate of my Content Strategy & Marketing Course, a reader of my books, a subscriber to my blogs at Content Hacker™, or even one of hundreds of thousands of readers on the frequent publications I guest write for, you know this.

And if there's one thing I know and love more specifically, it's SEO content. I'm a self-taught content writer who dropped out of college and built a business at 19 years old to pursue a dream of "writing for a living." Today, I love to play with the data around search algorithms and dig into what actually causes content to rise above the rest of the playing field, whether that's sitting in a hard-earned boss ranking spot on Google or "top-shared" in the BuzzSumo categories earning social love.

Why I especially love Google and studying how to ideate, create, and publish killer content around an ideal keyword is, simply put, how *amazing* the traffic gets when you start to earn those rankings. All it takes is to just glance at the numbers. Data speaks. I mean, hello, over 70% of *all traffic on the web* now originates from a "search." From a hungry passenger in a fast-moving car on a Friday night, asking Siri "what's the best restaurant near me?", to an eight-year-old craving seasonal sugar yelling from the living room, "hey Alexa! How do I make pumpkin cookies?", to the tired but curious marketer researching "how to start a blog" on a Thursday night while Netflix and Stranger Things plays in the background... You name it, the searches are happening. Every second. And if you're not even trying to get your website found in search, by golly, you're missing out.

I know the dollar-for-dollar worth of organic search traffic because, well, it's the main source of our revenue. For eight years, the majority of Express Writers' seven-figure revenue has come through traffic organically searching in Google, finding my content. Our site gets 100k visits per month, and has more than 20k keyword position rankings in Google. And we have over 1,000 published blogs. As I've said in my conference talks, "We never take a vacation from content." It's true. I've published a blog weekly for nine years straight.

With The SEO Blueprint, you're not just getting any old, regurgitated, done-a-million-times book on "search engine optimization" techniques. Heck no. I can personally vouch for this one.

I'd describe Ryan and his team's approach to search optimization as two-fold: first, he's insanely *thorough*. I have mad respect for Ryan because he doesn't treat SEO like 99.9% of the other SEO'ers out there. He goes *all in*. He's not wimpy about it. He gets thorough, and he's not afraid of digging deeper than the rest. And that's what it takes, to put it simply. Secondly, Ryan's a boss at those critical details that require strategic thinking. Doing it right matters to him. And not only right, *smart*. He's strategic. His frameworks and methodology are gold. Use them.

Read this book, highlight it, digest it, and *use* it.

In a world where Google is all about Expertise, Authoritativeness, Trust (EAT) in ranking websites *and* the content published on them, you aren't going to chance on a quick hack anymore and win some massive placement and traffic inflation overnight. Winning online in search and with your readers doesn't happen by using B.S. techniques and a superficial approach. Warning: if that's you, it might be time to put this book on the shelf--there's no quick hack for overnight success here. But if you *are* the reader in search of a long-term, evergreen approach to search engine optimization using strategic thinking and unique implementation methods that actually work, then you need to sit your butt down and read this book *all the way through*. Thank me later. Heck, your clients can even thank me later, if your implementation plan for these lessons goes beyond your website. Because that's how far Ryan's book and techniques will go. It will help you build your business, and that of your clients', too.

This monologue is getting long, but I already warned you that long-form content is my thing. If you ask me to write a foreword, it won't be short.

To sum up: Listen to Ryan. Use this book for your search engine optimization planning and implementation. Thank me later.

-- Julia McCoy

Express Writers

The Content Hacker™

Twitter: @JuliaEMcCoy

YouTube: @JuliaMcCoy

PHASE 0

An Introduction to SEO

An Introduction to SEO

Search Engine Optimization is not for the faint of heart. It's a lot more work than you think and it *never* stops evolving.

In this book, we're going to journey together from the most basic aspects of SEO to its more advanced aspects. We have a ton of information to go through, so I suggest you set some time aside and get comfortable.

If you already know the basics when it comes to SEO, feel free to skip right to phase 1. Even so, it never hurts to brush up on the fundamentals, so stick with me and you might learn a thing or two.

What Exactly is "SEO"?

Let's start from the very beginning. SEO stands for Search Engine Optimization - in short, it involves all the work you do to get your website to rank higher in search engines.

For example, let's say you own a website that sells watches. When someone searches "best women's watches" in Google, you want your products to appear within the search results, preferably near the top of the first page. If they do, it's basically a license to print money.

Keep in mind, though, following best SEO practices isn't the only way to show up at the top of the Search Engine Result Pages (SERPs). Google, Yahoo, and Bing will happily take your money and display "Pay Per Click" ads in exchange for it. As the name implies, everytime someone clicks on your ads, you pay the search engine.

It's easy enough to recognize ads because search engines disclose the difference in plain view: what's an ad and what's an organic search result, as you can see below. Google's little green "Ad" box next to each PPC ad gives it away.

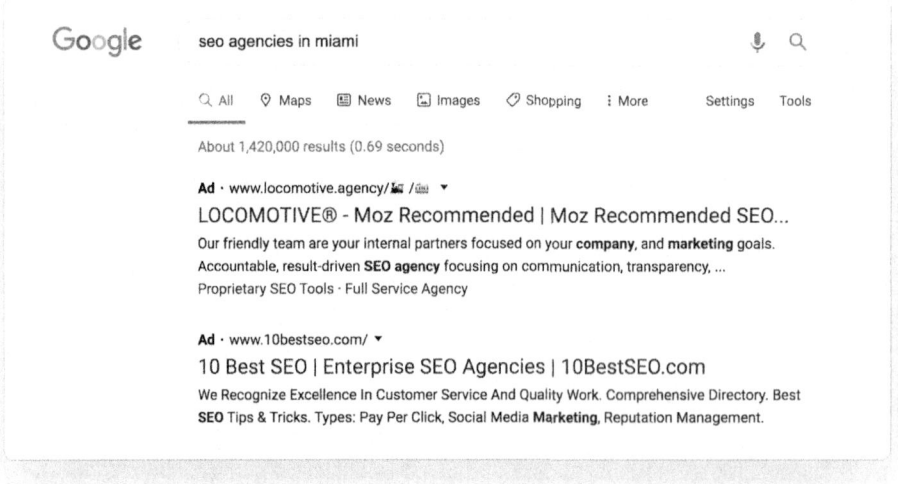

Since we're going to dig into the mechanics and benefits of SEO, it's important you understand how it differs from paid ads, as well as the benefits both options offer. Despite being an "SEO guy," I always tell clients Pay Per Click ads can be powerful marketing tools and they shouldn't shy away from using them. As long as they have the budget for a proper campaign, that is.

	SEO - Organic Search	**Pay Per Click - Advertising**
Benefits	The traffic is 100% free (unless you're paying an agency for SEO services). On top of that, organic traffic tends offers higher conversion rates on average, as users prefer real results to ads.	As long as you can pay for your ads, your website can show up at the top of the SERPs almost immediately. Paid ads are incredibly customizable and if you're a good marketer, they can drive amazing ROI.
Downside	Following best SEO practices requires a lot of research and work. The field is constantly changing and the competition is fierce for almost every type of website. It's also important to understand, SEO takes time to pay off, even if you do everything right. It can take months or even years before you see explosive results.	You need a high budget if you expect to see decent returns from your ads. In some verticals (I'm looking at you, insurance!), clicks can cost hundreds of dollars. As a rule of thumb, Pay Per Click ads don't scale as well as SEO. If you want to drive massive traffic, you need a massive budget, and you'll often need to spend a lot of money before you see an ROI.

If there's one thing SEO and online marketing experts have in common, though, is that they both understand the power of having a presence on search engines. Simply put, the easier it is for people to find you, the more sales, brand reach, and engagement you can get.

Why You Need SEO

Traditional marketing/advertising is outbound, meaning you have to disrupt people's attention in order to communicate your message (i.e. TV ads, radio, print, and even social media).

With search engine traffic, people are coming to you, which flips the script in your favor. Users look for specific products, services, and answers, and you have the power to help them. As far as I'm concerned, there's nothing more powerful than organic traffic from search engines when it comes to growing your business.

You don't have to take my word for it – the numbers speak for themselves.

Leads generated from search engines close at an average of 15% which is 12% higher than the conversion rate for outbound leads. (Hubspot, 2019)

In the same Hubspot study, only 9% of businesses using inbound marketing with SEO failed to see an ROI. If it works for 91% or businesses, it is very likely to work for you too. Blogging is a leading source of leads and traffic for businesses when each blog is properly optimized for search.

On a more personal note, our agency has blossomed into $120,000 MRR in just 18 months time. All of that revenue comes from organic channels (Google Search and YouTube).

There's a million things to do as a business owner - having a steady, automated stream of highly qualified leads frees up a ton of time and resources for me and we can get your business to that point as well.

Imagine how much your business could grow if you had a free flow of customers coming to your website, day after day, month after month. It sounds too good to be true, but if you put in the work when it comes to SEO, it can pay off for years to come.

I want you to be excited about that idea, because the road ahead when it comes to SEO involves a lot of work and patience. If you don't have a clear picture of the benefits of SEO, at some point you might begin to wonder *"is all this work even worth it?"*

My answer is yes. Overwhelmingly yes.

A Breakdown of How Search Engines Work

When I say search engine, I bet the first word that comes to your mind is Google. That makes sense, since Google owns over 90% of the search engine market share (Oberlo, 2019) and doesn't show any signs of slowing down.

With that in mind, let's make our lives simpler. From now on, I'm going to focus on talking about Google instead of using the broader term 'search engines'.

I mean, let's be serious - the *only* reason you've used Bing or Yahoo is because they come as the default option in some cases. Even so, most of us replace them as soon as possible.

You know what you want from Google (traffic!) but what does Google want from you? Google Search has two simple goals and the first one is to keep its users happy. That means serving the best possible search results, as quickly and accurately as possible, so they don't flock to Bing, Yahoo, or whatever else people aren't using these days.

Goal number two is to sell advertising. Google is a $50B company - they make 90% of that revenue from selling advertising (Investopedia, 2018). As long as people are using Google Search, that revenue stream is safe (hence why #1 is so important).

Bottom line, Google needs to keep users coming back, and they do so by making sure their search algorithms delivers the most relevant results.

For your website to show up higher in search results, you need to understand how Google ranks websites.

At the fundamental level, Google uses a 3-step process:

1. Crawling
2. Indexing
3. Ranking

Google "crawls" billions of pages, both new and old, every single day, using automated programs called 'bots' or 'spiders'.

These bots follow links from page to page (crawling the 'web' as they go, so to speak) and then index them into Google's database. These days, that database contains trillions of pages and it occupies more than 100,000,000 gigabytes in storage. It literally never stops growing.

How search engines work (nutshell version).

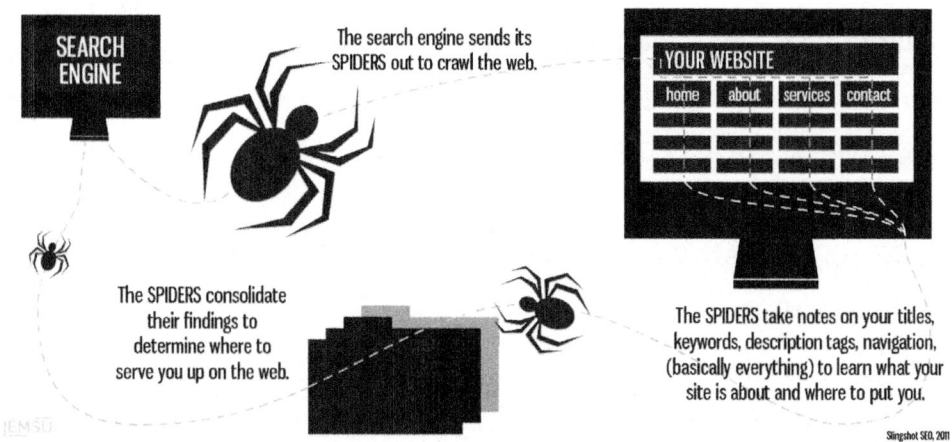

Search algorithms then sift through the data within the index and rank the pages almost instantaneously based on over 200 signals, according to Google (Backlinko, 2019).

These algorithms are Google's secret sauce, and they determine which pages it shows for any particular query.

It's important you understand that although we know what most of those signals are – no one outside of Google can tell you precisely how their algorithms work, and that's a topic we'll be touching again soon.

That means there's no magic recipe when it comes to SEO, but there are definitely best practices.

At the time of this writing, Google's infrastructure handles 63,075 searches every second (Bluelist, 2019), and that volume will increase by the time you finish reading this sentence.

While you don't need to be an expert in algorithms, it's important you have a grasp on how Google works below the hood.

What Makes Websites "Rank"?

Contrary to popular perception, Google doesn't have one single monolithic algorithm working behind the scenes, indexing pages, and delivering results. Instead, Google employs an army of algorithms they tweak constantly.

Some of those algorithms are now smart enough to:

- Correct your spelling mistakes.
- Understand if you want to know more about Mustang the breed of horse vs Mustang the car brand.
- Show you a list of coffee shops near you if you type "coffee shops".
- Display information about Barcelona the soccer club if you typed "Barcelona" after "Barcelona vs Arsenal."

So, how do these algorithms work?

No one except a select few inside Google has answers to that billion dollar question. If someone tells you they have a method to beat Google's algorithms, they're lying to your face.

Even so, we can make educated guesses about the relative impact of the over 200 signals Google uses to rank pages.

To name a few:

- **Number of "links" pointing to your website.** Google crawls websites through links and they count those links as they would the votes in a popularity contest. A link is when another website talks about yours and links to you as attribution. There are dozens of factors that go into links, but generally speaking, if your website attracts a lot of links from 'high-quality' sites, your ranking improves.

- **Keywords in important places on important pages.** It's important to have your keywords in titles, URLs, subheadings, and body text. While you don't want to overdo it, these keywords help Google associate your pages with searcher's queries.

- **Content quality and depth.** Google looks heavily at the quality of your content when deciding if you're worthy of being ranked. You want to make sure you're covering topics to the best of your ability and staying away from 'thin' content that does not provide any value to searchers.

- **Website speed and page load times.** All things being equal, a page that loads faster will be ranked higher than pages that take more time to load.

- **Mobile optimization.** In 2015, Google announced that the number of searchers on mobile phones surpassed that of desktop for the first time (Search Engine Land, 2015). They've also stated repeatedly that sites that fail to optimize for mobile devices will receive decreased rankings.

You might be asking yourself, how do we know these things to be true if no one is privy to the composition of Google's secret algorithms? The answer lies in years of experience, testing, and the pooled knowledge of a highly-active SEO community on the web.

When you combine all those signals together, you get a highly-curated list of results that should give you an answer to whatever it is you're looking for (unless it's the meaning of life). That's what lies at the heart of Google's success, and what makes search engines such awe-inspiring tools.

The Evolution of SEO

SEO has changed a lot in the last few years.

I started learning about SEO in 2012. Back then, it was really easy to rank a website. Basically, all I had to worry about was:

1. Identifying my main keywords

2. Putting those keywords in the page titles, URLs, and all over the body text

3. Building a lot of links to your pages (it didn't even matter if they were links from reputable sources)

Needless to say, I miss those days. You could literally rank a website in less than a week - it was amazing.

Now? Not so much.

It takes months of hard, consistent work to get results. There are simply no shortcuts in SEO anymore. Google's algorithm is incredibly intelligent, and in most cases, it can tell when you're trying to game the system, and it'll punish you accordingly.

That makes life harder for us, but it's not necessarily a bad change. After all, that dedication to improving the quality of its search results is what makes Google such a valuable tool for people all over the world.

Google is constantly looking for ways to improve the quality of their search results. The way they do so is by making constant tweaks to their algorithms. In some cases, that means adding new signals or changing the 'weight' each one has for their final results.

Here's a quick rundown of some of the major updates Google has made to its algorithm over the years:

- **Panda (February 2011).** Impacted sites with low-quality, duplicate, keyword-stuffed content. This update also brought quality scores to pages and multiple versions of Panda have rolled out since.

- **Penguin (April 2012).** Penalized sites with bad linking practices. Some of those bad practices include spamming links or over-optimized anchor text.

- **Hummingbird (August 2013).** Sites with low-quality content and poor keyword spread were hit by this update.

- **Pigeon (July 2014) and Possum (September 2016).** Affected sites with poor on-page and off-page SEO, and had a massive impact on location related search.

- **Mobilegeddon (April 2015).** This update punished sites not optimized for mobile.

- **RankBrain (October 2015).** This update added machine learning capabilities to the algorithm, and impacted sites with poor UX and lack of relevant, query-specific content.

- **Fred (March 2017).** This update eliminated sites with content created only to drive ad revenue.

- **Maccabees (December, 2017).** With this update, Google hit websites that tried to game the system by forcing multiple keyword permutations.

- **Mobile-first index rollout (March 2018).** This update didn't get its own fancy name, but it marks a before and after in search engine history, as Google shifted its focus to mobile-friendly websites.

- **Bert (October 2019).** With this update, Google sought to dramatically improve its understanding of 'natural-sounding' search queries.

The trend is clear. Over the years, Google has made it harder for websites to rank by punishing low-effort SEO tactics at the same time it keeps improving its algorithms. Plus, as time goes by, the competition among websites only gets fiercer, which is another reason you need to step up your SEO game.

Where SEO is Heading

If you're brand new to SEO, I can imagine your head is probably spinning at this point. I'm not going to lie to you, SEO is hard - and no bullshit, it's getting harder.

Working with so many clients means we get access to concrete data on what's working and what isn't. Aside from the 'traditional' SEO ranking factors, we're seeing a lot of new elements come into play:

- **Machine learning is now a part of Google's algorithms.** It's not as scary as it sounds - basically it means the algorithms are learning on the fly what a quality result should like and adjusting accordingly.
    - **Search satisfaction**. When a user clicks on a result in Google, how do they behave? Did they leave right away and go back to Google

to find another result? Did they refine their search query to find something else? This data is valuable to Google's understanding of what searchers are really looking for. What this means is you have to be fully aware of the quality of your pages, to make sure they satisfy searcher intent to the fullest.

- o **Query level algorithms**. This is mostly speculation on my part, but I believe there are mini algorithms triggered at a query level. Google is 'learning' what a good result looks like based on the search query. For example, the payday loan industry is riddled with web spam. I believe the algorithm understands how to sift through the crap to get to the top sites, and it measures you against them. What this means is you need to understand your industry and which players are killing it when it comes to SEO. That information alone will tell you a lot about how to improve your website.

- **Approaching SEO from a more holistic standpoint**. In some spaces, SEO is just too competitive for small websites. If you just launched a website that sells jeans, it's nearly impossible to outrank The Gap for "jeans" related keywords. It's an iconic brand, online and offline, that has a proven track record with consumers. You can still build a profitable organic presence in Google, but if you want to maximize your chances of success, you'll need to get creative. While you're following traditional SEO practices on your site, look into building organic channels **off site**. Some ways to do that include:
  - o Sites like Yelp are a gold mine for local businesses - having a page with a ton of positive reviews will drive a lot of customers to your business.

- o Platforms like Avvo and Clutch also provide opportunities for organic exposure. These sites rank really, really well for high-intent searches - getting ranked on top of those platforms is just as powerful as ranking your website there.
- o Video views on YouTube are just as important if not more than someone reading a blog post.

The point is, don't limit your thinking to only 'ranking' for your main keywords. In some cases, that may be nearly impossible, or it can take years, so don't be afraid to shift your focus to other organic opportunities for exposure.

Google has stated publicly they believe brands are good for SEO, as people trust them and want to see them in search results. For example, if you're shopping for TVs and you see two results, one from Best Buy and another from Cheap-O-TVs, which one are you most likely to click? Brands carry a certain level of trust with consumers that gives them weight within search engines.

For us peasants, powerful branding is a difficult thing to overcome, as you just can't compete with the likes of Best Buy. However, we've seen some of our clients rank very quickly without being household brand names and it comes down to the way that Google thinks about branding.

Google doesn't determine what a brand is the same way we would. What the algorithm does is look at quality signals that dictate the authority or 'brand power' of a website. Traditional aspects like links and content are still major factors, but we've seen clients with no links and no content rank #1 for incredibly competitive keywords.

The reason is they have a ton of 'branded search'. In other words, every month tens of thousands of people are searching directly for their product and website.

There is no higher quality signal than branded search. Unlike other ranking factors, branded search is impossible to emulate. It's a clear sign to Google that when people are looking for a certain product, they want to see yours. What Google sees is your product is so popular that people don't care about other search results, so you get that sweet sweet number 1 place in the rankings.

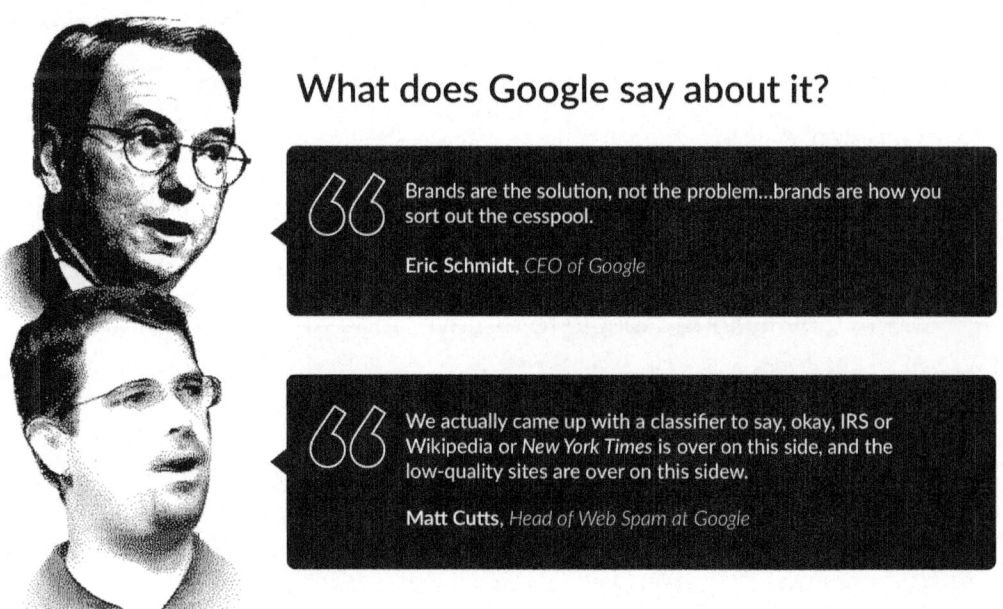

Building branded search is no different than building a traditional brand, with a few caveats:

- **Offline advertising (i.e. radio, TV, etc)**. When people hear an ad they like, one of the first things they do is head to Google to search for you.

- **Influencer advertising (Instagram, YouTube)**. This is one of the methods we employ for our clients and it's powerful. Instagram does not have the ability to link to a website from individual posts. When Instagram users repeatedly see people they follow talking about a product, they head to Google to look for it. Some influencers can reach millions of people within hours, which makes this by far the best way to increase branded search. However, influencer marketing can be incredibly expensive. This is an interesting topic, which we'll cover in depth later in the book.

- **PR**. Getting consistent coverage in media outlets, both online and offline. If you don't have access to outlets or the resources to work with an expert, start at the bottom and do it yourself. Apply to write at big sites, hustle to get on podcasts, and start your own blog filled with great content.

- **Having a great product / service**. It sounds cliche, but nothing is more powerful than word of mouth. When people hear about how great you are, they head to Google to discover more. As a smaller business, you may be able to provide a much better quality of product/service than your big-brand competitors.

You've been hearing it for years that "content is king" and Google loves "quality content", and so has every other marketer on the planet. Because of this, content is being crapped out at an alarming rate and over the course of the next few years, most of it will be written by automation bots (Wired, 2015).

With so much crap content on the web, Google doesn't want to waste space indexing it. To beat this back, the algorithm has become incredibly adept in understanding what 'quality' really looks like.

While we don't have official word from Google (we never do), a lot of industry experts are in agreement that Google builds an overall quality score for your website. There are, in all likelihood, a lot more factors involved in that score. However, it's clear that having too much thin, outdated, or low-quality content can build a negative perception about your site's quality.

In essence, Google's algorithms may be just as good as your or I are at spotting crappy websites.

When this happens, Google loses trust in your website and that means that your website gets crawled less and less. In time, your website starts to lose indexed pages and it begins to slip through the rankings. That's not a good look for anyone.

In this book, we're going to talk about exactly how to create, clean up and maintain the highest quality content (on a budget) among many other topics.

Here are some things you should keep in mind as we move ahead:

Links are important, but you need to pay just as much attention to quality. We *know* that links have to be high quality, and we can prove that assertion with data we've collected from hundreds of campaigns throughout the years.

We're lucky to have helped websites acquire over 10,000 links over the last 2 years. We alo have access to the organic traffic data for all of those campaigns. In other words, we're able to understand the true impact of links on organic traffic. Here's what we've found (in a nutshell):

- **Links have a positive impact on organic traffic.** 75% of the time, we found the pages we built links to increase in organic traffic (over a 6 month period).

- **The quality of the website matters.** When analyzing sites we want to build links on, we look at much more than just Domain Authority (DA). We look at:
    - Social following
    - The quality of the articles they publish
    - Topical relevance of the website
    - What type of websites they are currently linking out to (are they random?)
- **The quality of the link matters.** I can easily identify a paid link by just looking at the article - they all look the same. No images, 500 words or less, and a random link to a site. If I can tell this, so can Google. Our data shows these kinds of low-effort links have no impact on rankings, even if they're coming from high-authority websites.
- **What you link to matters.** Google is very smart at not only sniffing out low quality and paid links, but also irrelevant links.
- **When building your links, you have to match link type to content type.** For example, if you're linking to a product page, you need to ask yourself, "What kind of content would organically link to this item?".

We found that product pages did not react overly well to direct links. Instead, Google paid attention to 'best-of' listicles, Quora, Reddit, blog, and forum comments. In theory, those are all places where product mentions come up organically, which gives them more value in the eyes of search engines.

Content (i.e. in-depth articles) react much more positively to links. We believe it's because getting a link to an in-depth piece of content is much more natural than with a product/service page. The blog posts that we built links to ranked very well, and they drove a ton of traffic for our clients.

What I suggest is that you start thinking about links as 'citations', like footnotes in your high school essays. Great content serves as a much better citation than a sales page.

Google doesn't penalize, it just loses 'trust' in your content. As mentioned, we used to build a lot of guest post links to ecommerce product pages. In hindsight, those pages could have been penalized. I mean, out of nowhere, a page with no links starts getting contextually mentioned in a bunch of blog posts? Not likely.

Instead of penalizing the page, the links just won't have any effect. They get ignored, which isn't the worst possible outcome, but it does mean you wasted a lot of time building links with no value.

In my opinion, Google learned their lesson from penalizing websites. I mean, most websites outsource their SEO to an agency - it's just not cool ripping down someone's online presence for actions they did not take.

Link building is a lot of work (and it's expensive), so you don't want to waste resources on tactics that won't impact your traffic. We'll be talking about this in great depth in the link acquisition section.

We'll also talk about how to target the right pages on your site with the right type of links and how you can secure them.

3 Core Concepts for an Evergreen SEO Strategy

I get asked by family and friends all the time for help with their website and SEO. Since I'm not getting paid, what I tell them is to focus on these three things:

1. **The technical aspect**. Build a well organized, fast website that follows Google's guidelines. If it's a 'small' website, build it using WordPress. You'll save a lot of time and you will be able to do most of the work yourself if you're so inclined.

2. **The core content**. Populate that website with the content your audience wants, needs, and is searching for. Make it a point of pride to not publish any pages that aren't helpful to your customers. Quality is very, very important. By the time you're done reading this book, we will have drilled that concept home.

3. **The links**. You need to figure out a way to get other websites to talk about you. First, you will need to do this manually. Become active in platforms such as Reddit, Quora, Facebook Groups - find your voice and provide value. Look for the best blogs in your industry and ask them if you can write a post for them. If you can do this, people will discover your site, and assuming you have quality content, they will begin to talk about you organically.

We do advanced SEO for Fortune 500 websites and our methods are built on these principles, even for our larger clients. These concepts aren't (just) something I tell friends and family to get them off my back. What they are is the pillars upon with all SEO work is built and they're a core part of my sales pitch.

The remainder of this book will run you through our agency's proven process for higher rankings and more organic traffic from search engines.

Our Evergreen Approach to SEO

While every website needs its own strategy for optimization, we follow the same template process regardless of industry. Whether you're trying to get more clients for your law firm or customers to your ecommerce store selling candy, the cornerstones of good SEO remain true.

Throughout this book, I will teach you how to run an SEO campaign from start to finish, as if we were working for a Fortune-500 company. The process we use is incredibly thorough and it leaves nothing to chance. You might think it's overkill if you're just working on a small website, but if you understand how big businesses approach SEO, you're going to be miles ahead of most of your competitors. That's exactly where I want you to be and I bet you do as well.

With that out of the way, let's talk about the 5-phase project WEBRIS uses:

Phase 1: The Discovery Process

- It's critical to understand as much as possible about the website, its past SEO efforts, and the industry it's part of. This knowledge helps us determine the best strategy to pursue.

- That same principle comes to play with clients, as you need to understand precisely what they want, so you can meet their demands. Our process helps you manage expectations while delivering high quality work, on time.

- How we onboard new projects quickly and effectively through questions and custom built reports.

Phase 2: The Improving Process

- The fastest turn around in organic traffic comes from small tweaks to existing pages. What we do is run a number of audits to identify which existing pages can give us the best short-term returns when it comes to traffic.

- In this section, we'll also discuss the tools we use to crosswalk data and decide which pages hold the most value. We will also go over how we do keyword research for existing pages, 'on-page' SEO corrections, schema markup, and more.

Phase 3: The Building Process

- By analyzing competitors and industry leaders, we can identify keyword 'gaps' on your website. These gaps represent opportunities to claw away some of your competitors' traffic once you build content that can target them.

- In this section, we will discuss how we do keyword gap analysis, keyword intent mapping and how we build new pages on a website, both content (i.e. blog posts, resource guides, etc) or landing pages (i.e. sales based content). We will also discuss how to manage large-scale content campaigns across dozens (hundreds) of websites.

Phase 4: The Promotion Process

- As you know, it's not enough to just do on-page corrections and create quality content. To get explosive traffic gains, you need to promote your website by getting links and mentions from relevant industry websites.

- In this section, we will not only discuss how our agency secures high quality links at scale, but also the content promotion tactics we recommend to increase the reach of your brand.

Phase 5: The Evaluation Process

- After an SEO campaign, we evaluate the whole process. This step is key since it enables you to see how far you've come. If you're doing SEO for clients, then in-depth reports are essential.

- For this section, we'll show you the reports we use for our clients and cover all the metrics you need to track to measure your campaign's success.

PHASE 1

The Discovery Process

Whether you're working on a client campaign or trying to improve the rankings of your own website, you can't overlook this period.

"Discovery" refers to the process of gathering the information you need to understand the website you're working on and its industry. That knowledge is key to planning what your steps should be.

The last thing we want is to invest 6 months of time, resources, and money into a campaign only to realize we were optimizing the wrong aspects of the website. By asking the right questions, analyzing the data, looking at competitors, and building a solid project plan we minimize that risk.

The discovery process goes beyond gathering information, though. In SEO, a lot of the work we do involves numbers. We gather data, zero in on the metrics we know are important, and we make decisions based on them. However, when you're working with clients instead of using that information to improve your own website, the dynamic changes.

Working in SEO isn't just about poring over data, it's also about making sure your clients are happy. That means keeping them in the loop about what you do, what the next steps are, and managing expectations. To succeed and thrive in this line of work, you need more than just smarts, you need to incorporate a "service" layer.

It took me a while to figure out how essential that service layer is when it comes to managing clients. Once I left my corporate job, I hustled to find my first SEO clients, until I finally landed a big whale – a hosting company based in the UK.

The job was mostly link building and I knew precisely what I had to do to get the results they needed. I was confident, but the problem was, I was so focused on getting results, I didn't realize I was getting paid for more than just results, I was getting paid for a *service*.

After about a week of work, I got that dreaded email that said "Hey Ryan, this isn't working out. It's not you, it's us". I had been so focused on planting new trees, I forgot I needed to water the lawn.

Although losing my first big client was a significant hit. I didn't let it slow me down. The way I see it, I lucked out by learning a critical lesson right when my SEO journey was starting.

These days, whenever we sign a new client, we never skip the discovery process. I'd go as far as to say it's the most essential step when it comes to building a long and stable working relationship.

Not only do we spend a lot of time analyzing where our clients are and what they need, we also put a lot of effort into communicating that information. A lot of businesses know they need SEO, but they have no idea what actually happens in the background when they spend big bucks on an agency to take care of it for them.

It's my job and my team's to communicate with clients often and to have the data to back up the plans we put in front of them. It's that layer of extra service that makes the difference between a small agency and a multimillion dollar business, but you don't have to take my word for it. 82% of consumers in the US admit they've stopped doing business with a company because they felt the service was lacking. The number one cause for lost businesses for companies is poor customer service.

When the people you do business with know you have their best interests in mind, they tend to stick around, so that needs to be one of your guiding principles if you want to break into the SEO industry.

Throughout the rest of this book we're going to tackle a lot of technical processes and talk about data, but I wanted to take this time to impress upon you one of the most important lessons when it comes to the world of SEO (and pretty much any other industry): you're not just getting paid for results, you're getting paid for making sure your customers are happy. If you internalize that lesson and you pay attention to the SEO blueprint I'm going to lay out for you, you'll be miles ahead of most other agencies in the world.

Now let's get to work.

> ### AGENCY NOTES.
> Sometimes, clients can push back on "too much research" and "not enough action". Do not get flustered and skip it. You need to explain the importance of this period and emphasize patience. SEO is won through good strategy, not haphazard execution.

What we're going to cover in this phase:

- **1.1 - 7 Types of Questions You Need to Ask Before You Start a Campaign**

- **1.2 - How to Analyze Your Website's Numbers**
- **1.3 - Taking a Close Look at Your Competitors**
- **1.4 - How to Manage Your SEO Campaigns**

1.1 - 7 Types of Questions You Need to Ask Before You Start A Campaign

As soon as a new client signs a contract we send them a list of onboarding questions. These questions help our team understand the most important aspects of a client's business and website.

We don't take any immediate action based on the information we get. What we do is come away with key insights we can use down the road, such as:

- **Understanding the client's/your internal expectations from a campaign.** This information can help you shift around your project plan to ensure you meet your goals.

- **Getting a sense of the resources you have available.** There's a significant overlap between SEO and marketing. Getting an idea of what your client is already doing and what tools they have access to will make your life a lot easier (social, lead generation campaigns, PPC ads, etc).

- **Formulating your initial plan of attack.** Once you understand what your client's primary value proposition is, you can formulate a plan built around it.

We break down the questions we ask down into 7 'buckets', which we'll cover now.

NOTE: Most of these questions are geared towards working on a client campaign, but it's a checklist you can easily modify to work on your own site as well.

1. Accesses to your platforms
Do you have **Google Analytics**[1] setup on your website? *If so, please share access with youremail@gmail.com*
Do you have **Google Search Console**[2] setup on your website? *If so, please share access with youremail@gmail.com*
Do you have **Google Tag Manager** setup [3]on your website? *If so, please share access with youremail@gmail.com*
We might need to make edits to your website throughout this campaign. Can you provide us a login to your website, control panel, and hosting? We will not make any changes without your permission.

2. Questions about your business
What are your goals for the company and what are the challenges you face in meeting your goals?
When was the company founded?
How many employees do you have?
What do you estimate your revenue will be in the next 12 months - how does this compare to past years?
Are there any market trends we should know about?

---

[1] https://analytics.google.com/analytics/web/
[2] https://www.google.com/webmasters/tools/home
[3] https://developers.google.com/tag-manager/

What's your top acquisition channel to date? How did you build that pipeline?

Can you outline your ideal customer? Who are they?

Is there anyone out there that you'd like us to take a look at (in terms of what they're doing for marketing)? Please give us at least 3 competitors to review.

What KPIs are most important to you (i.e. phone calls, leads, sales, etc)?

What's your value prop against your competitors?

What are your customers' pain points? Have you gotten any negative feedback?

What is the average life of a customer and how exactly does the customer cycle look like?

Is your business cyclical or seasonal (i.e. are there periods of natural dips in traffic and sales)?

Do you have an internal developer / developer team (or external)? If we needed to modify code on the website, who would handle it? If we want to modify page titles and body text, who would handle it?

What marketing specific resources (people) do you have internally? Do they support you full time? Are they part-time? Contractors? Offshore workers?

What type of resources (people) do you have internally that KNOW the your industry inside and out? Can we leverage them for certain aspects of the campaign (i.e. coming up with topics for content marketing that ONLY insiders know about)?

3. Questions about content

What websites do you use / trust for the best information in your industry?
Are there any content topics you'd like us to focus on specifically?
Are there any content topics you'd like us to NOT cover?
Do you have a content writer you'd like us to work with? Please provide contact info if yes.

4. Questions about link building

Are you currently doing anything to acquire links? Do you have a list of websites you'd like us to start with?
Has your website had any issues with link (Penguin) penalties?
Has your website had any issues with manual link warnings?
Are you currently doing PR (or have you in the past)?
Has your website had any issues with link (Penguin) penalties?
Do we have permission to do email outreach on behalf of your brand? Or, use someone in the company as the outreach person. (Sending emails from WEBRIS drives down success rates)

5. Questions about SEO

Can you provide us with keyword research done by previous agency / staff?
Can you provide us with reports / work done by previous agency (we don't want to waste time with duplicate efforts)?

Do you do any "offline" marketing / advertising?
Are you currently doing PR (or have you in the past)?
Are you running paid search ads? If so, can you provide us access to the data (for KW research)?
Do you have a list of target keywords or pages you'd like us to focus on? Please list them out.

6. Questions about email marketing

Are you capturing emails (on your website, paid campaigns, etc)?
What email platform do you use? How many subscribers? Open rate? CTR?
Are you utilizing any automation sequences or funnels?
How often do you send emails?

7. Questions about social media marketing

Are you currently spending any money on social advertising? Could you provide us with details on the campaigns?
For social media management, do you use an agency or internal team?
What social networks are you most active on (please provide profile URLs)?
Have you done any influencer campaigns? How did they end up?

As you can see, we're thorough. Once we have access to that treasure trove of information, we store the answers to those questions within the client's Google Drive folder. That way, we can refer to them during the life of a campaign.

With all those answers at your fingertips, you should have a thorough understanding of the website you're working on. That knowledge is essential so you can make sense of what the numbers tell you, which we'll discuss during the next step of phase one.

1.2 - How to Analyze Your Website's Data

Your website's data tells a story we need to listen to. Before diving head first into a campaign, we need to take a look at the following:

1. Website analytics (Google Analytics, WebTrends, etc)
2. Google Search Console
3. Keyword rankings (SEMrush, Ahrefs, Moz, other rank tracking software)

Asking the right questions gets you off to a great start whenever you start working on a new project. As you've seen by now, we ask new clients a lot of questions. It can be overwhelming at times, but the more you dig, the more likely you are to find the little details that can make a huge difference for a campaign.

Something you need to keep in mind, though, is sometimes clients might be unwilling to share information or maybe they just don't understand what you're asking.

Early on in WEBRIS' life, we dealt with a client that wasn't comfortable sharing access to some of the analytics tools they used. Right off the bat, that tells you they didn't understand why that data was so important and that we didn't do a good enough job explaining why we needed that information.

Like any young and plucky agency, though, we got to work, and we busted our butts trying to get results. It took us four months to realize we weren't seeing the results we wanted because the client's website had been hit by an algorithm change before the project even started.

The client wasn't even aware of it.

All they knew was suddenly, their website wasn't getting the traffic it used to, so they sought the help of experts. During the onboarding questionnaire, they didn't tell us about that algorithm hit because they weren't aware what had happened in the background.

Had we had access to their analytics accounts, we would've been able to sniff out the problem from the get go, saving us time and cutting down costs for them. However, as the "SEO-guys" we also let them down by failing to convey the importance of having access to the data we needed to get the full picture.

Needless to say, they weren't happy it took us so long to figure out the problem. That's four months of work we had been billing for and we failed to do our due diligence.

These days, we have a much more streamlined process in place. We use Google Data Studio to pull data we need from all the tools we mentioned earlier. With Data Studio, we can build reports that enable us to analyze all the data we need, without poring through pages and pages of analytics.

We use a report template that's polished enough to submit to clients. By presenting data the right way, we can make sure they understand what their weak points are and where we want to focus.

Not only does that standardized approach save us time, it also boosts our service layer. Although initially, we built that report to save us time and prevent the same mistake from occurring again, we stumbled into a synergy that's helped the business tremendously. The more work you put into optimizing your process, the better service you can provide, and in turn, the more you can charge. If that's not enough to convince you of how essential service is in this industry, I don't know what is.

NOTE: Since most of you are using Google Analytics, that's what we'll be using as an example throughout this section.

> **Visit www.theblueprint.website**
> **to check out the Data Studio kickoff report.**

The goal of this report is to uncover as much information as possible, in the shortest amount of time. We do so by asking a specific set of questions and using the data from the report to answer them. This section will run you through our evaluation process.

1. How is overall marketing performance trending?

We can uncover the answer through Google Analytics. Digging through GA manually takes hours, but the dashboard we built allows us to analyze progress instantly.

TRAFFIC AND CONVERSION TRENDS

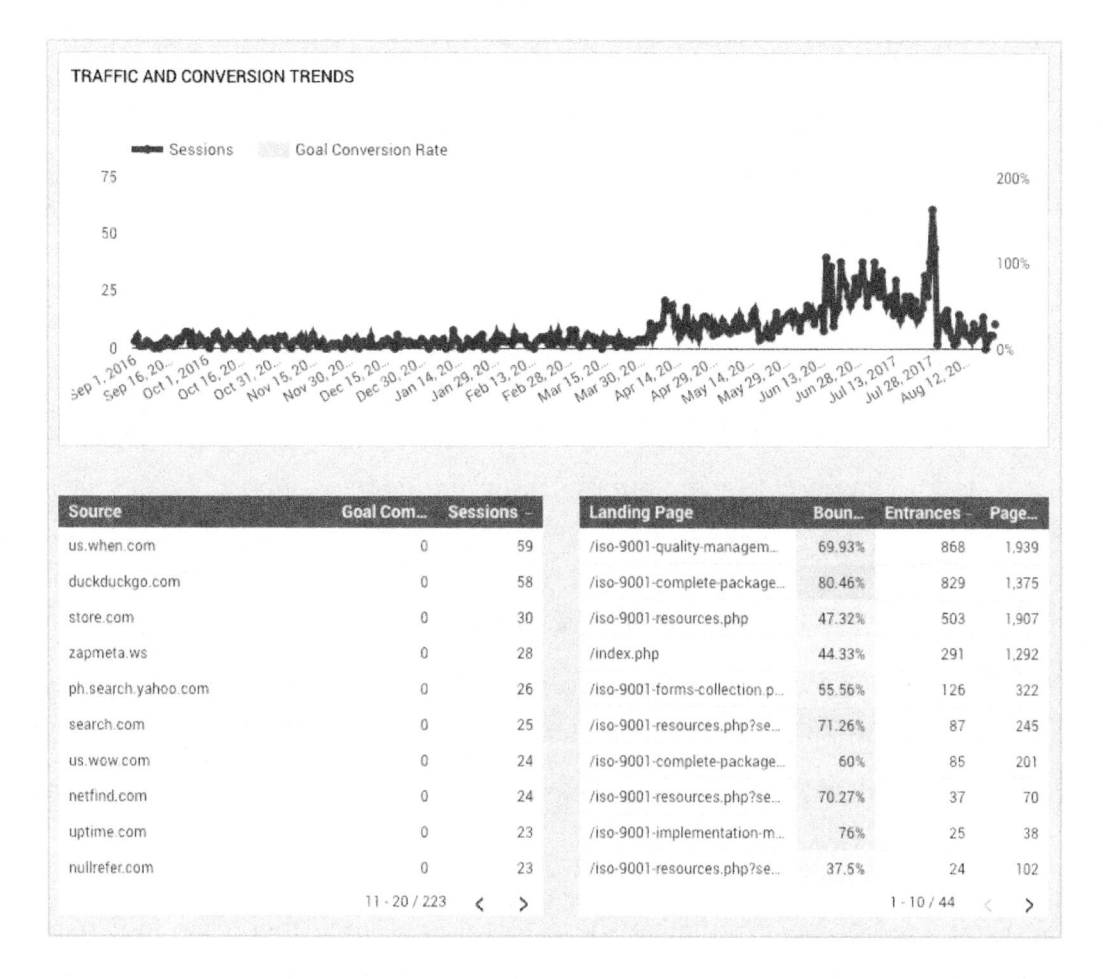

Source	Goal Com...	Sessions	Landing Page	Boun...	Entrances	Page...
us.when.com	0	59	/iso-9001-quality-managem...	69.93%	868	1,939
duckduckgo.com	0	58	/iso-9001-complete-package...	80.46%	829	1,375
store.com	0	30	/iso-9001-resources.php	47.32%	503	1,907
zapmeta.ws	0	28	/index.php	44.33%	291	1,292
ph.search.yahoo.com	0	26	/iso-9001-forms-collection.p...	55.56%	126	322
search.com	0	25	/iso-9001-resources.php?se...	71.26%	87	245
us.wow.com	0	24	/iso-9001-complete-package...	60%	85	201
netfind.com	0	24	/iso-9001-resources.php?se...	70.27%	37	70
uptime.com	0	23	/iso-9001-implementation-m...	76%	25	38
nullrefer.com	0	23	/iso-9001-resources.php?se...	37.5%	24	102

I like to look at a full year's worth of data - it gives a sense of overall growth but also seasonality trends.

What we're looking for is patterns, trends and information from *non-organic channels* that could be impacting their *organic* performance.

- **Paid search**. If you're spending a good amount of money on Search Engine Marketing (SEM), you will see an increase in organic traffic. Generally speaking, this is people returning back to the site through "branded keywords" (i.e. they clicked your ad for "Miami attorney" then returned to Google the next day to search for your website directly). This is pertinent information because changes in SEM spend will cause a fluctuation in organic traffic that you could misdiagnose.

- **NOTE:** You can also layer on NEW vs. RETURNING to understand visitor behavior.

- **Social**. While social links and traffic doesn't [officially] impact organic rankings, those numbers are still a critical part of an integrated digital strategy. If you're going to be focusing on content creation, you need to know which social platforms your audience prefers.

- **Referral**. Referrals directly impact your rankings and organic traffic, so you want to monitor the quality of your inbound links.

Referral traffic data gives us critical insights for link building strategy. If you know what links are driving the most traffic to your website, you know where to focus your efforts and look for scaling opportunities.

We're not going to analyze these too much since there are too many factors that could cause changes. The idea, at this point, is to use this report to get an overall understanding of traffic trends from all sources.

2. What are your website's top pages?

This page is still looking at 1 year trends, but now from *organic search only*. We're now analyzing the top landing pages from organic search by sessions count, change in traffic (year over year), bounce rate, and conversion rate.

NOTE: If you run an online store website, you can configure your dashboard to focus on ecommerce conversion rates instead of less specific goals.

Jan 1, 2016 - Dec 31, 2016					WEBRIS
Traffic Performance, Year over Year Comparison					Data From Google Analytics

Default Channel Grouping: Organic Search (1) — Device Category

Landing Page	Sessions	% Δ	Bounce...	% Δ	Goal Conve...	% Δ
/iso-9001-resources.php	14,874	-3.2% ↓	47.71%	-1.5% ↓	0%	
/iso-9001-resources.php?section=2	5,815	-25.5% ↓	74.53%	-1.4% ↓	0%	
/iso-9001-resources.php?section=3	1,559	-20.8% ↓	75.88%	-0.2% ↓	0%	
/iso-9001-resources.php?section=1&implementation_ste...	815	-8.2% ↓	41.1%	2.5% ↑	0%	
/iso-9001-complete-package.php	536	21.0% ↑	68.47%	3.5% ↑	0%	
/index.php	322	-19.9% ↓	28.88%	-12.7% ↓	0%	

We're looking for a few key insights here:

- **What pages are performing the best.** Look at the sessions - this data along will tell you what your most popular pages are. If you look at conversions next, you can understand how valuable that traffic is.

- **What page type is performing the best?** For example, home page, blog posts, product pages, etc. This gives you insight into areas to initially focus on. For example, if content is your primary source of traffic, you should focus heavily on commercial pages and remarketing strategy (and vice versa).

- **What's the share of traffic?** Do some of those top pages tower over the rest in terms of sessions? The site may be doing 1M visits a month, but if 94% of the traffic is going to a blog post with no commercial value, those visits are *a lot less meaningful.*

- **Are key pages gaining or losing traffic?** If you look at traffic fluctuations over the long term (think year by year), you can easily tell if the website (or specific pages) are in a downward spiral.

- **At a glance, do their pages satisfy searcher intent?** Bounce rate is a crude way to judge engagement, but it does give you a topical overview. Generally speaking, you can expect content (blog posts) to have a higher bounce rate since the intent behind a lot of these searches is purely informational. If you have a page that serves up good information, a high bounce rate is not necessarily indicative of poor performance.

To fully answer this, we need to dive deeper inro Google Analytics and look at the Content Drilldown report (Behavior > Site Content > Content Drilldown). Here, you can check out your Avg. Time on Page numbers, which are the counter to bounce rate.

Page path level 1	Pageviews	Unique Pageviews	Avg. Time on Page	Bounce Rate	% Exit
	22,058 % of Total: 100.00% (22,058)	6,398 % of Total: 100.00% (6,398)	00:00:53 Avg for View: 00:00:53 (0.00%)	52.28% Avg for View: 52.28% (0.00%)	21.54% Avg for View: 21.54% (0.00%)
1. /link-building-strategies-that-work/	2,374 (10.76%)	276 (4.31%)	00:00:40	49.56%	9.94%
2. /services/	2,221 (10.07%)	295 (4.61%)	00:00:30	40.26%	6.71%
3. /	2,043 (9.26%)	543 (8.49%)	00:00:30	29.80%	12.63%
4. /how-to-perform-a-technical-seo-audit/	2,023 (9.17%)	219 (3.42%)	00:01:01	36.55%	9.99%
5. /youtube-seo/	1,671 (7.58%)	699 (10.93%)	00:01:23	59.00%	38.72%
6. /tools/	1,229 (5.57%)	445 (6.96%)	00:00:33	53.08%	20.75%
7. /training/	1,041 (4.72%)	263 (4.11%)	00:00:43	46.61%	18.83%

- **Is there a drop off or increase in mobile traffic?** By adding a filter for MOBILE, we can see the impact of desktop vs mobile on your website. Our agency website does about 90% desktop organic traffic. Our ecommerce website does about 70% mobile organic traffic. There's no issue with the way our agency site is optimized, but the audience is completely different, which impacts their online behavior.

3. Does your website have any organic traffic trends?

A series of charts using sessions data from Google Analytics.

Chart #1: Year over year traffic comparison, by month

This chart lets you compare each month's organic session count to the previous year. This is also a great growth forecasting report.

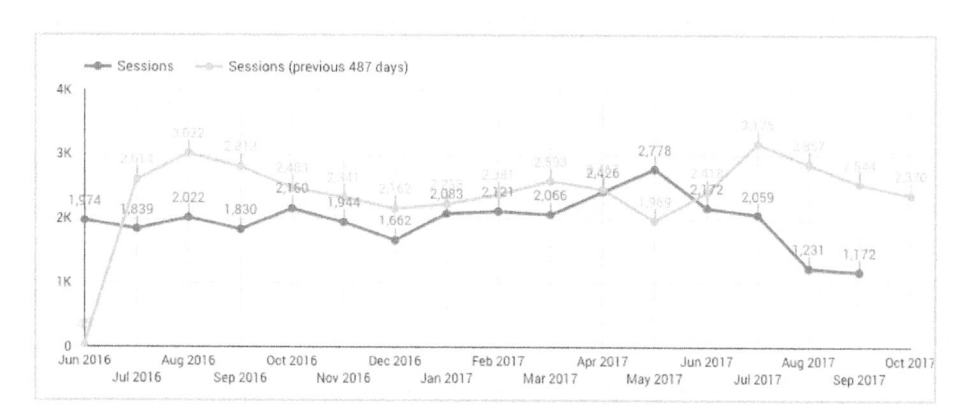

Chart #2: History of organic traffic by month

You can use this chart to track your website's growth since its inception. This report is also pivotal for understanding seasonality and if your site got hit by an algorithm update.

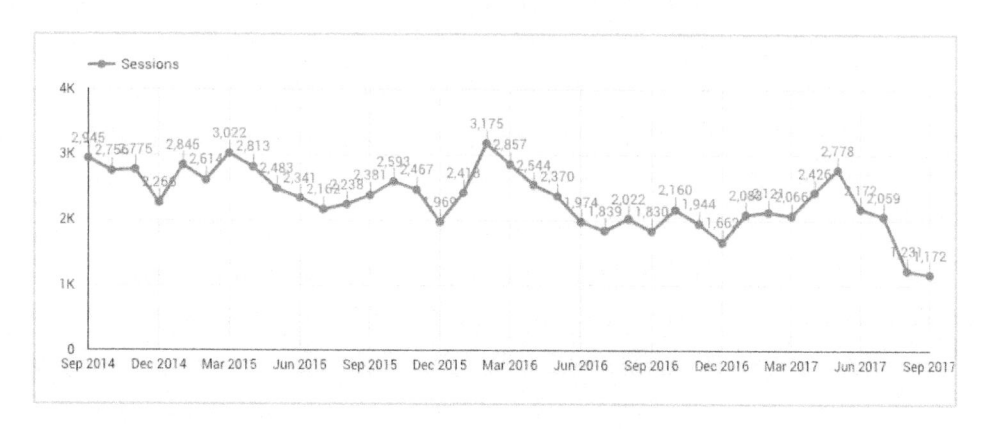

Chart #3: Organic traffic trends by day

This isn't what I'd call a critical report. However, it's still worth a glance since it helps you understand which day of the week is most popular for searchers.

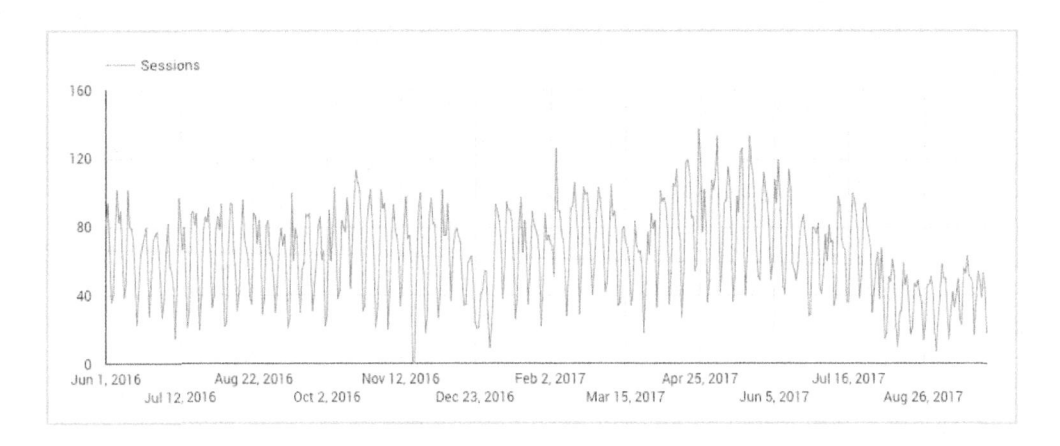

4. How many keywords does your website rank for?

More charts, this time using data from a keyword tracking tool (we like Ahrefs and SEMrush).

Chart #1: Keyword visibility chart

If you enter your website in SEMrush (or Ahrefs), you will get a chart that includes a "keyword visibility" report. That report includes:

- The number of keywords the entire website is ranking for.
- The ranking / position for each keyword.
- The search volume of those keywords.
- The AdWords cost per click for those keywords

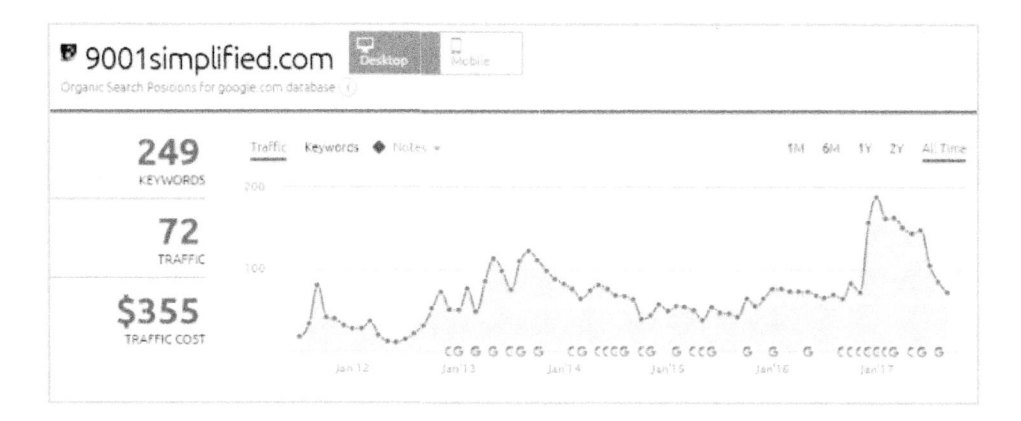

[Screenshot: 9001simplified.com — 249 Keywords, 72 Traffic, $355 Traffic Cost, with organic search positions chart from Jan '12 to Jan '17]

This data gives me a great idea of how "visible" the website is. Generally speaking, the more keywords you're ranking for (regardless of position), the easier it is to find the website. In other words, it's easier to find.

It's also important to understand, the easiest way to get more traffic isn't to rank for new keywords, but to **improve** your existing rankings.

Chart #2: Organic position distribution

This chart shows ALL keywords a website is ranking for, including details about their position. In my experience, keywords ranking below position 7 don't have much value. That means you have to take that previous number about the total of keywords you're ranking for with a grain of salt.

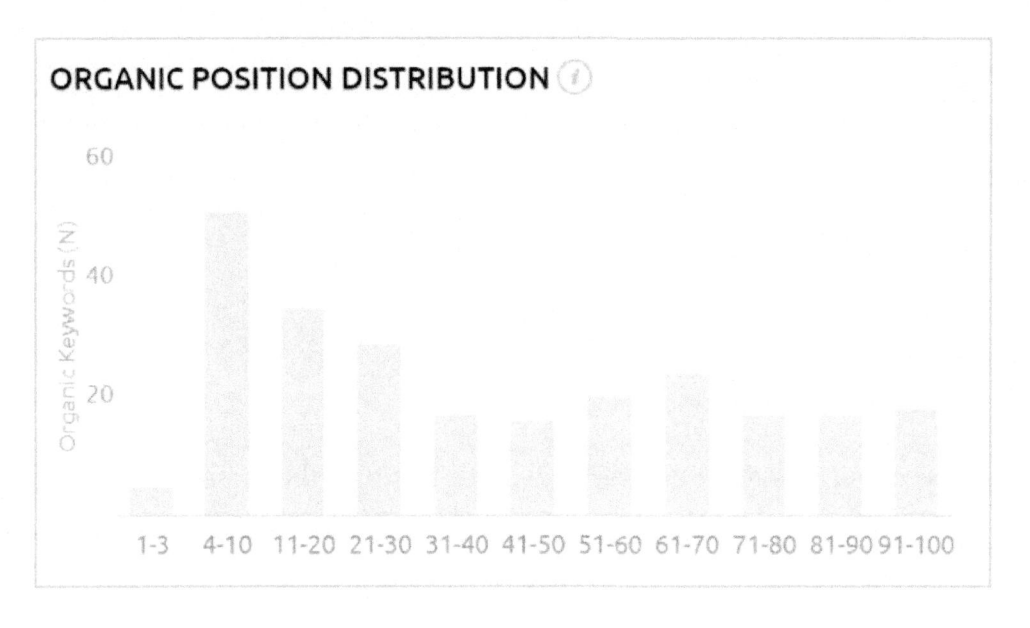

Chart #3: All keyword rankings

When you're ready for a closer look at the data, this chart gives you a list of every single keyword you're ranking for. That includes the URL, the exact position you're ranking for, and how much traffic it's sending you.

Remember – keywords ranking below position 7 might not bring in all that much traffic, but if you can improve them, you can change that.

5. How is your website performing in Google?

Unlike Google Analytics, Google Search Console only reports on your website's performance in Google Search. We can get more granular data like SERP position, impressions and Click Through Rate (CTR). This data is invaluable to bring us up to speed on a website's current and past performance within Google.

Chart #1: Branded vs non branded search

"Branded search" is when someone uses your business name, brand or website URL to find your website. This happens when someone is aware of your site or returning for another visit (a blog post they read before, a product they looked at previously, etc.).

This metric is incredibly important, for a couple reasons:

- **Branded search is a powerful ranking factor**. It's the hardest thing to replicate (no, search bots don't work) and therefore is a huge quality signal to Google. There's nothing more powerful than someone searching for you "your product / service + your brand name".

- **It helps you better understand your traffic**. While branded search is important, the majority of an SEO campaign should focus on driving non-branded search (aka ranking for new, high intent keywords). That means branded search needs to be factored out for reporting and measurement purposes.

Branded Search	Non Branded Search
30 Clicks	**712** Clicks
5% % of Traffic	**95%** % of Traffic

Chart #2: Clicks from Google

While similar to sessions, GSC only looks at unique clicks. Sessions, on the other hand, groups new and returning clicks into a single metric.

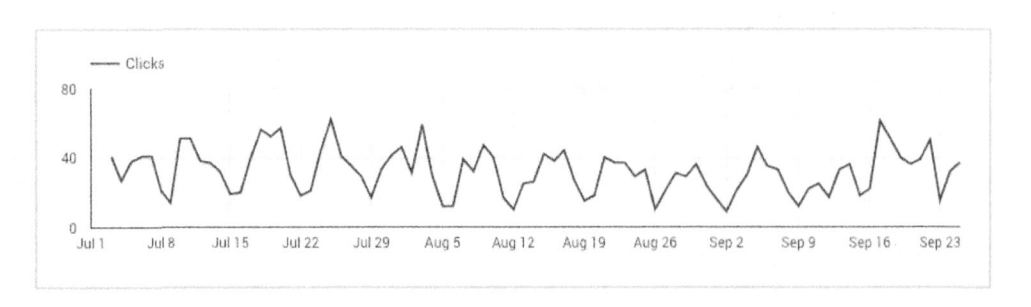

Chart #3: Impressions from Google

GSC counts impressions as anytime your website shows up in a search result, no matter if that person clicks on it or not. Regardless, this report gives me a good idea of how search intent for a keyword fluctuates. Plus, if you're not getting that many clicks, it can point towards any number of issues, such as:

- Competitors stepping up their game and taking over the landscape

- Technical issues that are impacting your SEO
- Increased "noise" in the SERPs at a query level (i.e. more ads, knowledge graphs, etc)

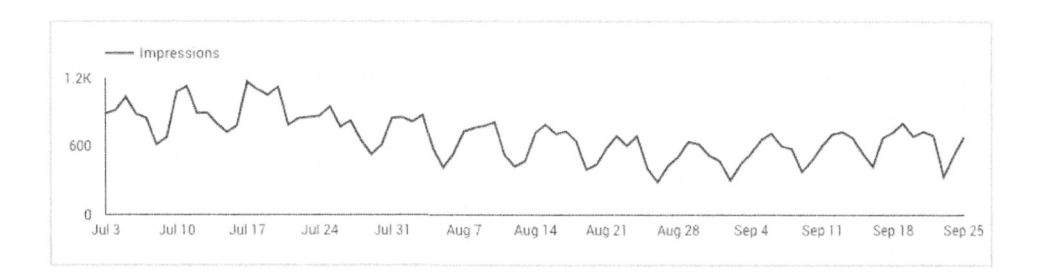

Chart #4: Click Through Rate (CTR) from Google

CTR tells you what percentage of searches clicked on your links within the SERPs. Needless to say, the higher it is, the better.

The most important factor when it comes to CTR is the position of your results. Top results show significantly higher CTRs. In any case, there are several actions you can take to increase your pages' CTR, such as:

- Rewriting page titles to be more "click worthy"
- Rewriting meta descriptions to be more "click worthy"
- Looking into Structured Data markup options to add to pages to increase SERP real estate (i.e. review stars, event tables, etc)

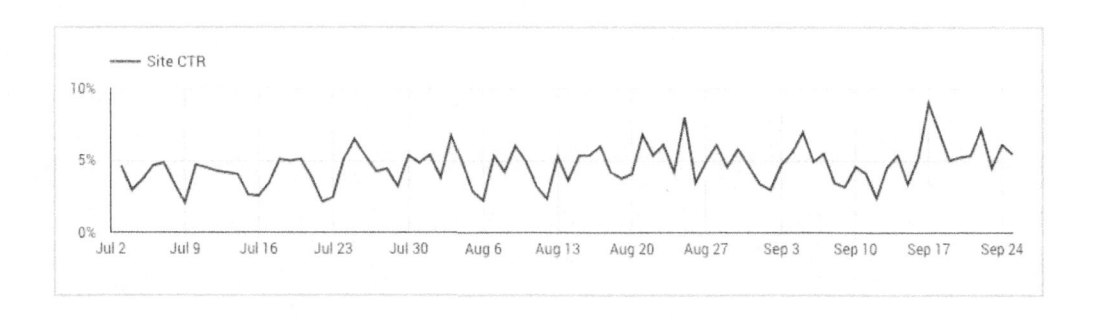

6. Where is organic traffic coming from?

Google Search Console has a powerful tool called "Search Analytics" that allows you to segment your traffic based on what aspect of Google Search people are finding your site through:

- Desktop
- Mobile
- Images
- Video

This is essential information, as it allows us to understand opportunities using different types of content geared for each audience.

For each of the 4 options, our report breaks down:

Clicks vs. average position

Filtered for desktop/mobile/image/video only, this chart shows you how average keyword rankings (for all your pages) affect traffic.

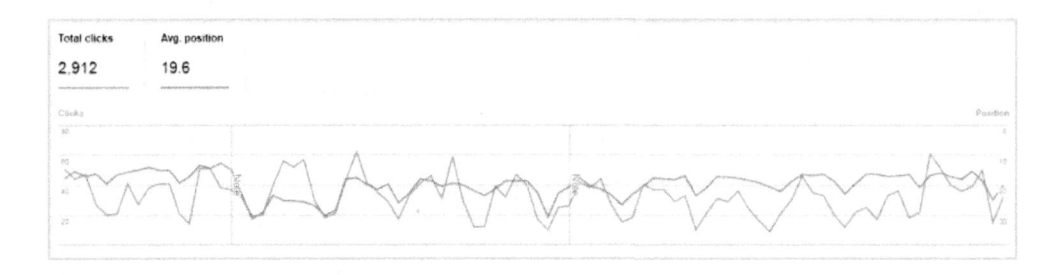

Remember, your rankings on mobile could be significantly different than desktop (and vice versa) based on how your content / site is built. If you find major discrepancies, you need to analyze what's causing them.

Exact search queries driving traffic to your site

Filtered for desktop/mobile/image/vide, this chart lists out the exact search queries people are using to find your website.

	Queries	Clicks ▾	Impressions	CTR	Position
1.	iso certification process steps	73	673	0.11	3.6
2.	iso 9001 certification kit	66	365	0.18	1
3.	how to get iso certification	56	2,961	0.02	8.7
4.	what is the last step in iso 9001 registration	41	165	0.25	1.5
5.	how to get iso 9001 certification	37	1,110	0.03	6.7
6.	iso 9001 certification process	25	925	0.03	8.7
7.	how to become iso 9001 certified	15	519	0.03	7.7
8.	iso 9001 compliance	14	586	0.02	6.7

This chart gives you an interesting insight into how people use different queries depending on the platform.

For example, I particularly love the report on image search, because it gives us a brand new opportunity to score traffic. Most marketers undervalue image search traffic, but in some cases, it can drive a ton of users to your website.

Real estate is a prime example of such a situation. When you're searching for a new home, you're going to want to see pictures and Google Images may be your first stop. If you see something you like, then you're going to visit the parent website. In other words, image SEO can become a powerful funnel for traffic.

7. What did you learn?

This report is key for forming your initial strategy. What I like to do is take notes of everything I see while going through it. Those notes often make it into the first page of the reports I'll show clients.

Here are some ideas of the types of insights the numbers can give you, depending on what type of website you're analyzing:

- Traffic tends to dip around the holiday season.

- Sessions were trending up until February of 2017, since then, traffic began to dip at a rate of 40% per month. That indicates that algorithms are impacting your rankings, so we need to zero in on why that is.

- One image on their site is driving over 100 visits a month, which means there could be an opportunity to exploit more images for similar intent keywords.

- Xyz.com linked to the site back in February and has since driven over 700 visits. We visited the site and they accept guest posts, so we want to add them to our list of outreach contacts.

Insights like these are gold, so you need to carry them into the next phase, which involves building and executing your campaign. We'll get to that soon.

1.3 - Taking a Close Look at Your Top Competitors

I get asked all the time - *"**Ryan, what is XYZ.com doing that we aren't? Tell me why they're ranking 1st for this keyword and we are not!**"*

There's so many algorithmic factors that we can't see, it's literally impossible to answer that question with full certainty.

What I tell clients is, it's important to understand what your competitors are doing, but it's equally crucial you don't obsess over it. Their website is different than yours and they have different resources than you - spending too much time trying to reverse engineer their success is not a good use of your time.

Even so, a cursory analysis is still in order. Why? Because Google considers them a "quality" result or else they wouldn't outrank you. Getting an idea of how they operate gives you an insight into the way Google thinks.

How to find your competition

You can probably rattle off a list of your competitors off the top of your head. However, there's a big difference between regular and SEO competitors. For example, there might be a store across the street that sells the same products you do at lower prices, but they don't have an online presence.

They're certainly a competitor, but not in the SEO landscape, which is what we're here to talk about.

What we need to do is find competitors at the keyword level - aka the people you're competing against for Google's love and attention.

a. Use Google Search + MozBar

This first part is simple. All you have to do is search for the keywords you're ranking for and take a look at what the top results are. If you want more information on them, you can also use MozBar, a free browser plugin that displays on SEO metrics below each result, which you can download from this URL:

https://moz.com/products/pro/seo-toolbar

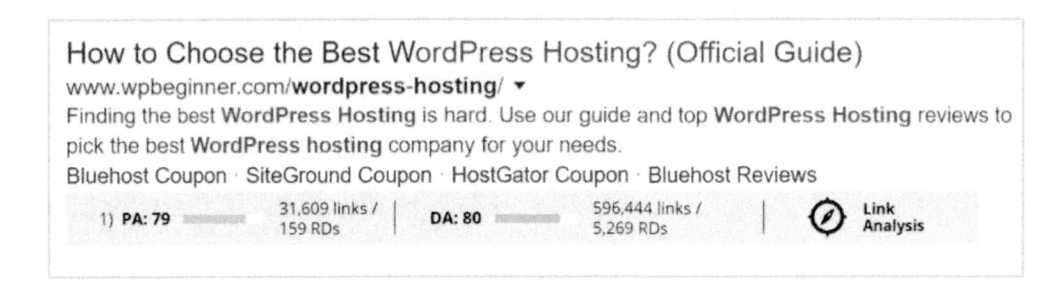

Google Search with Mozbar

Having that information right there saves you a ton of time when it comes to analyzing each result. Here's what each metric tells you:

- **The PA (or Page Authority) of the result.** PA is a metric that Moz developed to tell you how authoritative a page is. The higher the PA, the harder it is to outrank it.

- **The DA (or Domain Authority) of the result.** PA looks at the specific page result - DA looks at the entire domain. DA is a solid metric to understand the overall ranking power of an entire website. You should be comparing your DA / PA to the top results to see how you measure up.

- **Number of links and referring domains to that particular page.** Generally speaking, the more the links the harder that result will be to outrank.

You probably rank for a lot of keywords, so I suggest you start with the ones that have the highest conversion rates. They're the most valuable for your business, so if there are websites that outrank you for those terms, those are your nemeses.

b. Use SEMrush to find common keywords

SEMrush is a paid tool, but it's worth the price tag due to the great competitive analysis it provides you (**NOTE:** you can use Ahrefs as well).

All you have to do is enter your domain into SEMrush and it will give you a list of your 'top' competitors based on shared keywords.

Competitor search in SEMrush

Not only does SEMrush tell you who your competitors are, it also shows you their monthly traffic volume and how many keywords they're ranking for do you have a list of your competition, you also can determine the monthly traffic and the number of keywords they're ranking for in high positions within the SERPs. It even tells you what those keywords are.

It's easy to become overwhelmed with all this information, so I recommend you stick to analyzing the top three domains you're competing with. You can always dive deeper into the rest later during the campaign.

What to look for in competitor websites

Once you have a list of your top 3 competitors, we can take a look at the factors that contribute to their success.

1. Understand a competitor's site build by crawling it

We like to use DeepCrawl, but Screaming Frog and SiteBulb are both awesome tools as well. A full crawl through tells us a ton of information about a website, including:

- An overview of their website's architecture and setup
- A full list of all the pages on their site
- Title tags, meta tags and other "on page" elements

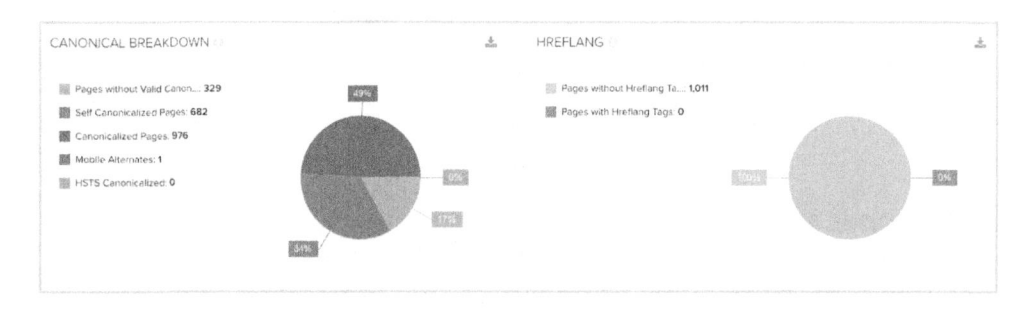

This is a somewhat advanced tactic when it comes to SEO. Generally speaking, a site crawl provides you insight into the technical aspects of website's build, so you can identify problems with your own.

2. Number of indexed pages

Go to Google Search and type in -> site:competitor.com. This will pull back the number of pages that Google is indexing on that site.

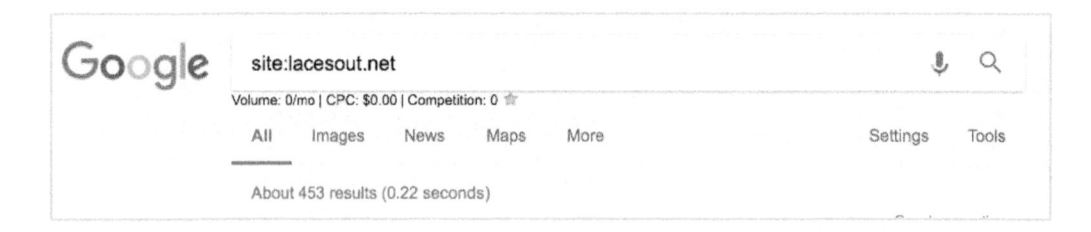

This tells you a number of things:

1. How much content / type of content they have on their site.

2. A high level overview of how Google is indexing their website (in comparison to yours).

3. A high level overview of the authority and indexation power that site has.

4. The size of their website in comparison to yours. This can give you an idea of how much work you have ahead of you if you want to knock them off their perch.

A good rule of thumb is to dig a little deeper here based on your vertical. To give you an example, if you're running an online store, you won't just care how many pages your competitors have. What you care about is *how many of those are product pages.*

In that case, what I would do is click around their site to find out if they're using a subfolder architecture for products, then repeat that as a Google search.

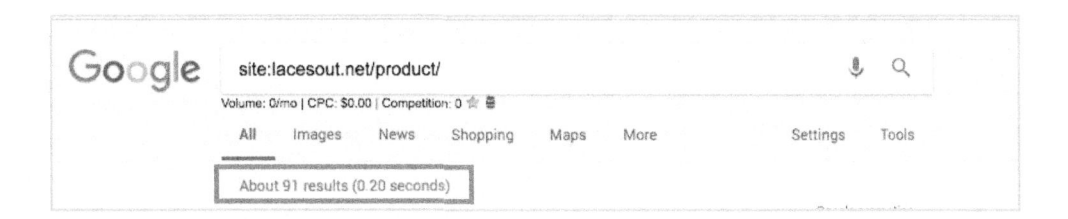

```
Google    site:lacesout.net/product/
          Volume: 0/mo | CPC: $0.00 | Competition: 0
          All   Images   News   Shopping   Maps   More        Settings   Tools
          About 91 results (0.20 seconds)
```

Now you have a full list of all their product pages, all in a few minutes' work.

3. Keyword rankings

It's important to know the keywords your competitors are using to drive the most traffic to their site. SEMrush (and Ahrefs) is a fantastic tool to find that information, as it can show you the top keywords by search volume for any website.

Keyword	Pos.	Volume	KD	CPC (USD)	URL	Traffic %	Costs %	Com.	Results	Trend	SERP	Last Update
laces out	1 (1)	9,900	77.50	0.00	www.lacesout.net/	25.03	0.00	0.01	1,040,000			40 min ago
fake jordan 11	1 (1)	1,300	73.24	0.06	www.lacesout.net...-real/	3.28	0.86	0.98	5,970,000			1 day ago
how to clean jordans	1 (2)	1,000	76.29	0.00	www.lacesout.net...akers/	2.52	0.00	0.07	26,200,000			Sep 2017
lacing jordans	1 (1)	880	88.28	0.00	www.lacesout.net...dan-1/	2.22	0.00	0.11	470,000			1 Oct 2017
how to tell if jordan 11 are fake	1 (1)	880	70.05	0.00	www.lacesout.net...-real/	2.22	0.00	0.04	1,660,000			2 Oct 2017
how to tie nike shoes	1 (1)	880	87.80	1.38	www.lacesout.net...guide/	2.22	13.74	0.01	5,010,000			1 Oct 2017

Spying on the competition can give you great insight into new keywords to you might want to target as well as opportunities to improve existing rankings.

4. Top pages

SEMrush (and Ahrefs) will also tell you the top pages based on the number of keywords they're ranking for. That information can aid you in:

1. Finding additional keywords for pages

2. Finding keywords for content creation

3. Visiting those pages manually and deconstructing their on page elements to understand how they're ranking for so many keywords

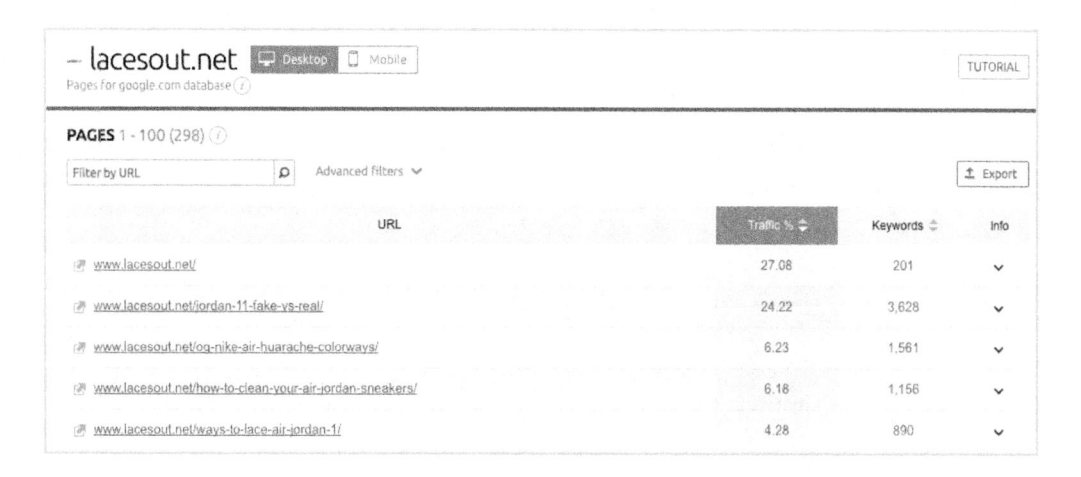

URL	Traffic %	Keywords	Info
www.lacesout.net/	27.08	201	
www.lacesout.net/jordan-11-fake-vs-real/	24.22	3,628	
www.lacesout.net/og-nike-air-huarache-colorways/	6.23	1,561	
www.lacesout.net/how-to-clean-your-air-jordan-sneakers/	6.18	1,156	
www.lacesout.net/ways-to-lace-air-jordan-1/	4.28	890	

Using that data, you can break down the value of the top pages within any competitor's website, as well as run a keyword gap analysis, which tells you where you're falling short against them.

5. Type of content

Looking at the same "pages" report, you can understand the type of content your competitors are using to drive so much traffic.

- Blog posts
- Resource guides
- Product / service pages

Understanding page type helps you get an idea of what your audience might want, as well as how valuable the traffic they're getting is.

For example, if a large majority of their traffic is going to pages with low purchase intent, it's not all that valuable. Ideally, you'll analyze websites that have both great content and sales pages to understand the full scope of pages you need on your site.

The SEO Blueprint

6. Quality of content / "On Page" optimizations

Looking at the top pages in SEMRush of Ahrefs, visit some of them to review them manually:

- How many words are on the page?
- Are they using images? Video?
- How good is the content (i.e. well written, informative, in depth, etc)?
- How are they optimizing their page titles? Subheadings?
- Is the site / page visually appealing?
- What type of call to actions are they using on their pages?
- Are they using internal links?
- Are they using external links?

Even with all the amazing SEO tools at our disposal, that doesn't mean you don't need to roll up your sleeves from time to time. If you're relying solely on numbers to analyze your competitors, you might miss a lot of factors a simple cursory visit would reveal. For example, their website design might just be **amazing**, but you'd never know if you didn't see it for yourself.

7. Backlink profile

I like to look at links at the page level as opposed to domain level. The information is a lot easier to digest and you can derive far better insight for the types of links that are working in your industry.

For this type of analysis, we like to use Ahrefs. We look at the "Backlinks" report, filtered for "One Link Per Domain" and "DOFOLLOW" only (which are the types of links that crawlers move through).

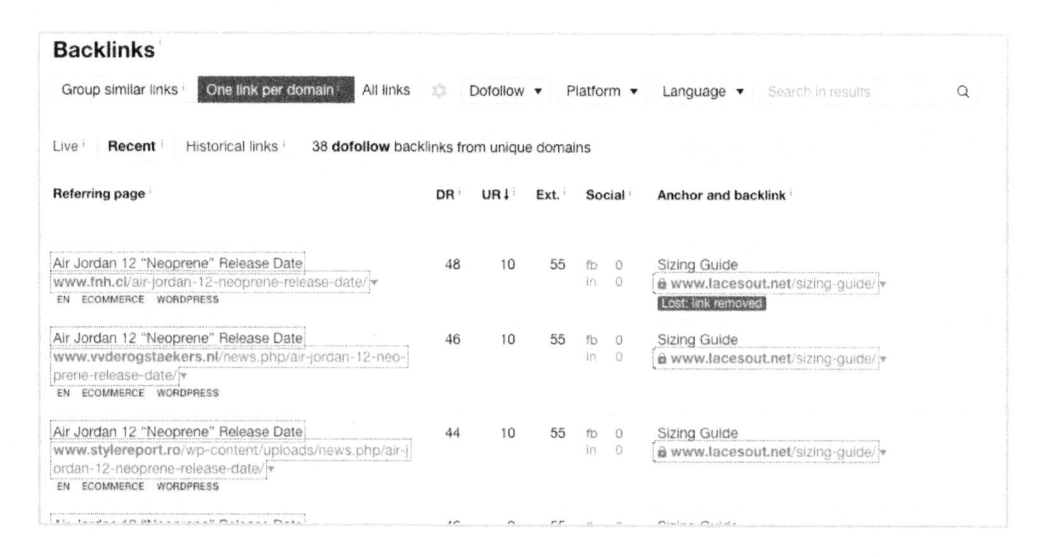

With that information, you can do a quick analysis that includes:

- **What types of links are these pages getting** (i.e. Huffington Post press mentions, forum comments, directory spam, blogger reviews, etc). This tells you a lot about the types of links you need to target for your pages.

- **How often are these pages getting links (i.e. link velocity)?** When we get to building links to your site, we want to create a natural pattern. We determine what's "natural" based on the acquisition patterns of your competitors.

- **Are there opportunities for you to steal the links?** With a little extra digging, you can find out if you can score the link for your site too.

When you're first beginning the campaign, this information helps you to understand how competitive the industry is. Plus, it's also valuable once we get to the link building phase.

8. Branded search

Branded search means the number of times a Google user searches for your company's name or product. This is a HUGE indicator of quality to search engines, and it's one that most SEO professionals overlook, which makes it a goldmine.

Branded search comes from a number of places:

- General market awareness and reach
- Offline advertisements (TV, radio, print, etc)
- Online advertisements (influencers, video views, social ads, etc)

I like to use Ahrefs to uncover the data.

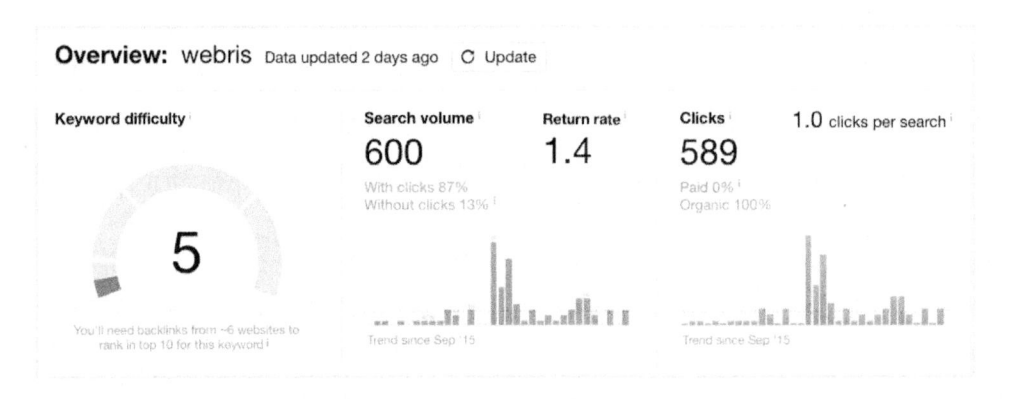

Overview: webris Data updated 2 days ago ↻ Update

Keyword difficulty	Search volume	Return rate	Clicks	1.0 clicks per search
5	600	1.4	589	
You'll need backlinks from ~6 websites to rank in top 10 for this keyword	With clicks 87% / Without clicks 13%	Trend since Sep '15	Paid 0% / Organic 100%	Trend since Sep '15

It not only gives me an accurate search volume for the brand's main keywords, but other semantic ones as well.

Keyword ideas

Having same terms

webris	600
ryan stewart webris	40
webris review	10
webris white hat training	0-10

This helps you complete the picture for the popularity of a brand overall and their specific products.

Putting this analysis to work

We like to record all of our findings in a Google Sheets template that tracks our site vs. 3 competitors.

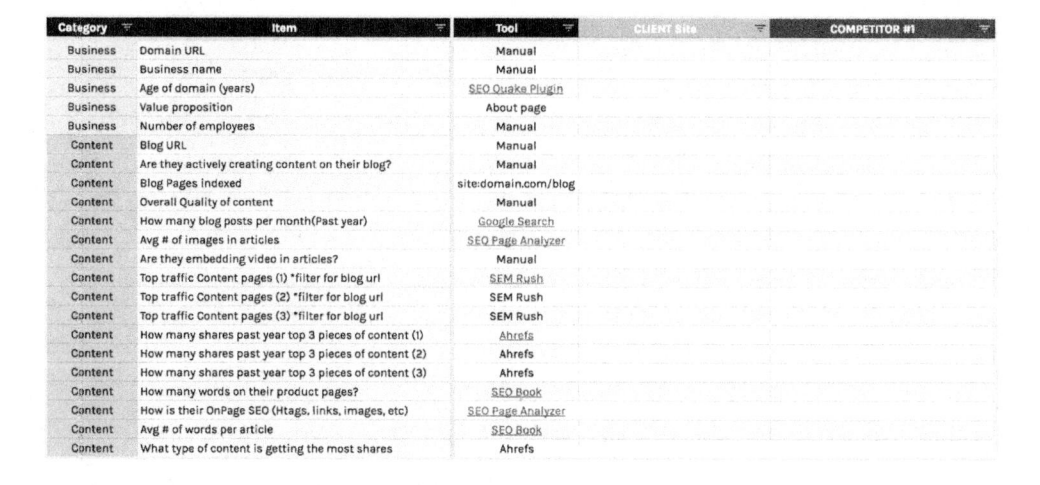

Category	Item	Tool	CLIENT Site	COMPETITOR #1
Business	Domain URL	Manual		
Business	Business name	Manual		
Business	Age of domain (years)	SEO Quake Plugin		
Business	Value proposition	About page		
Business	Number of employees	Manual		
Content	Blog URL	Manual		
Content	Are they actively creating content on their blog?	Manual		
Content	Blog Pages Indexed	site:domain.com/blog		
Content	Overall Quality of content	Manual		
Content	How many blog posts per month(Past year)	Google Search		
Content	Avg # of images in articles	SEO Page Analyzer		
Content	Are they embedding video in articles?	Manual		
Content	Top traffic Content pages (1) *filter for blog url	SEM Rush		
Content	Top traffic Content pages (2) *filter for blog url	SEM Rush		
Content	Top traffic Content pages (3) *filter for blog url	SEM Rush		
Content	How many shares past year top 3 pieces of content (1)	Ahrefs		
Content	How many shares past year top 3 pieces of content (2)	Ahrefs		
Content	How many shares past year top 3 pieces of content (3)	Ahrefs		
Content	How many words on their product pages?	SEO Book		
Content	How is their OnPage SEO (Htags, links, images, etc)	SEO Page Analyzer		
Content	Avg # of words per article	SEO Book		
Content	What type of content is getting the most shares	Ahrefs		

It's not enough to just have this data, the analysis is where the magic really happens. That means that we need to spend a lot of time internally reviewing the data and using that to build actionable insights from it.

A few examples:

- Understanding how much content you should create
- Understanding how many links you'll need to acquire
- Understanding if you should alter pricing, play with coupons, free giveaways, etc
- Understanding how long you'll need to invest in solid SEO to overtake competitors (THIS IS KEY)

It's difficult to read spreadsheets - if you're working with a client or internal leadership team, we recommend using a slidedeck with visuals to help communicate what the data's saying.

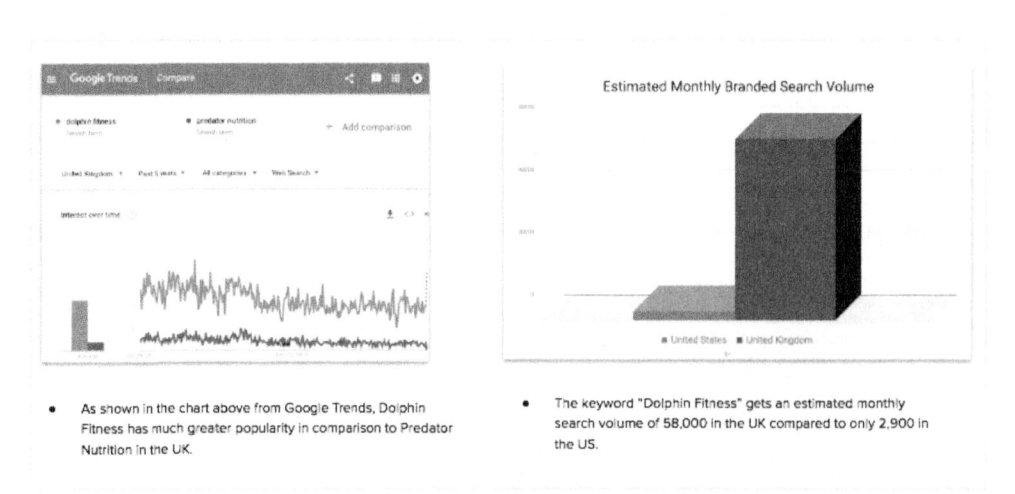

- As shown in the chart above from Google Trends, Dolphin Fitness has much greater popularity in comparison to Predator Nutrition in the UK.
- The keyword "Dolphin Fitness" gets an estimated monthly search volume of 58,000 in the UK compared to only 2,900 in the US.

Detailed analysis should be pushed into the execution phase of your campaign. Our team does so by keeping a simple matrix in Google Sheets that has all of our findings, which are ready to be added to a client's project plan at a moment's notice.

A	B	C	D	E	F
Date	Client	Bucket	Item	Discussed w/ Team?	Added to Plan?
10/9/2017	WEBRIS	Links	Need to review ALL anchor texts and article quality	No	No
10/9/2017	Predator	SEO	Predator keywords that Phil sent over need to be integrated into our targets for them. https://docs.google.com/spreadsheets/d/1d4sSifn--Cy6wn5HLUOKSlppPT0d-FvLDtsdwcJA|yc/edit#gid=0 What are we doing with? https://docs.google.com/spreadsheets/d/1IU0mJgXKFzRYWKX6SyIqnCDESgSv7i70JB6VRyHCeos/edit#gid=1218751978 The plan was to turn these into target pages and do the WQA which is in our Task schedule for Maria. We need to reconcile what Phil sent over with our KW gap analysis. There's too many keyword spreadsheets floating around and I'm not sure what to set as target pages. Currently there's 15 target pages for which we haven't built much links to - Cesar	Yes	Yes
10/9/2017	Banana Print	Content	Status on content going live? Do we have access to their blog?	Yes	Yes
10/9/2017	Truval	Links	Difference between what's showing in LIVE (outreach file) and what's in their client folder. Check to make sure live links are tracking properly.	Yes	Yes
10/9/2017	Aid In Recovery	Links	Review link plan, strategy, targets https://docs.google.com/spreadsheets/d/1cWxv95WebvEhGA_u214SB9wZb2yB	No	No

If you're using our project management system, we record our notes in the "Actions" tab. That way we can review internally and build an action plan based on our findings. It also ensures we're taking these insights and pushing them into our client's individual project plans for execution in the future.

As I mentioned before, it's important to understand your competitors, but *not obsess over them*. There are so many factors that we humans can't see. So, you can literally drive yourself crazy trying to deconstruct a competitor's website. You need to understand what the landscape looks like, but your primary focus should always be on **your site**.

> **Visit www.theblueprint.website**
> **to check out the competitive analysis template.**

1.4 - How to Manage Your SEO Campaign

Project management isn't all that sexy, so most SEOs overlook it. It has nothing to do with tactics, hacks or driving growth. **It's about being organized and holding your team accountable for what needs to be done.**

More importantly, a project plan can double as a roadmap. As a client, if you hire a company to do SEO for you, but you don't know what that involves, the project plan is your reference.

Back when WEBRIS was only a few months old, a prospective client approached us about doing SEO work for them. They found us because, at that time, I was highly active creating long-form content to market the agency.

The client loved my content and they assumed that was what our agency's SEO service entailed. While content is a cornerstone of any great SEO service, there's a lot of things that need to get done before we move to the content portion of the campaign.

Ideally, we would've made that crystal clear at the beginning of that relationship with a project plan the client could approve. Project plans are black and white – if the client says yes, you know they're on board. They won't have unrealistic expectations and it saves you from disputes down the line.

But it didn't work out that way in real life. At that time we were only using project plans to manage our internal team, the client had little visibility into what we were working on. This made it impossible to communicate effectively and manage expectations. Within 30 days of hiring us, they fired us.

Lesson learned. We started developing a detailed project management system that would keep clients informed and our team on track. Project management isn't just about being organized and providing an excellent service, though – it's the cornerstone of building a scalable business.

With all the moving pieces that go into an advanced SEO campaign, **you will fail if you don't have a system to help you manage everything.**

> **Visit www.theblueprint.website**
> **to check out our custom built project management system.**

Processes are critical to your SEO practice

One of the biggest challenges every SEO agency faces is scaling. Anyone can run a one-man show doing SEO for small businesses, but if you want to play in the big leagues, you can't approach the work without a gameplan.

If you do things right, at some point, you will have too many clients to manage without the help of a team.

With WEBRIS, that team building process happened almost all at once. One minute, we were hiring our second full-time employee, then a third. At the same time, we were laying the foundation for what would become an impressive offshore team and signing up two or three new clients per week.

It was madness.

One thing you notice real quick when you have new clients coming in all the time, is you can't reinvent the wheel with each campaign. Although every SEO campaign is unique, at a high level, there are a lot of processes that remain the same. Those processes are your framework.

If you look at it from a high level, this book is our framework. It covers every process we use from onboarding clients to successfully completing a campaign. The sheer amount of effort we've poured into perfecting every part of that process is one of the reasons we've been able to scale our business.

Without this framework, we couldn't handle as many clients as we do. We'd have to hire more people to do the same amount of work, and they'd likely be less efficient at it. The fewer details you leave in the air, the easier managing client work and your team becomes.

To manage SEO properly you need a process. *Why?*

1. **A process is your roadmap**. SEO is overwhelming, there's dozens of things that need to get done [yesterday]. A process gives you the framework to get from point A to Z and allows you to easily manage it without pulling your hair out.

2. **A process isn't set in stone, it's malleable**. Most people think a process forces you to do things a certain way - it's actually the opposite. No two SEO campaigns are the same, they vary depending on the site. It's much easier to *move* tasks than build from scratch. Having a set process / framework gives you something to start with on day 1, saving you time and headaches.

3. **A process let's you clearly see gaps**. With a process in place, you know that you need to do XYZ on a certain date. That means if you don't know how to do something, you can hire someone to take care of it. It's easier to hire someone to JUST do keyword research or write content than to take care of all your project's "SEO".

4. **A process saves you money**. A huge key to SEO (and life) is getting other people to do work for you. If you want to hire someone to do a technical audit, you're going to pay out the ass. If you want to hire someone to follow a specific process, you don't need to hire someone to "think", just to "do".

Now, in case you haven't noticed, this book is our process (at a high level) - I developed these "5 phases" over a long period of time. My primary goal with this book is help you adopt my 5-phase system, while giving you the tools to adjust it so it becomes unique to you.

Building your processes

It sounds basic, but the process is really just a step by step list. Our "5 phases" started as a list on a whiteboard. If you have one, it's a great place to start yours - a pen and paper will do just fine as well.

Your individual process will depend heavily on a number of factors:

1. Are you doing SEO for one website or hundreds?

2. How much do you really know about SEO?

3. Have you done SEO work in the past? Did it go well negatively?

4. Do you have enough resources (money) and a team to help you execute your process?

Not to over simplify it, but all you need to do is write down **what you need to do** - you should be able to derive almost everything from this book, but you'll still need it in your own formatting.

As mentioned earlier, the framework for SEO is simple:

1. Proper technical structure

2. Building pages with robust content, around the keywords you want to rank for

3. Promoting your website through acquiring links on relevant websites

With that in mind, you can begin to build a checklist, and this is where things get interesting:

1. Run a technical audit

2. Perform keyword research

3. Review use of keywords on website

4. Edit on page elements of key landing pages (titles, metas, etc)

5. Build topics for new content creation on blog

6. Build list of websites to guest post on

7. Build list of influencers to pitch sponsorships

Keep blowing it out – the more specific the better. Here's how I'd expand on item number one, to give you an idea of the level of detail you should be aiming for:

1. Run a technical audit

a. Review indexation status in Google Search Console

b. Review use of XML sitemaps in Google Search Console

c. Review directives in Robots.txt file

d. Review use of canonical tags

e. Review use of Schema on key landing pages

f. Review speed of key landing pages

Again, this is a grossly oversimplified list - the point is simply to get you thinking about your campaign in terms of a process. If you don't have the knowledge to build this list, just use this book - I'm literally giving you our process.

Building a project plan

There are certain elements you need in a project plan to ensure it runs smoothly.

We like to build our plans based on a *task + deliverable + action* schedule.

- **Deliverables.** These are the items that "move the needle" on the campaign and what we send to clients, as well as discuss with them. For example, our keyword research process produces a document the client can look at and understand how it will help them grow their traffic. That document itself is the deliverable, so it needs to be polished.

- **Tasks**. Carry out enough tasks and you've got a deliverable on your hands, baby. Tasks are what we track in terms of "status" and they map into the larger deliverable.

- **Actions**. Deliverables don't only give you the chance to touch base with clients. They also mean you've progressed enough to know what actions you need to carry out next. For example, if you complete an "on page" assessment for your website, that means the next step should probably be the need to change page titles, internal links, etc. If you don't manage these action items, things will fall through the cracks and your campaign will fail.

Example:

- **Deliverable** = Keyword research.

- **Tasks** =

    o Find primary and secondary keywords for impact pages

    o Assigned "journey" (aka intent) to each keyword

    o Analyze top 3 results for each keyword (links, DA, etc)

    o Build KW research deck + create analysis for client

- **Actions**

    o Approve list of keywords

    o Prioritize the list of keywords

    o Add keywords to rank tracker

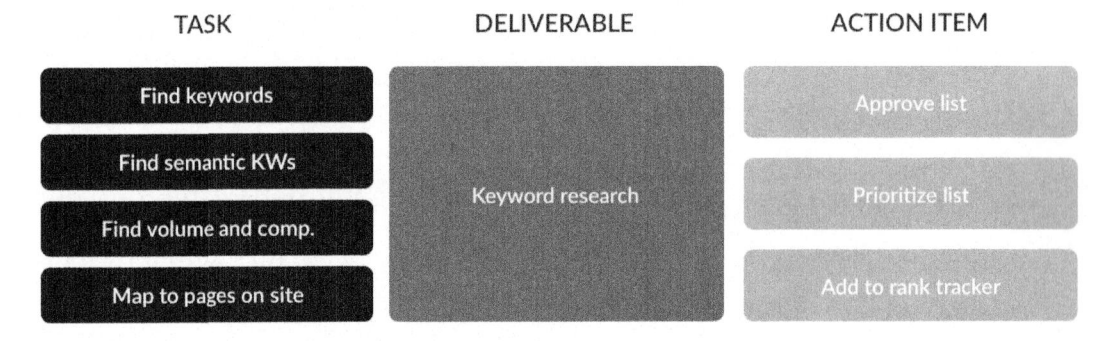

TASK	DELIVERABLE	ACTION ITEM
Find keywords		Approve list
Find semantic KWs	Keyword research	Prioritize list
Find volume and comp.		Add to rank tracker
Map to pages on site		

A look into our internal project plan

In terms of tools to use to manage your campaign, you have a wide range of options. If you are only working on 1 site (or in house), I suggest a tool like Trello, Basecamp or Asana. However, if you're managing multiple SEO campaigns I suggest you go with Google Sheets. Yes, there's dozens of project management tools out there but none are built for the specific needs of an SEO campaign.

There's a reason why the world runs on spreadsheets. They're flexible, cheap to use, and with Google Sheets, you can work in a shared environment. That's all you need.

Our entire project management system runs in Google Sheets. We use different tabs within the same file to stay organized.

Tasks tab

This is where we house the day-to-day tasks we need to take care of to move the needle - aka our project plan. It includes:

- **Task start date**. The date the task needs to begin.
- **Task completion date**. The deadline for that task to be completed.
- **Owner**. The person who is assigned to complete the task.
- **Project**. For us, this means the client that task is for. If you're an in-house marketer, you could use different marketing tactics (i.e. design, social, paid search, etc)
- **Deliverable**. The deliverable that the task maps to (i.e. keyword research).
- **Task**. Specific items needed to complete the deliverable.
- **Status**. Where that task is on the road to completion (i.e. scheduled, working, delayed, late, completed, etc).
- **Template**. In this column we drop a link to the template for that deliverable. All of our deliverables use a single template that we modify

for each client. It keeps us organized and it means we don't have to start from scratch with each deliverable.

- **Presentation**. If there is a presentation deck attached to the deliverable, the link goes here. For example, we don't like to just send a client a list of 1,000 keywords. A lot of clients need help visualizing the data, which is why also have a template Google Slides Deck that helps us communicate what that data means.

- **Training**. Everything we do has a training attached to it. This is a large part of building a functional process that scales. We don't just ask someone to do keyword research, we have a step by step process + video training series for them to learn our way to do (aka, the right way). This is why we're able to use so much offshore labor and still deliver better quality work than any agency in the world (yeah, I went there).

- **Notes**. Any internal communication that takes place between team members.

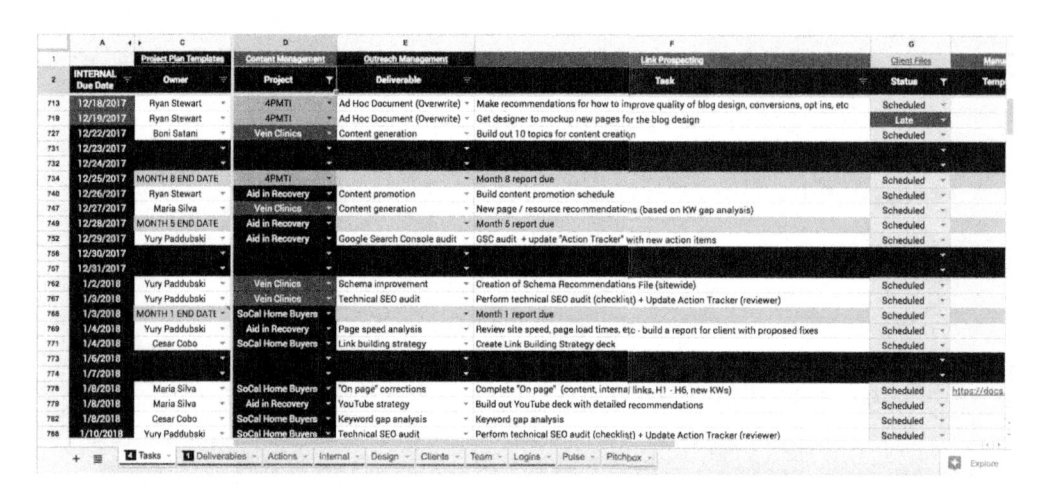

This is what our project management file looks like. It looks complicated, but I promise it's a simple solution. We track all of our clients / projects in a single file, this allows me to take a peek when I need to and understand where a client is in their campaign.

Deliverables tab

After a Task is marked as "completed", the Google Sheets file automatically moves it to the Deliverables tab for review (before sending to client):

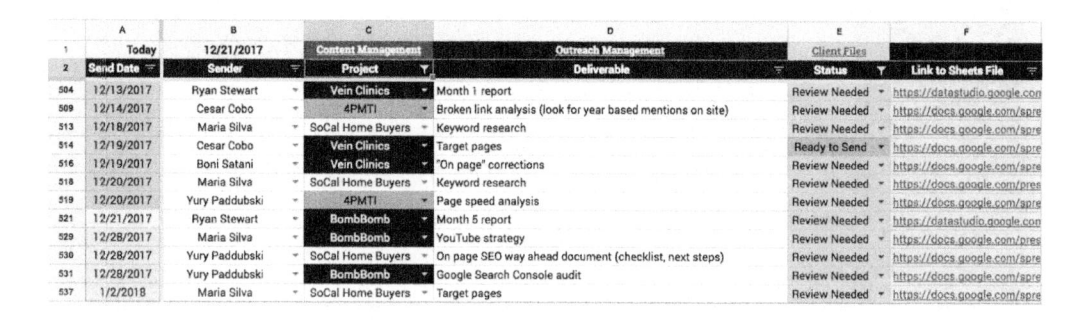

Actions tab

Anything that requires further action gets added to the next tab, Actions:

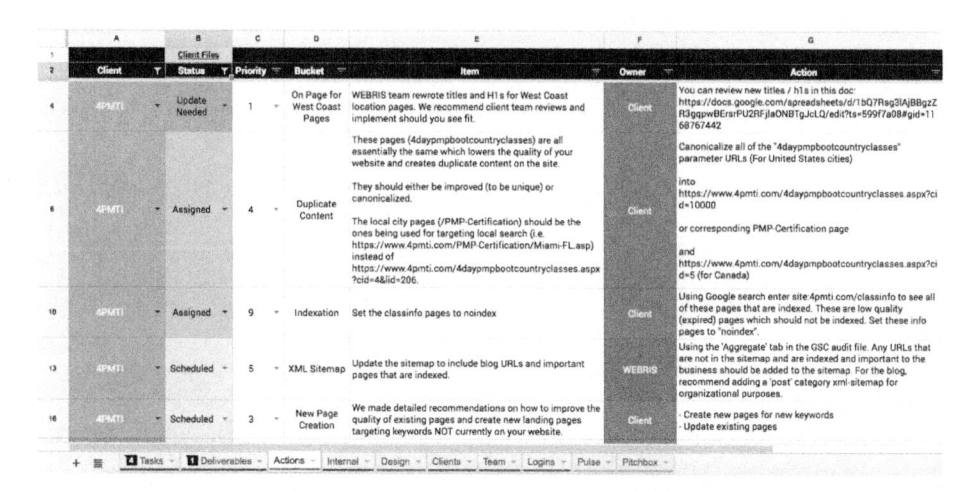

This has a nice built-in flow from Task -> Deliverable -> Action Item. It ensures nothing falls through the cracks.

Pre-building project plans

We have a pre-built project plan that we use to launch every client campaign, regardless what niche it falls under.

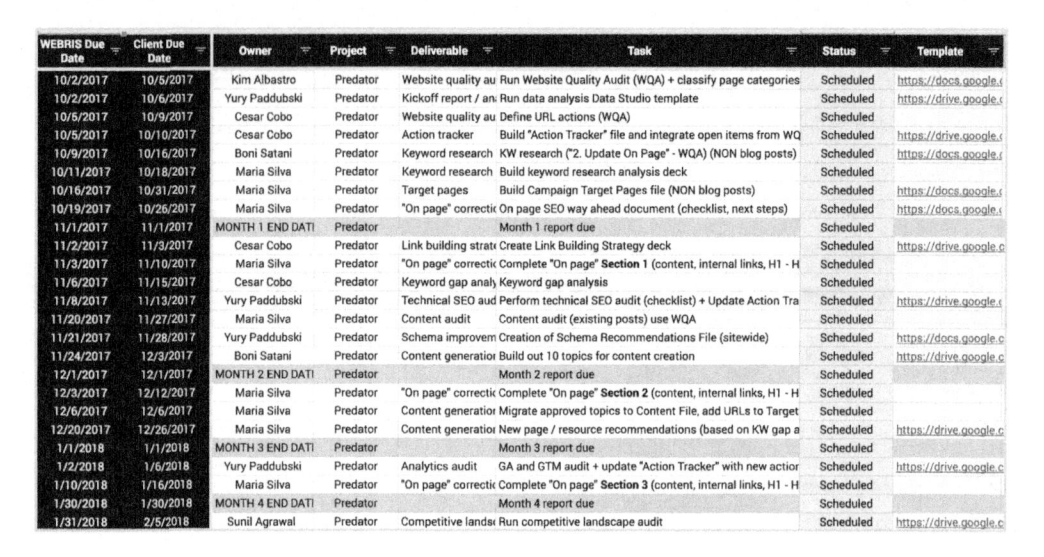

WEBRIS Due Date	Client Due Date	Owner	Project	Deliverable	Task	Status	Template
10/2/2017	10/5/2017	Kim Albastro	Predator	Website quality au	Run Website Quality Audit (WQA) + classify page categories	Scheduled	https://docs.google.c
10/2/2017	10/6/2017	Yury Paddubski	Predator	Kickoff report / an	Run data analysis Data Studio template	Scheduled	https://drive.google.c
10/5/2017	10/9/2017	Cesar Cobo	Predator	Website quality au	Define URL actions (WQA)	Scheduled	
10/5/2017	10/10/2017	Cesar Cobo	Predator	Action tracker	Build "Action Tracker" file and integrate open items from WQ	Scheduled	https://drive.google.c
10/9/2017	10/16/2017	Boni Satani	Predator	Keyword research	KW research ("2. Update On Page" - WQA) (NON blog posts)	Scheduled	https://docs.google.c
10/11/2017	10/18/2017	Maria Silva	Predator	Keyword research	Build keyword research analysis deck	Scheduled	
10/16/2017	10/31/2017	Maria Silva	Predator	Target pages	Build Campaign Target Pages file (NON blog posts)	Scheduled	https://docs.google.c
10/19/2017	10/26/2017	Maria Silva	Predator	"On page" correcti	On page SEO way ahead document (checklist, next steps)	Scheduled	https://docs.google.c
11/1/2017	11/1/2017	MONTH 1 END DATI	Predator		Month 1 report due	Scheduled	
11/2/2017	11/3/2017	Cesar Cobo	Predator	Link building strat	Create Link Building Strategy deck	Scheduled	https://drive.google.c
11/3/2017	11/10/2017	Maria Silva	Predator	"On page" correcti	Complete "On page" Section 1 (content, internal links, H1 - H	Scheduled	
11/6/2017	11/15/2017	Cesar Cobo	Predator	Keyword gap anal	Keyword gap analysis	Scheduled	
11/8/2017	11/13/2017	Yury Paddubski	Predator	Technical SEO aud	Perform technical SEO audit (checklist) + Update Action Tra	Scheduled	https://drive.google.c
11/20/2017	11/27/2017	Maria Silva	Predator	Content audit	Content audit (existing posts) use WQA	Scheduled	
11/21/2017	11/28/2017	Yury Paddubski	Predator	Schema improver	Creation of Schema Recommendations File (sitewide)	Scheduled	https://docs.google.c
11/24/2017	12/3/2017	Boni Satani	Predator	Content generatio	Build out 10 topics for content creation	Scheduled	https://drive.google.c
12/1/2017	12/1/2017	MONTH 2 END DATI	Predator		Month 2 report due	Scheduled	
12/3/2017	12/12/2017	Maria Silva	Predator	"On page" correcti	Complete "On page" Section 2 (content, internal links, H1 - H	Scheduled	
12/6/2017	12/6/2017	Maria Silva	Predator	Content generatio	Migrate approved topics to Content File, add URLs to Target	Scheduled	
12/20/2017	12/26/2017	Maria Silva	Predator	Content generatio	New page / resource recommendations (based on KW gap a	Scheduled	https://drive.google.c
1/1/2018	1/1/2018	MONTH 3 END DATI	Predator		Month 3 report due	Scheduled	
1/2/2018	1/6/2018	Yury Paddubski	Predator	Analytics audit	GA and GTM audit + update "Action Tracker" with new action	Scheduled	https://drive.google.c
1/10/2018	1/16/2018	Maria Silva	Predator	"On page" correcti	Complete "On Page" Section 3 (content, internal links, H1 - H	Scheduled	
1/30/2018	1/30/2018	MONTH 4 END DATI	Predator		Month 4 report due	Scheduled	
1/31/2018	2/5/2018	Sunil Agrawal	Predator	Competitive lands	Run competitive landscape audit	Scheduled	https://drive.google.c

Having a prebuilt solution allows us to quickly onboard new campaigns. What's more, using Google Sheets as our project management tool allows us to make changes on the fly.

After going through the discovery and data analysis phase, you should have a lot of new insights into the campaign and how to proceed. For example:

- You have a small website that's built on WordPress that you know has no technical issues. That means you can push the technical audit back 6 months and focus on content creation for the time being.

- You find that your website has weak authority compared to your competitors, which means link acquisition should be your top priority. In other words, you may want to begin prospecting for link opportunities on day 1 as opposed to day 50.

- You've noticed your top keywords are local, so you want to focus on optimizing your Google My Business Listing, building citations, and more.

Project management is an ongoing process. That means you need to adjust your plans as you move along depending on client feedback or new tasks you need to take care of. Without those plans, you're flying blind, so don't underestimate the importance of project management.

Once you have a process and plan in place, you can start to think about who will take care of each task, which is what we'll talk about now.

> **Visit www.theblueprint.website**
> **to check out our Project Management system.**

Assigning resources to tasks

You can do end-to-end SEO yourself (I used to). However, it's a tremendous drain on your time - I strongly suggest you look into hiring help (especially if you're a consultant / agency).

More importantly, doing everything yourself is not a scalable model. After all, no matter how knowledgeable you are, there are only so many hours in a day you can spend working.

The problem with hiring is most SEO professionals are self trained - there's no college degree for this (yet). That's not a bad thing, per se, but it means finding someone with reasonable rates and who knows what they're doing is even more difficult.

Luckily, you have this book. After you're done reading, you'll have a firm grasp on SEO and what it takes to run a successful campaigns. Armed with that information, and with this book as a reference, you'll be able to onboard new hires.

Personally, I'm a big fan of looking outside your borders for great talent. There's no reason why you should limit yourself to local hire only nowadays. Instead, look for the best possible hires, no matter where they're located.

Just to give you an idea, we have team members in Venezuela (design), Ukraine (technical SEO) and Philippines (general data entry type work) - **we wouldn't be where we're at without them.**

I don't want to get into the nitty gritty of outsourcing work, as I have a blog post that does it better.

> **Visit www.theblueprint.website**
> **to check out our video series on staffing an SEO team.**

For my agency folks reading this, I want to explore agency structure in more detail.

Traditional agency model

- **C Suite/VP/Lead.** Manages highest level of relationship, sales.
- **Account Manager.** Manages the client day-to-day, relationship, scope, etc.
- **Project Manager.** Oversees tasks, deliverables, communications with clients.

- **Consultants, Analysts, Specialists**. The people who execute the tasks in the project plan. They are generally responsible for a wide range of tasks within a certain bucket (i.e content specialists, technical specialists, etc).

- **Marketing.** These are the people in charge of finding new clients, building your brand, overseeing content, and social media. A lot of agencies overlook their work, but it's critical if you want a scalable business.

- **Finance.** Unless you're running a one-man operation, any agency can benefit from a dedicated finance specialist or bookkeeper. Don't read anything to the fact they don't show up on the graph below, I was just pressed for space!

C Suite / VP / Lead

Account Managers - Project/ Program Managers

Consultants / Analysts / Specialists

Naturally, this is grossly oversimplified, but it's the model most agencies use. However, I had a number of issues with it:

1. **It works better for large agencies with massive clients**. Large agencies can do it because they charge an hourly rate which is way more than what they pay that person (i.e. $350/hour for a junior analyst whom they pay $50k/year). When you're a small agency just getting started, your margins are much smaller (if there are any at all). You can't afford

to pay account people + position specialists a full time salary – it just doesn't add up.

2. **Clients weren't crazy about it**. Most account managers and analysts don't provide enough value for what you're paying. Once clients realize this, they start thinking, "Why am I wasting money on this?"

3. **If you lose a client, you need to cut people**. Two - three times a year that large agency would have mass layoffs when a big client decided not to renew their contract. When you have a team (i.e. a pyramid) of people working on just a single account, you don't have a choice but to let those people go if the account dies. It's the nature of the business, but it's a shitty, shitty thing to do. Moreover, if your business can't handle client turnover, then you're not building a sustainable model.

4. **It doesn't scale well**. This is by far my biggest issue. The traditional agency model means **when you take on new client accounts, you have to onboard new teams**. That means increased recruiting and HR costs, as well as all the other joys that come along with staffing. Another big problem with this model is you're not taking full advantage of your top talent since you're limiting them to one or two client accounts at the most. If you've ever employed a "superstar", then you know that's a problem.

The Blueprint Model

When I started my agency, I knew I had the tools to run successful campaigns for clients. The problem was, if I wanted to achieve real scale, I needed to find a model that was more sustainable and efficient than what traditional agencies use.

Here's what our modern organization chart looks like:

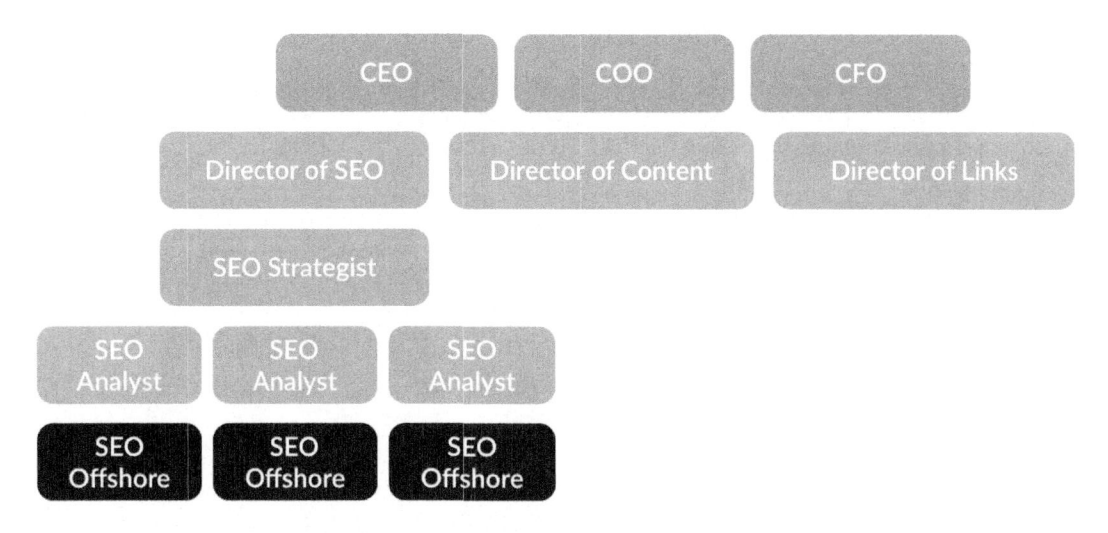

```
        CEO              COO              CFO

     Director of SEO    Director of Content    Director of Links

     SEO Strategist

   SEO         SEO         SEO
  Analyst     Analyst     Analyst
   SEO         SEO         SEO
  Offshore   Offshore    Offshore
```

At the top, you still have one or two people that manage all the big picture decisions. Although you're the CEO of your agency, I'm a big proponent of having dedicated Financial and Operations Officers, to help you handle the day-to-day tasks. Finance, in particular, isn't something you should tackle unless it's something you know inside and out (I'm talking payroll, taxes, invoices, and more).

Those are pretty traditional positions, though, so let's go a little deeper and talk about everyone else's roles in the agency:

- **Directors of SEO, Content, and Links.** We like to have a level of management in between specialists and the big picture decision makers. This helps filter the amount of work you have to do on a daily basis and frees you up to strategize. We like to tackle SEO, Content, and Links at a separate level because they each require such a specific set of tasks. This separation enables us to better train our specialists, which we'll introduce in a minute.

- **Strategists.** These would be the equivalent of project or account managers in a classic organization chart. They make sure that your specialists don't miss deadlines, that deliverables get out, and more. In short, they're the people that make day-to-day operations possible.

- **Analysts.** Our analysts are SEO specialists who know how we operate in-and-out. They manage tasks and deliverables for all our client campaigns and make sure everything is perfect. However, they're not the people that take care of all the small tasks that make up an SEO campaign.

- **Offshore or niche specialists.** These are the people who execute the day-to-day tasks. They are hourly workers, ranging from $5 - $15/hour depending on their skill set. They are highly trained in very specific subsets of our service and that's all they focus on. For example, we have specialists who only do keyword research - that's it. By narrowing down the tasks your team of specialists do, you allow them to hyper specialize, which can drastically increase productivity.

The primary takeaway from our model is, instead of asking one person to become an expert in dozens of tasks, we spread out the work among highly-specialized workers. As you move up the ladder, you have plenty of experts that do know SEO inside and out, who make sure that everything is up to our very high standards.

Our hyperspecialization model comes with plenty of other benefits:

- **Ability to be hyper productive without compromising the quality of the work.** In fact, the quality has gotten better because we're able to zoom in on inefficiencies in the process and make improvements instantly.

- **It's easier to manage.** Using our project management system, we have a pulse on everything going on. We always know where we're standing, which means clients also know everything that's happening (in fact, it's shared in real time via Google Sheets).

- **Hiring and new employee onboarding is a breeze.** When we bring on a new niche specialist, they know exactly what's expected of them and are able to fit into the process within a day.

- **It's cheaper, which makes our model more sustainable.** As a business owner, this is huge for me. I like to make money on the money we make - aka profit margins are crucial. While the pyramid model has more predictable margins, they can't be improved.

To be fair, we didn't reinvent the wheel, but we sure as hell made it roll more smoothly.

> **Visit www.theblueprint.website to check out our video series on who to hire first when building an SEO agency.**

PHASE 2

The Improving Process

The discovery process is over, so now it's time to start getting our hands dirty with your campaign. The first thing we like to do is start by existing pages on your website and get to work on improving them. After all, it takes a lot less work to improve on what's already there than to build from scratch. With that in mind, let's go over what you can do to improve your website right now:

- **2.1 - The Website quality audit.** This is a proprietary audit we designed to understand page level performance and issues on websites. It helps us understand the value of each page on a website and the exact "action" we need to take on it.

- **2.2 - Basic SEO Assets Audit**. Not to be confused with the website quality audit, this process looks at traditional SEO items like sitemaps, robots.txt and status codes.

- **2.3 - In-Depth Keyword Analysis**. We like to break down keyword research in two parts. First we take a look at the keywords you're already using and where we can improve them, then we identify new opportunities for you to target.

- **2.4 - Putting Together a List of "Target Pages"**. Nowadays, most websites are too big to keep track of every single keyword you use. The smart approach is to build a list of key pages where you want to focus your efforts on.

- **2.5 - "On-Page" SEO Audit.** The nuts and bolts of SEO still apply - titles, metas, keyword density, etc. This section looks at analyzing on page SEO for your existing assets and tweaking things to get better results.

2.1 - The Website Quality Audit (WQA)

As we covered in Phase 0, the main priority of search engines is keeping searchers happy by providing the best possible search results. For us as search professionals, that means we have to strive to make our websites "high quality" in Google's eyes. Here's what that means in practice:

1. Sites that are built according to their webmaster guidelines (Google Webmaster Guidelines).

2. Sites that are organized well and provide for easy pathing, both for visitors and search engine spiders.

3. Sites that make searchers happy by **providing content that matches what they're looking for**.

4. Sites that are popular, aka getting mentioned across the web (i.e. on blogs, social media, forums, press sites, etc).

In other words, if Google views your website as "low quality" you may experience lower crawl frequency, indexation and rankings.

> **Over the last few years a number of leading SEO experts have come out to express just how important "search satisfaction" is.**
>
> - Google's Quality Score (Moz Whiteboard Friday): moz.com/blog/organic-quality-score
>
> - Brian Dean (ecommerce case study): backlinko.com/ecommerce-seo#chapter-4-technical-seo
>
> - Bill Sebald (how to prune your website for SEO): moz.com/learn/seo/what-why-how-pruning-website-seo

Analyzing a website for these factors requires a lot of SEO data. Since there's no software in the market that can help with all these, we had to build our own using API data from a handful of tools.

Hence, we built "The Website Quality Audit". I can honestly say the buildout of this audit changed the trajectory of our agency. This gave us something proprietary to show to prospective clients that no other agency could. Now it's yours to use as you see fit.

One of the first things that we look at during our website quality audit are pages that Google might consider low quality. Then we can decide how to improve that content.

Let's break down what the audit encompasses:

1. A crawl of every page on your website

2. Each page on your website is crosswalked against vital SEO data

3. Analysis of the performance of each page on your website (in regards to "quality")

4. Analysis of the "value" of each page on your website, both to search engines and users

5. A decision about what action to take to improve the value for each page

With that in mind, let's talk about how we build, run, and analyze this report for your website.

NOTE: Things are about to get a bit technical. We're going to teach you step by step how to run your very own Website Quality Audit. The version we use everyday runs in Google BigQuery - it's fully automated and, well, amazing.

You can run a [modified] Website Quality Audit using Google Sheets, so don't worry, you don't need access to any premium tools to make this process work. If you need help, contact us about running the Google BigQuery version for your site.

> **Visit www.theblueprint.website to check out the Google Sheets free version of The Website Quality Audit.**

Gathering all the data inputs

To analyze the quality of your website, we need to compile "SEO data" from multiple sources. The sources we like to use are:

1. XML Sitemap(s)

An XML sitemap tells search engines what pages make up your website and where to focus their crawling efforts. Some websites have more than one sitemap, depending on what kind of content they focus on (for images, video, site sections, etc).

We like to start with sitemaps to check if they're missing any key pages from the website we're working on. If there are any key pages missing, adding them to your sitemap is a simple way to get a quick SEO win.

Assuming you have a one-sitemap setup, you can access it via Google Search Console (Crawl > Sitemaps).

For the next steps, we recommend you extract this data and use Excel to navigate it. You can extract your sitemap in *.xml* format using this awesome free tool from Rob Hammond:

https://robhammond.co/tools/xml-extract

2. Screaming Frog Site Crawl

Whereas your sitemaps only includes the URLs you add to it - Screaming Frog will return every single URL on your server. With this data, we can quickly find out if there are any gaps or pages we didn't know about.

On top of having an awesome name and providing you with a list of every URL on your website, Screaming Frog also extracts the following SEO data from each page:

- Title

- Meta description

- H1

- Word count

- Canonical link element

- URl status code

- NOINDEX directives

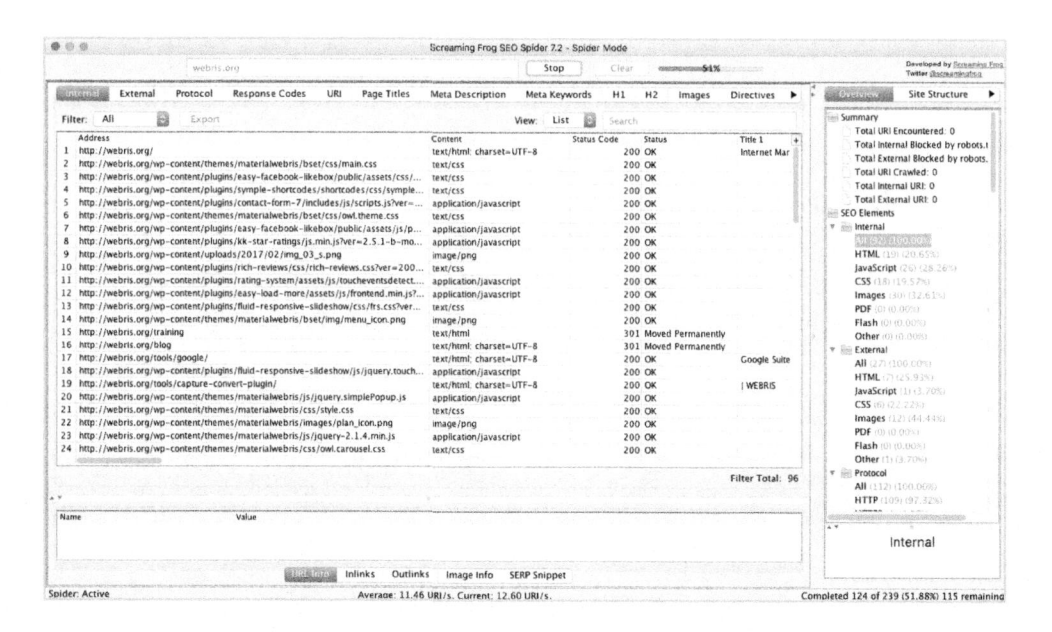

3. Ahrefs DOFOLLOW Links Report

Links are one of the top ranking factors in Google's algorithm, which means we need to understand how many links each page on your website has.

To do so, we can use Ahrefs, a tool that lets you check who's linking to your website, and provides you with a handy report that includes all those links.

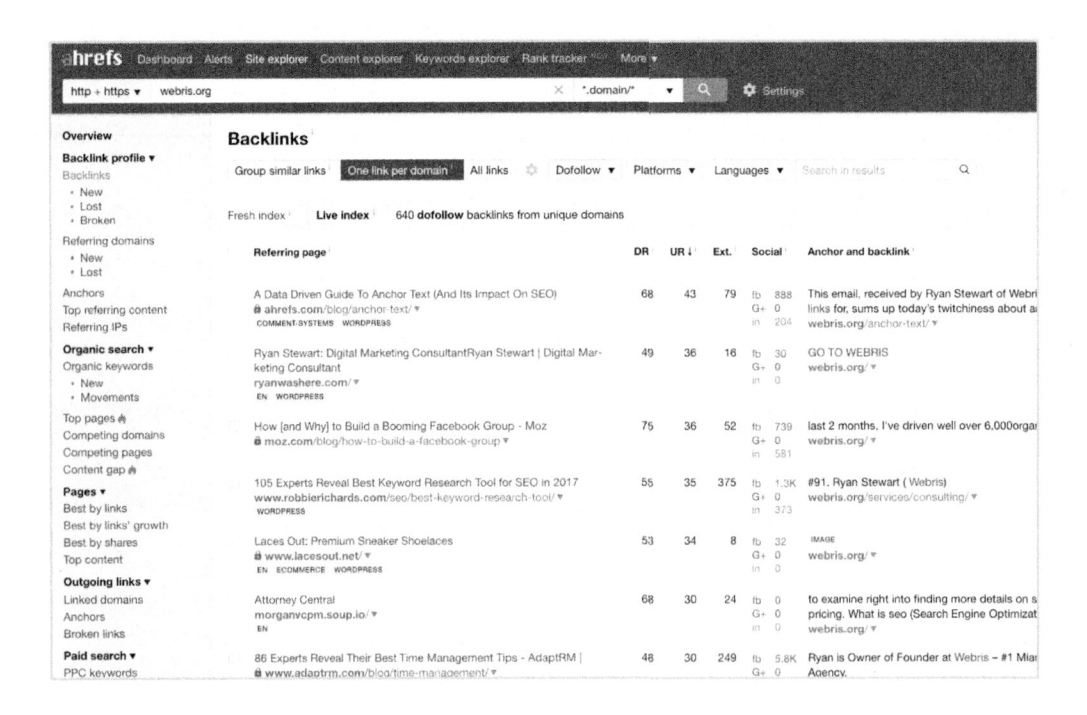

4. SEMrush

SEMrush is a tool that lets us check the keyword rankings of all the pages on your website. We can use SEMrush to tell us the "top" keyword for every page on your website. For every report, you also get specific rankings and search volume, which makes SEMrush one of our favorite tools.

With this information, we can quickly figure out what pages have real value when it comes to organic traffic. More importantly, it tells us what pages we shouldn't waste too much time on, as we mentioned in the beginning of this section.

5. Google Analytics

We use Google Analytics data to give us insights into each page's:

- Organic sessions over the last 12 months

- Organic sales over the last 12 months (if ecommerce site)

- $ conversion value over the last 12 months (if ecommerce site)

- Goal conversion rate over the last 12 months

- If that page is losing traffic over the last month (tool calculates it)

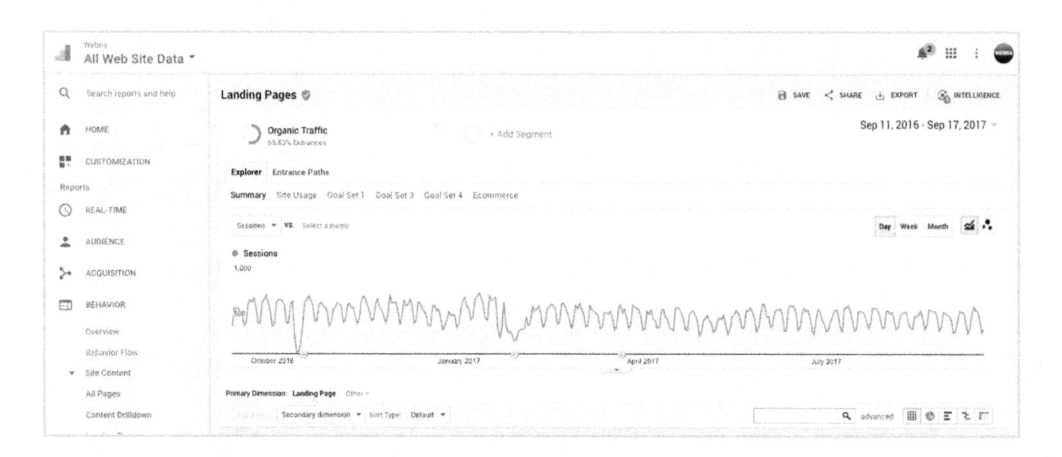

Organic traffic, conversions, or sales are the fastest way to tell the quality of a page. Simply put, the higher the numbers, the better the quality. With this tool you can quickly aggregate all that data.

6. Google Search Console

We use Google Search Console data to give us insights into each page's:

- Impressions in the SERPS over the last 90 days

- SERP Click Through Rate over the last 90 days

Crosswalking the data

We could have built this tool on a server and put it online with a nice UI. However, we chose to go with Google Sheets instead, for a number of reasons:

1. As SEO professionals, 99% of what we work on ends up in Excel or Google Sheets. That makes it much easier to submit deliverables using Google Sheets.

2. Google Sheets can connect to APIs, which means we can extract data from any source that has one.

3. Google Sheets has incredibly powerful formulas and data formatting capabilities.

With our tool, all we have to do is get the CSV file inputs from Screaming Frog, Ahrefs, and SEMrush, and let all that information pour in.

What you're left with is an itemized list of URLs with the necessary list of SEO data to make an educated decision about what to do with that page.

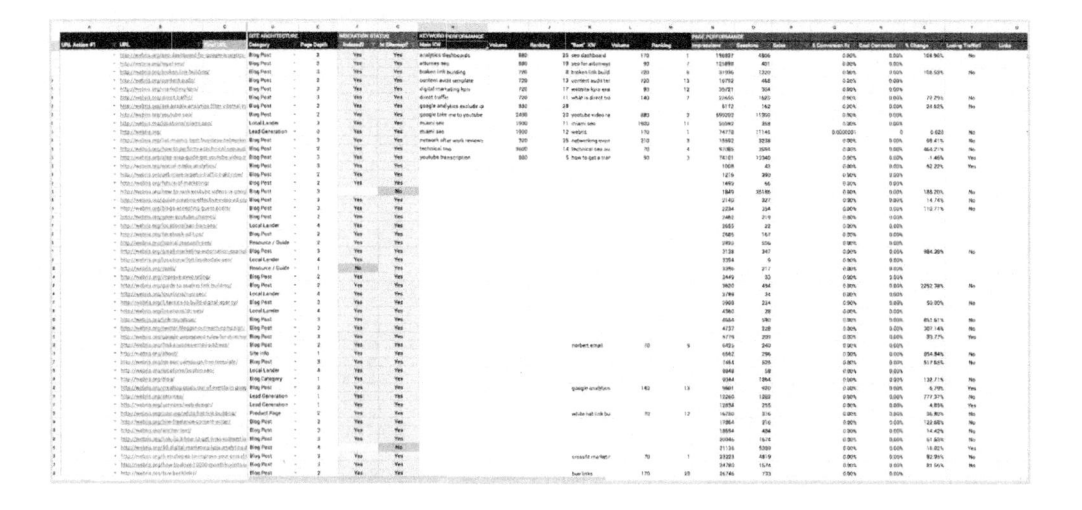

Let's take a look under the hood...

Since you have access to a version of the WQA, I'm not going to go into too much detail on how we pull, process and format all this data.

Here's a quick synopsis of the Google Sheets formulas running behind the scenes to make this powerful audit work:

IMPORTXML, which pulls in URLs from your sitemaps

=importxml("https://webris.org/post-sitemap.xml","//*[local-name()='url']/*[local-name() ='loc']")

- QUERY, which filters out only the columns you'll need from those CSV exports above

> =query('CSV Import'!A1:G,"select G, A, D, B where G != '' and B <= 30 and D >= 300 order by D desc",1)
>
> - VLOOKUP, which is used to aggregate data on a URL-level
>
> =vlookup('CSV Import'!A1:Z, Aggregation!B3, 4, 0)
>
> If you're interested in learning more about how to write advanced Sheets formulas for SEO, check out www.codingisforlosers.com[4]

Classifying website section

With the data in place, we can start evaluating the results. First, we need to understand what ***type*** of page each URL is.

Our BigQuery version automates this, but if you're running the free version you will need to do this manually. That means tagging each URL under a specific section or category (i.e. product page, product category, etc.). It's a tedious process, but once it's done, you will be able to filter all that data by section in a matter of seconds.

Ae classify pages using 8 different tags:

Tag	Detail	Examples
Product Page	This tag applies to *eCommerce websites only*. A product page is where they are selling the product (i.e. cart, price, etc).	- Product page 1[5] - Product page 2[6]

---

[4] http://www.codingisforlosers.com/
[5] https://www.lacesout.net/product/jordan-2-laces/
[6] http://www.predatornutrition.com/protein-powder/optimum-nutrition/gold-standard-100-whey.html

		- Product page 3[7]
Product Category	This tag applies to *eCommerce websites only*. A product category page is where the website lists their products based product type. For example, a website that sells shoes could have category pages for brands like Nike, Reebok, etc. Each of these pages will filter products to show them based on category.	- Product category page 1[8] - Product category page 2[9]
Local Lander	This tag applies to *local websites only*. A local lander is the dedicated page to a given location. If the business has multiple locations, each store should have it's own dedicated landing page. If the business only has 1 location, this can apply to the home page.	- Local lander 1[10] - Local lander 2[11] - Local lander 3[12]
Lead Generation	This tag applies to pages on a site that are geared towards generating leads. For example, an attorney's website could be trying to rank for keywords related to the different services they provide (DUI attorney, Criminal defense attorney, etc). Each of these keywords should have a dedicated landing page targeting those keywords. NOTE. There is a lot of similarity between Local Lander and Lead Generation pages. In fact, the pages	- Lead generation 1[13] - Lead generation 2[14]

---

[7] http://jrdunn.com/michele-watch-cape-topaz-powder-pink-watch.html
[8] https://www.lacesout.net/product-category/sneaker-replacement-laces/
[9] http://www.predatornutrition.com/shop-by-brand/fusion-supplements
[10] http://webris.org/locations/miami-seo/
[11] http://drsmood.com/cafes/wynwood-fl/
[12] https://www.24hourfitness.com/Website/Club/624
[13] https://www.moonclerk.com/payment-solutions/accept-donations-online/
[14] https://www.opiates.com/rapid-detox/

	are the same with a simple distinction - if the page is targeting local terms, tag it with Local Lander. If the page is targeting national or NON-geo fenced terms, make it Lead Generation.	
Blog Post	This tag applies to blog posts. Some sites will have /blog/ or /news/ (or something similar) built into the URL structure.	- Blog post 1[15] - Blog post 2[16]
Blog Category	This tag applies to categories of blog posts. These are generally used on bigger sites that publish a lot of content in order to better organize posts.	- Blog category 1[17] - Blog category 2[18]
Resource / Guide	Similar to a blog post, but more in depth and robust. Resources or guides NOT connected to the blog, but instead are stand alone pages or site sections.	- Resource guide 1[19] - Resource / guide 2[20]
Site Info	This is a broad tag that applies to a wide range of pages. Essentially, these are the required pages to build out a full site but generally have little SEO (i.e. traffic potential) value. This can include cart pages, terms and services, contact page, shipping, FAQ and more.	- Site info 1[21] - Site info 2[22] - Site info 3

---

[15] https://www.lacesout.net/how-to-clean-your-air-jordan-sneakers/
[16] http://www.predatornutrition.com/articlesdetail?cid=mr-olympia-winners
[17] http://searchengineland.com/library/channel/seo
[18] https://www.forbes.com/leadership/
[19] https://moz.com/beginners-guide-to-seo
[20] https://www.quicksprout.com/the-advanced-guide-to-seo/
[21] https://www.lacesout.net/about/
[22] http://www.predatornutrition.com/customer-service/shipping-and-returns/shipping.html

While this is a manual process reviewing each page, you **can** use the power of Google Sheets to filter by URL structure and bulk your analysis. Usually, it's pretty easy to spot what section each page falls under by taking a look at its URL structure, which makes your life a lot easier.

For example, filter by URL and look use folder structure as a guide (i.e. /blog/, /services/, /products/, etc). This will greatly speed up the process.

Analysis of the report results

At this stage, your head might be spinning due to all the information we've gone over so far. Let's stop and recap for a second.

Here's what we we're working with at the moment:

- Every URL on your website laid out in Google Sheets

- Every URL on your website with a ton of valuable SEO data like "page type", keyword rankings, organic traffic, links, page title and more

- Every URL on your website classified by page type

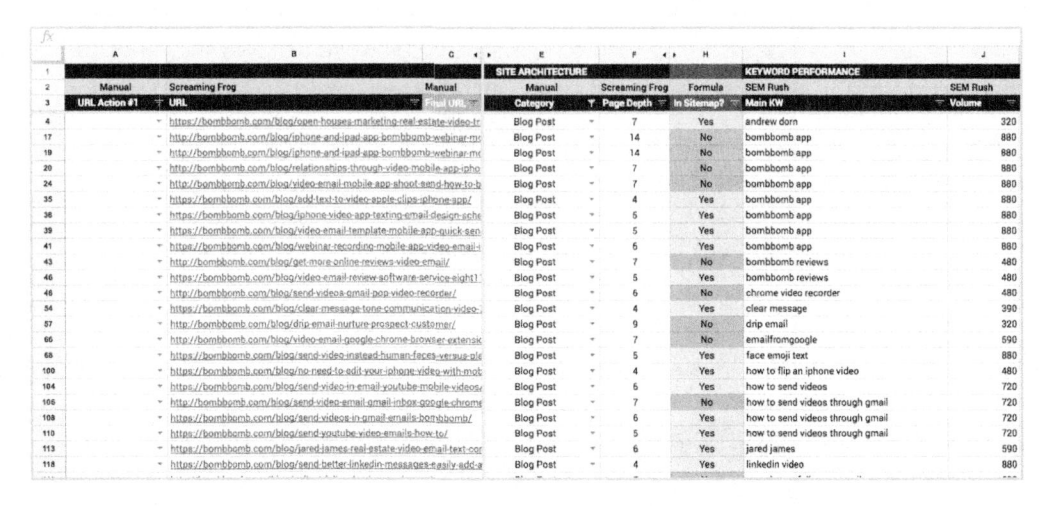

From an SEO point of view, we have everything we need to analyze the quality of each page on your website, all laid out in a single spreadsheet.

Gotta love spreadsheets.

At WEBRIS, we like to assign what we call "URL Actions" to every page on the website. That URL action covers what you have to do to improve it from an SEO standpoint.

We use 9 different URL actions tags which I will break down for you now:

Tag	Logic
1. Leave As Is	No further action needed on the page.
Use case	Some pages have no SEO value - this is not to say they aren't important to the website, but rather it's a waste to spend resources on. You can use this tag for pages performing well or for pages you simply want to ignore because they are irrelevant to your SEO (contact page, etc) or the pages are already well optimized.
2. Update "On Page"	Use this when you want to review the keywords, titles, meta and on page content for that URL. This can also be used for older blog posts / resource guides that you want to update with more recent information.
Use case	We will review the keyword targeting of any important page on a website. Product pages, service pages, resource guides - anything that has large SEO potential needs to be reviewed for keyword targeting. This tag simply helps us classify those pages for deeper review during keyword research.

3. Target w/ Links	If everything checks out with the page but it doesn't have rankings, the best solution is to target it with links. You can also double up to "Update On Page" and "Target w/ Links" using both action columns.
Use case	When the page is targeting the right keywords, has good on page (titles, content, etc), the main thing holding it back is likely a lack of inbound links. We use this tag sparingly, as we will like to review the keyword targeting in detail before building links to it.
4. 301	When a page serves no value to the website (both for search engines and users) you will want to 301 redirect it into a more relevant page.
Use case	301 redirects are Google's preferred guidance on removing pages from your website. If a WQA turns back duplicate content, "thin" pages, CMS auto generated cruft pages or anything you need low quality, clean it up with a 301 redirect. Yes, that's right - deleting pages can result in increased organic traffic. Ross Hudgens, CEO of Siege Media wrote in a recent blog post: *"An example of a recent audit we ran involved pruning over 3,000 pages, which resulted in organic traffic improvements. Outdated and low performing pages were removed from the site.* *The number of pages pruned was equal to roughly 15% of the entire site at the current time. Organic traffic after the project went up about 50% and has sustained itself since then, helping provide evidence of the benefits of a proper content audit and content pruning."*

5. Canonicalize	If you have similar pages targeting the same topic but you NEED both pages (i.e. you don't want to remove the page), set a canonical tag that points to the page you want to rank.
Use case	Chris Long, SEO Manager at Go Fish Digital wrote about how implementing canonical tags improved organic traffic 47% to his target pages: *"As Google gets better and better at understanding semantically related topics, the search engine is starting to return more results that contain topics outside of the initial query. For instance, in a search for "braces near me," I see a lot of results for orthodontists, even though the term "orthodontist" wasn't in my original search. Google is most likely doing this type of consolidation for some of your core keywords, and you should be aware of what it's grouping together.* *The client mentioned above has done a good job of building out landing pages that target different industry options (Auto Franchises, Cleaning Franchises and so on). This included the following two pages: Food Franchises and Fast Food Franchises.* *At first glance, it might seem obvious that searches for these two terms might yield different results. However, when [we Google the keywords] we see that Google is treating the keywords differently.* *It appeared that Google had collected enough user data to determine that searchers wanted similar results for these two queries. Because neither of their pages were ranking well at the time, and they both contained very similar content, we recommended that they consolidate the ranking signals.*

	Our client still wanted users to be able to access both pages, so we recommended they implement a canonical tag instead of a 301 redirect. They added the canonical tag on the "Fast Food" page that pointed to the "Food" page because the latter gave users a list of all the franchises under both categories. Organic traffic to the page has improved by 47 percent since implementation. This shows us that it's important to not only consolidate pages where standard keyword targeting and content overlap, but also where there might be conflict with other semantically related pages."
6. Block Crawl	If you have a group of pages that serve NO value to search engines (but have value to website visitors), the best option is to block that section from being crawled. This works best when pages are grouped by URL structure (i.e. /archives/).
Use case	This option is really only to be used to block pages at scale, aka entire sections of a website that serve no value. Use this option sparingly and only in the right situations.
7. No Index	If you want to stop Google from indexing a low quality page, use this tag. Blocking Crawl is reserved for a number of pages or site sections, No Index is reserved for individual or stand alone pages.
Use case	Inflow, a leading eCommerce marketing agency, was hired to help an auto equipment vendor fix a sharp decline in revenue and organic traffic. The team at Inflow began with an audit to see exactly where the problem was. There were thousands of

	pages that had not driven any organic traffic Year to Date (YTD) by the end of September. The audit uncovered 20k+ product pages, and 11k+ did not get any organic traffic. Inflow started to improve the product pages that were good. So, Inflow experts set the pages with no traffic to "noindex". A few weeks later they saw a lift in organic traffic per article. Then they began planning to rewrite the top product pages (1,300), which started 1-2 months after the pruning and continued for months. The "noindex, follow" tag tells the robot to noindex, but the user can still access it they know the link through the follow tag. The results were impressive. For the rewritten product pages, the company saw: Organic search traffic: +35,668 visits Organic search transactions: +112 transactions Organic search revenue: +$40,421.87 revenue (source)[23]
8. Delete (404)	If a page no longer serves a purpose to the website, has NO links, NO traffic and the keywords are no longer relevant, we can delete it.
Use case	As previously mentioned, Google advises webmasters to use 301 redirects when removing pages from their website. A 301 redirect preserves SEO equity and helps users discover a more relevant page. However, 301 redirects can be tricky to track after implemented. In some cases, it's best to just delete the page and let it 404. Those cases are when the page has no value whatsoever and is better off dying than being pushed back in with a redirect.

---

[23] https://cognitiveseo.com/blog/17548/content-pruning-for-seo/

9. Update Content	If a piece of content (blog post, guide, video) is underperforming it needs further attention. This tag will push the page to the "content audit" part of the process, which we will cover in Phase 3.1.
Use case	The WQA can be used as a content audit, but we prefer to push that down the line. We like to use the WQA to focus on bottom funnel pages (product pages, landing pages) and use a content audit to focus on top funnel pages (blog posts, guides, etc).

The bottom line here is simple - use this data to find pages that:

- Are not performing well (no organic traffic, no keyword rankings) and decide whether you want to update that page, remove it (301 redirect), or update it.

- Do not add value to search engines or users (orphaned pages, thin content pages, etc) and make a decision if you want to update that page, remove it (301 redirect), or update it.

- Have issues with technical roadblocks (pagination, canonicals, NOINDEX directives) and make recommendations to clean up.

- Should be moved to another part of the SEO process (keyword research, link building, content audit).

Once we have action tags for every page, we have an initial action plan for your campaign.

I like to call the WQA the "swiss army knife" of SEO audits because it serves so many purposes for us. Not only does it help with technical cleanups, but it serves as a strategy for the next phases in the campaign.

Final actions and next steps

At this stage, we know what actions we need to do for each page. Here's how we like to move forward with that information:

- **Clean up low quality pages.** If you run this properly, you should have a list of pages that you want to "clean up" using 301 redirects, canonical tags, NOINDEX tags, or using your Robots.txt file to stop them from getting crawled.

- **Build technical project management file.** We call it the "Action Tracker" - it helps our team stay in sync with clients for all the technical changes we recommend. Any URL that requires developer assistance gets added here with a date, detailed comments and status for project tracking. This "Action Tracker" gets updated throughout the life of a campaign as we perform more technical deliverables like a full audit, Search Console audit and more.

- **Initial evaluation of which pages to focus on for campaign.** Anything we tag with Update "On Page" tells us it's an important page that we want to review in more detail. This set of pages gets passed to the next phases of the campaign.

- **Keyword research + intent mapping.** Once more, any pages marked Update "On Page" are important and need further review. The first thing we do for these pages is keyword research, which is a time-consuming process, but it pays off later on.

- **"On page" improvements (titles, metas, internal links, body text, schema).** After we find keywords, we crosswalk those keywords against the "on page" elements of that URL. Again, on page SEO requires a lot of resources - our Website Quality Audit hacks down the work by giving us the important pages to focus on.

- **Perform an in depth content audit.** We make a copy of this file and filter for blog posts / resource pages only. Then, we do a deep audit to review which topics they cover. Our goal is to find content overlap, opportunities to merge pages, and posts that need to be rewritten from the ground up.

Developing this report changed the way we do SEO. Replicating it takes a bit of work, but once you have the process down, it gives you a replicable and scalable roadmap you can use for any SEO projects.

Limitation of Google Sheets

The upside of using Sheets for this analysis is that it's easy to get started - but that does come at a cost.

Sheets workbooks are limited to a total of 2,000,000 cells. If your website has more than 3,000 or so pages, when you add up all that data, you get a massive file that Google Sheets may not be able to handle.

If the website you're working on has more pages, it's time to bring out the big guns. For us, that means exporting all that data to BigQuery and performing the audit using SQL models. It's not as easy to set up as Google Sheets, but this approach will work for sites of any size, rather than being capped at a few thousand.

> If you need help gathering all the data inputs for a massive website, our other agency (www.codingisforlosers.com) can handle it for you.

2.2 - Technical SEO Audit

Technical SEO varies in importance depending on a project-by-project basis. Newer, smaller websites built on platforms like Shopify or WordPress generally don't have as many technical issues, which makes them easier to work with.

Larger, older websites built on clunky platforms tend to accumulate issues over time. That means you may spend a *lot* of time and effort analyzing and fixing technical issues that impact SEO.

Here's one upside, though – when you have a large website, fixing even small errors can have a massive impact because it's amplified across thousands of pages.

For smaller websites, we use the WQA in lieu of a technical audit. For larger enterprise websites, we run a deep forensic technical SEO audit.

Those of you who are experienced technical SEOs know there's no way I could possibly cover how to run a forensic SEO audit here - that wouldn't fit into a chapter in a book, it needs its own graduate level course.

Instead, we will be walking through the top technical issues we've found after auditing 100+ websites this past year.

Common technical SEO mistakes

As mentioned, we've run over 100 audits for clients over the last year. This section will highlight the most common issues we see and the ones that have the most positive impact on organic traffic when corrected.

1. Mismanaged 404 errors

This happens quite a bit on ecommerce sites. When a product is removed or expires, it's easily forgotten and the page "404s".

Although 404 errors *can* erode your crawl 'budget', they won't necessarily impact your SEO all that much. Google understands that sometimes you HAVE to delete pages on your site.

However, 404 pages can be a problem when they:

- Are getting traffic (internally and from organic search)
- Have external links pointing to them
- Have internal links pointing to them
- Have a large number of them on a larger website
- Are shared on social media / around the web

The best practice is to set up a 301 redirect from the deleted page into another relevant page on your site. This helps preserve SEO equity and make sure users never get stuck on 404 pages.

How to find this error:

The SEO Blueprint

- Run a full website crawl (SiteBulb, DeepCrawl or Screaming Frog) to find all 404 pages

- Check Google Search Console reporting (Crawl > Crawl Errors)

How to fix this error:

- Analyze the list of "404" errors on your website

- Crosscheck those URLs with Google Analytics to understand which pages were getting traffic

- Crosscheck those URLs with Google Search Console to understand which pages had inbound links from outside websites

- For those pages of value, identify an existing page on your website that is most relevant to the deleted page

- Setup "server-side" 301 redirects from the 404 page into the existing page you've identified - If you are going to use a 4XX page - make sure that page is actually functional so it doesn't impact the user experience

2. Website migrations

When launching a new website, design changes or new pages, there are a number of technical aspects that should be addressed ahead of time.

Common errors we see:

- **Use of 302 (temporary redirect) instead of 301 (permanent) redirects.** While Google recently[24] stated that 302 redirects pass SEO equity, we

---

[24] https://searchengineland.com/google-no-pagerank-dilution-using-301-302-30x-redirects-anymore-254608

hedge based on internal data that shows 301 redirects are the better option

- **Improper setup of HTTPS on a website.** Specifically, not redirecting the HTTP version of the site to HTTPS which can cause issues with duplicate pages

- **Not carrying over 301 redirects from the previous site to the new site.** This often happens if you're using a plugin for 301 redirects - 301 redirects should always be setup through a website's cPanel to avoid issues

- **Leaving legacy tags on the site from the staging domain.** For example, canonical tags, NOINDEX tags, etc. that prevent pages on your staging domain from being indexed

- **Leaving staging domains indexed.** The opposite of the previous item, when you do NOT place the proper tags on staging domains (or subdomains) to NOINDEX them from SERPs (either with NOINDEX tags or blocking crawl via Robots.txt file).

- **Creating "redirect chains" when cleaning up legacy websites.** In other words, not properly identifying pages that were previously redirected and moving forward with a new set of redirects.

- **Not saving the force www or non www of the site in the .htaccess file.** This causes 2 (or more) instances of your website to be indexed in Google, causing issues with duplicate pages being indexed.

How to find this error:

- Run a full website crawl (SiteBulb, DeepCrawl or Screaming Frog) to get the needed data inputs

How to fix this error:

- Triple check to make sure your 301 redirects migrated properly

- Test your 301 and 302 redirects to make sure they go to the right place on the first step

- Check canonical tags in the same way and ensure you have the right canonical tags in place

- Given a choice between canonicalizing a page and 301 redirecting a page - a 301 redirect is a safer, stronger option

- Check your code to ensure you remove NOINDEX tags (if used on staging domain). Don't just uncheck the options the plugins. Your developer may have hardcoded NOINDEX into the theme header - Appearance > Themes > Editor >header.php

- Update your robots.txt file

- Check and update your .htaccess file

3. Website speed

Google has confirmed[25] that website speed is a ranking factor - it expects pages to load in 2 seconds or less. More importantly, website visitors won't wait around for a page to load.

In other words, **slow websites cost you money.** You don't have to take my word for it either. Over a decade ago, Amazon published a study that found a 100 ms increase in loading times for their pages translated to a drop in sales of around 1%.

---

[25] https://searchengineland.com/8-major-google-ranking-signals-2017-278450

Even if you don't come close to Amazon's volume (and who does, really?) that's still a scary figure.

When it comes to long loading times, some of the most common causes include:

- Large, unoptimized images
- Poorly written (bloated) website code
- Too many plugins
- Heavy Javascript and CSS

Here's the problem – fixing these issues usually requires a background in web development. That means you may need to hire outside help, but as the numbers tell us, it's well worth the cost to improve your loading times.

How to find these errors:

- Check your website in Google PageSpeed[26] Insights, GTMetrix[27] or Pingdom[28]

How to fix these errors:

- Hire a developer with experience in this area. We like to post the EXACT errors into Upwork[29] and hire a freelancer to handle it
- Make sure you have a staging domain setup so website performance isn't hindered

---

[26] https://developers.google.com/speed/pagespeed/insights/
[27] https://gtmetrix.com/
[28] https://tools.pingdom.com/
[29] https://www.upwork.com/

- If you're using a PHP-based CMS such as WordPress, make sure it's running on the latest version of PHP. The jump in performance in PHP 7 alone is staggering.

4. Not optimizing the mobile User Experience (UX)

Google's index is officially mobile first[30]. That means the first thing the algorithm looks at is the mobile version of your website. If you offer a terrible mobile experience, it's going to impact your rankings, no matter how amazing your website looks on desktops.

What you want is a fully responsive website that delivers a similar experience both on desktop and mobile devices. If you serve pages dynamically and have a fully responsive site, you're good to go.

How to find these errors:

- Use Google's Mobile-Friendly Test[31] to check if Google sees your site as mobile-friendly

- Check to see if "smartphone Googlebot" is crawling your site - it hasn't rolled out everywhere yet

- Does your website respond to different devices? If your site doesn't work on a mobile device, now is the time to get that fixed

- Got unusable content on your site? Check to see if it loads or if you get error messages. Make sure you fully test all your site pages on mobile

---

[30] https://techcrunch.com/2017/12/20/googles-mobile-first-search-index-has-rolled-out-to-a-handful-of-sites/
[31] https://search.google.com/test/mobile-friendly

How to fix these errors:

- Understand the impact of mobile on your server load

- Focus on building your pages from a mobile-first perspective. Google likes Responsive sites and is their preferred option for delivering mobile sites[32]. If you currently run a standalone subdirectory, m.yourdomain.com look at potential impact of increased crawling on your server

- If you need to, consider a template update to make the theme responsive. Just using a plugin might not do what you need or cause other issues._Find a developer[33] who can scratch build responsive themes

- Focus on multiple mobile breakpoints, not just your brand new iPhone X. 320px wide (iPhone 5 and SE) is still super important

- Test across iPhone and Android

- If you have content that needs "fixing" - flash or other proprietary systems that don't work on your mobile journey - consider moving to HTML5 which will render on mobile -_Google web designer[34] will allow you to reproduce FLASH files in HTML

---

[32] https://developers.google.com/search/mobile-sites/mobile-seo/
[33] https://www.upwork.com/
[34] https://www.google.com/webdesigner/

5. XML Sitemap issues

An XML Sitemap lists out URLs on your site that you want to be crawled and indexed by search engines. You're allowed to include information about when a page:

- Was last updated
- How often it changes
- How important it is in relation to other URLs in the site (i.e., priority)

While Google admittedly ignores a lot of this information, it doesn't mean you should. Large websites with complex architectures can benefit particularly from a thorough sitemap.

Beyond that, sitemaps come particularly handy for websites where:

- Some areas of the website are not available through the browsable interface
- Webmasters use rich Ajax, Silverlight or Flash content that is not normally processed by search engines.
- The site is very large, and there is a chance for the web crawlers to overlook some of the new or recently updated content
- When websites have a huge number of pages that are isolated or not well linked together
- Misused "crawl budget" on unimportant pages. For any pages you consider to be unimportant, you should go ahead and block crawlers by using the NOINDEX function

How to find these errors:

- Make sure you have submitted your sitemap to your GSC
- Even though we focus mostly on Google, it can also pay off to submit your sitemap to Bing webmaster tools
- Check your sitemap for errors Crawl > Sitemaps > Sitemap Errors
- Check the log files to see when your sitemap was last accessed by bots

How to fix these errors:

- Make sure your XML sitemap is connected to your Google Search Console
- Run a server log analysis to understand how often Google is crawling your sitemap. There are lots of other things we will cover using our server log files later on
- Google will show you the issues and examples of what it sees as an error so you can correct
- If you are using a plugin for sitemap generation, make sure it's not outdated and that the file it generates works by validating it
- If you don't want to use Excel to check your server logs - you can use a server log analytics tool such as Logz.io, Graylog, SEOlyzer (great for WordPress sites) or Loggly to see how your XML sitemap is being used

6. URL Structure issues

As your website grows, it's easy to lose track of URL structures and hierarchies. A poor URL structure makes it difficult for both users and bots to navigate your website , which can and will negatively impact your rankings.

By a poor URL structure, I mean:

- Issues with website structure and hierarchy
- Not using proper folder and subfolder structure
- URLs with special characters, capital letters or anything that would baffle a human

How to find these errors:

- 404 errors, 302 redirects, issues with your XML sitemap are all signs of a site that needs its structure revisited
- Run a full website crawl (using SiteBulb, DeepCrawl or Screaming Frog) and do a manual review of the results to find any errors
- Check your Google Search Console reports (Crawl > Crawl Errors)
- User testing - ask people to find content on your site or make a test purchase. Something we like to do is use a UX testing service so users can record their experience (although these can be a bit pricey)

How to fix these errors:

- Plan your site hierarchy - we always recommend parent-child folder structures
- Make sure all content is placed in its correct folder or subfolder
- Make sure your URL paths are easy to read and make sense
- Remove or consolidate any content that looks to rank for the same keyword

- Try to limit the number of subfolders / directories to no more than three levels, anything beyond that tends to be too convoluted to navigate

7. Issues with robots.txt file

A Robots.txt file controls how search engines access your website. It's a commonly misunderstood file and if you don't understand how it works, it can affect your site's indexation.

Most problems with the robots.txt stem from not updating it when you move from a staging environment to a live website or by using the wrong syntax.

How to find these errors:

- Check your site stats - i.e. Google Analytics for big drops in traffic
- Check your Google Search Console reports (Crawl > robots.txt tester)

How to fix these errors:

- Check your Google Search Console reports (Crawl > robots.txt tester), doing so will validate your file
- Check to make sure the pages/folders you DON'T want to be crawled are included in your robots.txt file
- Make sure you are not inadvertently blocking any important directories (JS, CSS, 404, etc.)

8. Too much thin content

Cranking out "low-effort" pages just to try and rank is a terrible idea for SEO purposes. What Google wants are pages with in-depth, high-value content.

In other words, having too much "thin" (i.e. less than 500 words or text with no media) content can negatively impact your SEO. Here's why:

- Content that doesn't resonate with your target audience will kill conversion and engagement rates
- Google's algorithm looks heavily at content quality[35], trust, and relevancy, so thin content can kill your rankings
- Too much low quality content can decrease search engine crawl rate, indexation rate, and traffic

As a rule of thumb, if you can't build enough content one keyword, your best bet is to build those thin slices of content into a massive pie. That approach helps us generate incredibly engaging and in-depth content, and it's fantastic for your rankings.

How to find these errors:

- Run a crawl to find pages with word count less than 500
- Check your GSC for manual messages from Google (GSC > Messages)
- Not ranking for the keywords you are writing content for or suddenly losing rankings

---

[35] https://moz.com/blog/google-search-quality-raters-guidelines

- Check your page bounce rates and user dwell time. A high bounce rate might be related to thin content (among other reasons, including poor UX and high loading times)

How to fix these errors:

- Collate keywords[36] into themes so rather than writing one keyword per page you can place 5 or 6 in the same piece of content and expand it

- Work on pages that try and keep the user engaged with a variety of content - consider video or audio, infographics or images. If you don't have these skills, you can hire people to create that media for in places such as Upwork, Fiverr, or PPH

- Think about your user first - what do they want? Your primary goal should be to create content that fulfills those needs

9. Too much irrelevant content

In addition to "thin" pages, you want to make sure your content is "relevant". Pages that don't help the user or provide them with any value, can also detract from the good stuff you have on site.

This is particularly important if you have a small, less authoritative website. Google crawls smaller websites less often than more authoritative ones. That means we want to make sure we're only serving Google our best content to increase that trust, authority, and crawl budget.

---

[36] https://imfromthefuture.com/bigfoot-strategy/

Some of the most common ways people fall into this trap include:

- Creating boring pages with low engagement
- Letting search engines crawl irrelevant pages

How to find these errors:

- Review your content strategy. Focus on high-quality content instead of a rapid-fire low-effort strategy
- Check your Google crawl stats and see what pages are getting crawled and indexed

How to fix these errors:

- Don't focus on quotas when it comes to content planning. More content is good, but you want to make sure every single piece you publish offers real value
- Add pages to your Robots.txt file that you would rather not see Google rank. That way, you ensure Google focuses on the good stuff

10. Misuse of canonical tags

If you have two pages that are the same (or similar), you use canonical tags to (which are HTML code) to tell search engines which of those pages you want to appear in search results. Canonical tags look like this:

"rel=canonical"

If your website runs on a CMS like WordPress or Shopify, you can set canonical tags using a plugin, so you don't have to tinker with any code (we're big fans of Yoast[37]).

We often run into websites that misuse canonical tags in a number of ways:

- Canonical tags pointing to the wrong pages (i.e. pages not relevant to the current page)
- Canonical tags pointing to 404 pages (i.e., pages that no longer exist)
- Missing a canonical tag altogether
- eCommerce and "faceted URLs."
- When a CMS creates two versions of one page

Misusing canonical tags is a big deal. When you do so, you're telling search engines to focus on the wrong results and if that happens to any of your high-value pages, you may miss out on a lot of traffic due to a simple technical error.

How to find these errors:

- Run a site crawl using Screaming Frog
- Compare "Canonical link element" to the root URL to see which pages are using canonical tags to point to a different page

---

[37] https://yoast.com/

How to fix these errors:

- Review pages to determine if canonical tags are pointing to the wrong page

- Also, you will want to run a content audit to understand pages that are similar and need a canonical tag

11. Misuse of robots tags

As well as your robots.txt file, there are also robots tags you can add to your page headers. The problem comes when you add multiple tags to the same pages, which can prevent even well-optimized pages from ranking.

How to find these errors:

- Check your source code in a browser to see if it contains more than one robot tag

- Make sure you're not confusing nofollow link attributes and nofollow robot tags.

How to fix these errors:

- Decide how you want to manage robots activity. Yoast SEO[38] gives you some pretty good options to manage robots at a page level

- Make sure you're using at least one plugin to manage robot activity (this is for WordPress users, if you're not a fan of Yoast)

---

[38] https://yoast.com/

- Make sure you amend any WordPress templates where robot tags have been added manually Appearance > Themes >Editor >header.php

- Add Nofollow directives[39] to the robots.txt file instead of going file by file

12. Mismanaged crawl budget

Crawling the entire web is a tall order, even for Google. To save time, Google allocates a 'crawl budget' to each website. Ideally, you want that budget to cover all your pages, so all your content is ranking. In practice, that budget depends on a number of factors.

More authoritative sites will have a bigger crawl budget than lower authority alternatives. Google itself defines this budget as "Prioritizing what to crawl, when and how much resources the server hosting the site can allocate to crawling" (Google Blog, 2017).

How to find these errors:

- Find out what your crawl stats are in GSC Search Console > Select your domain > Crawl > Crawl Stats

- Use your server logs to find out where the Googlebot is spending its time on your site. That information should tell you if it's targeting the right pages (you can use a tool such as botify if spreadsheets make you feel ill)

---

[39]https://www.deepcrawl.com/blog/best-practice/robots-txt-noindex-the-best-kept-secret-in-seo/

How to fix these errors:

- Minimize the number of errors on your site by covering all the other factors we've gone over so far

- Block pages you don't want Google to waste time crawling

- Minimize any existing redirect chains on your website

- If you're working on an ecommerce website, block the parameter tags that are used for faceted navigation

13. Not leveraging internal links to pass equity

Internal links help to distribute "equity" across a website. Lots of sites, especially those with tons of thin content, tend to have fewer internal links. That's because you don't have that much content worth linking to, which is a big issue.

Cross-linking articles and posts helps visitors move within your website by pointing them in the direction of more content they may want to consume. That traffic can help improve your keyword rankings.

How to find these errors:

- For pages you are trying to rank, look at what internal pages link to them (you can do this with Google Analytics)

- Run an internal links crawl using Screaming Frog

- You will know yourself if you actively link to other pages on your site

- Are you adding internal nofollow links via a plugin that automatically applies the attribute to all links? Check your source code to find out

How to fix these errors:

- Focus on pages you're trying to rank and go through your content to find internal linking opportunities you may have overlooked

- Use the crawl data from Screaming Frog to identify opportunities for additional internal links

- Don't overcook the number of links and the keywords used to link. As a rule of thumb, only add internal links when it makes sense to do so

- Check the nofollow link rules for any plugin you're using to manage links

14. Errors with page "on page" markups

Title tags and metadata are some of the most abused code on websites and have been since Google has been crawling websites. A lot of people know this, so a lot of site owners have begun ignoring the importance of on page markup. That's a mistake.

How to find these errors:

- Use Yoast to see how well your site titles and metadata work - red and amber mean there's room for improvement

- Don't take advantage of descriptions for keyword stuffing (once is fine if it makes sense within the context)

- Use SEMrush and Screaming Frog to identify duplicate and missing title tags

How to fix these errors:

- Use Yoast to see how to rework titles and metadata , especially the meta description, which has undergone a bit of a rebirth thanks to Google's increase of the overall character count. Meta description data used to be set to 255 characters, but now it averages over 300 characters in length. You should be taking advantage of that extra room

- Use SEMrush to identify and fix any missing or duplicate page title tags

- Remove any non-specific keywords from the meta keyword tag

Structured data

As Google grows more sophisticated and it enables webmasters to add more markup to their websites, the whole thing can start to become a bit messy on your end.

Here are some of the types of markup data you can add to your content:

- Map data
- Review data
- Rich snippet data
- Product data
- Book Reviews

When used properly, markup data can give you a distinct edge on the SERPs. However, if you go about adding that markup wrong, it can negatively impact your site's SEO.

We like to tackle schema markup optimization during the "on page" section of our optimization process, so we'll return to this topic later on in the book.

How to find these errors:

- Use GSC to identify what schema is being picked up by Google and if it includes any errors. Search Appearance > Structured Data.
- Test your schema using Google's markup helper[40]

How to fix these errors:

- Identify what schema you want to use on your website, then find a relevant plugin to help you insert it. The All in One Schema or RichSnippets plugins are excellent tools to help you generate and manage schema for a broad range of content types. Once the markup is in, remember to test it
- If you aren't using Wordpress, you can get a developer to build this code for you. Google prefers JSON-LD, so you need to make sure whomever you hire knows their way around that method

2.3 - In-Depth Keyword Analysis

Keywords are the foundation of any great SEO campaign. They dictate the quality of traffic we will receive from search engines.

---

[40] https://www.google.com/webmasters/markup-helper/u/0/

We like to break keyword research into 2 sections:

1. Finding keywords for existing pages on your website

2. Finding keywords you can develop new content around

In this section, we'll focus on finding keywords for the existing pages on your website. We'll talk about how to review each page to discover the best keywords to target - based on search volume, relevance and competition.

We will talk about identifying new keywords in section 3.2.
Our keyword research process:

1. Review existing pages on a website to identify the "**Main KW**" for every page.

2. Review existing pages on your website to identify the "**Secondary KWs**" for every page. These keywords support the "Main KW" by adding contextual support as well as "long tail" searches to the page.

3. Review the top **3 SERP results** (in Google) for each of the "Main KW" to understand the type of content Google wants to rank for that query (i.e. searcher intent + content type).

4. Review the **referring domains** of the top 3 SERP results (in Google) for each "Main KW". This helps us to understand the competition for each query we want to rank for.

5. Analyze the results and prioritize accordingly.

2.3.1 Intro to keywords.

For the beginner's reading this book, here's what you need to know about "keywords".

Keywords are what users type into search engines (we also call them "queries") in the hopes of finding specific information, products, services, etc.

In other words, keywords are an integral part of SEO and they dictate the kind of content you want to focus on. For the best possible results, you want to optimize your content around keywords you know users are looking for.

There are a lot of tools we use to help us understand keywords and optimize our websites around them. Let's go over a few terms you need to understand if you want to use any of those tools:

- **Keyword search volume**. How many times a certain keyword is being searched for each month. The higher the search volume, the more potential visitors we can get to our website if we get to the top of the SERPs.

- **Keyword / searcher intent**. While we want to find keywords with a large search volume, it's even more important to understand the intent behind the keyword. In other words, when someone is searching using a certain keyword, what are they really looking for?

Let's go back to our watch business example by breaking down a few relevant keywords:

- **"Pictures of Armani watches"**. Monthly search volume = 10,000. Intent = low. While there's a ton of volume, the intent is for window shoppers. If you sell Armani watches, you still want this traffic, but expect conversions to be low.

- **"Best watches for summer"**. Monthly search volume = 120. Intent = moderate. This keyword has "discovery" intent, i.e. this person is in the market for a watch but is still determining the brand, model, size, color, etc.

- **"Gold large face men's watches"**. Monthly search volume = 2,400. Intent = high. This searcher has educated themselves on the exact type of watch they want. At this point, it's just a matter of matching price / style for them to purchase.

The key here is to rank for ALL of these keywords, using different types of content to nurture that searcher into your funnel. These are advanced (but critical) concepts that we will cover in depth later in this book.

What we want is to optimize our website for keywords that won't just increase traffic, but also sales and leads. Understanding how keywords relate to search intent is a powerful skill to add to your SEO arsenal.

When it comes to search intent, there are a few more points we need to go over:

- **Keyword competition**. As a rule of thumb, keywords with high purchase intent tend to be harder to rank for. Here's when the quality of your results versus those of your competitors come into play.

- **Competitor keywords**. The keywords your competitors are using to drive traffic to their website.

"Keyword research" is the process of identifying the **ideal search queries** we want people to discover your website with. "Ideal" keywords have the following characteristics:

- **High monthly search volume**. We want to find the searches that people are performing a lot. The more searches, the more traffic potential. The more traffic potential, the more leads or sales for your business.

- **Low competition.** We want to find keywords that are not dominated by large brands and powerful websites. While this is not always the case (we often have to target competitive keywords), it is ideal, especially when finding keywords for content creation (we'll talk about this later).

- **Relevant to your business**. We want to drive qualified traffic to your website. To do so, the keywords we find must be related to **your business** *or* **your customer**.

We don't do KW research for every page on the site - only the pages that target valuable keywords to the business (i.e. doing KW research for a "contact" page is a waste of resources).

Internally at WEBRIS, we only do keyword research for pages categorized as **"Update On Page"** from the **Website Quality Audit.** If you want to save time, you should also develop a process to weed out low impact pages from your keyword research efforts.

Organizing your keywords

Before we talk about how to find keywords, let's talk about recording them. We have a done-for-you keyword research template (included in free The Blueprint bundle) that I'll be using to demonstrate.

70% of the inputs to our template are copied and pasted from The Website Quality Audit.

- URL
- Category
- DA / PA
- Sessions
- Links to page
- Main keyword, volume and current ranking

Priority	URL	Category	DA	PA	Sesions	RD Links (DOFOLLOW)	Target Main Keyword	Volume	Ranking	Intent
1	https://www.site.com/Teami_Energy	Product Page	41	42	2477	8	energy tea	720	3	2. Consider
1	https://www.site.com/increase-energy-level	Blog post	41	42	2477	8	how to increase energy	2,000	14	4. Awareness
2	https://www.site.com/Teami_Detox_30_Day	Product Page	41	48	45312	32	detox tea	49,500	4	2. Consider
3	https://www.site.com/matchami_strainer	Product Page	41	22	66	0	matcha strainer	30	7	2. Consider
4	https://www.site.com/Teami_Relax	Product Page	41	42	1547	5	relax tea	2,400	3	2. Consider
5	https://www.site.com/Teami_Profit	Product Page	41	41	2353	1	immune boosting tea	90	36	2. Consider
6	https://www.site.com/teami_focus	Product Page	41	22	813	0	tea to focus	320	3	2. Consider
7	https://www.site.com/green_tea_detox_ma	Product Page	41	22	2694	1	green tea face mask	1,900	22	2. Consider

Since the WQA pulls keyword ranking data from SEMrush, we already have a head start. It's important to note, this will likely not be the final keyword we're targeting. We still have to go through and refine that keyword with additional research (we will get to that shortly).

The "Main keyword" that pulls through from the WQA gives us a head start. It provides us contextual overview for what the page is (and should be) about.

There will also likely be a lot of URLs without a "Main keyword", as that page may not have any existing keyword rankings. We will need to start from scratch on those pages.

> Note: If you are not using our WQA, you can get the existing keyword rankings manually from SEMrush or Ahrefs.

The next part of our keyword research template gathers data from the SERPs on the top 3 websites ranking for each keyword.

1st Google Result for Main KW	1st Result Content Type	RD to 1st Result (DOFOL LOW)	RD Velocity (Monthly)	PA of 1st Result	DA of 1st Result	2nd Google Result for Main KW	2nd Result Content Type	RD to 2nd Result (DOFOL LOW)	RD Velocity (Monthly)	PA of 2nd Result	DA of 2nd Result	3rd Google Result for Main KW	3rd Result Content Type	RD to 3rd Result (DOFO LLOW)	RD Velocity (Monthly)
https://www.yogiproducts.com/teas/energy-teas/	Product Category	1	0	1	58	https://www.teamiblends.com/Teami_Energy	Product Page	17	1	42	41	https://yourtea.com/products/energy-tea	Product Page	0	0
https://www.yogiproducts.com/teas/energy-teas/	Product Category	1	0	1	58	https://www.teamiblends.com/Teami_Energy	Product Page	17	1	42	41	https://yourtea.com/products/energy-tea	Product Page	0	0
https://www.yogiproducts.com/teas/best-selling-teas/detox/	Product Page	12	1	42	58	https://www.yogiproducts.com/teas/detox-wellness-teas/	Product Category	5	1	1	58	https://www.teamiblends.com/Teami_Detox_30_Days_Pack	Product Page	68	7
https://www.amazon.com/Aiya-America-Matcha-Sifter-Accessory/dp/B006I	Amazon Product Page	0	0	1	98	https://www.amazon.com/Matcha-Strainer-Can-1-Cou/dp/B006	Amazon Product Page	0	0	1	98	https://www.amazon.com/Strainer-Marukyu-Koyamaen-Magus-Brands/dp/B0	Amazon Product Page	0	0

This data is critical to help us understand what it will take to rank by telling us exactly what Google wants to rank for each query we're targeting.

- The type of page ranking (product page, blog post, Amazon listing, etc) helps us formulate the type of content to create for each Main keyword

- The collective authority to the top 3 results helps us understand how much effort we'll need to place on link building

Gathering this data is a bit of a manual slog, we leverage our offshore team to build these files for clients.

We wrote some nifty formulas to calculate keyword "opportunity" scores to help determine the level of effort to rank.

DA Opportunity Score	PA Opportunity Score	Links Opportunity Score	Opportunity to rank	Priority SCORE	Content Type Recommendation	Content Analysis	Target Page
33	71	63	56	54	Product Page	Optimal Content Type	Yes
33	71	63	56	48	Product Page	Different Content Type	Yes
24	68	56	50	48	Product Page	Optimal Content Type	Yes

If you're a spreadsheet nerd like us, this file is amazing. If you're a client, it's overwhelming.

To make this easier to digest we simply create charts using the data. We then drop it into a presentation deck to send with our findings, recommendations and the data.

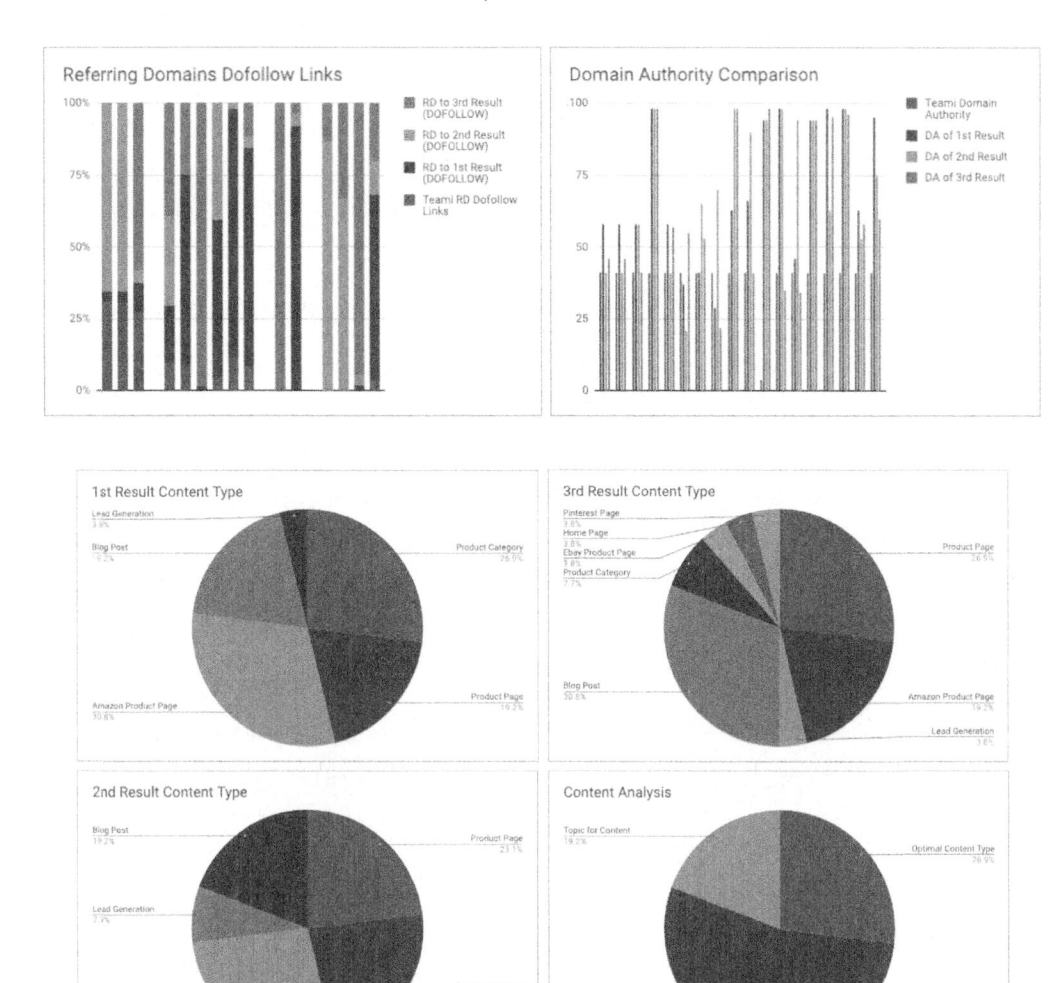

This deliverable template makes it easy to have conversations with clients who have unreal expectations about the results of their campaigns.

For example, we had a client in the loans industry - one of the most competitive niches. They hired us wanting to rank 1st keywords like "sba loans". After completion of this exact file, we were able to deduce:

1. It would take them years to rank (if ever) 1st for "sba loans"

2. Long form content (i.e. "SBA Loans: Are You Qualified?") was dominating the SERPs, we'd have to pivot the focus from landing pages to blog content to get the fastest results

If we went to the client without this data, they'd have fired us on the spot. You can't argue with data - they bought in to our plan and as a result increased organic traffic 120% in 10 months.

Now that we've covered the template, let's talk about how to populate it with the optimal keywords.

Finding the Keywords

While there's amazing tools out there to help you, keyword research is still a time consuming process. There's no hacks or shortcuts, we need to put in the time doing, well, *research*.

We don't want to just identify a handful of keywords, we want to identify (and understand) all the keywords that will make the page contextually relevant. That's why we structure our keyword research documents to discover 2 types of keywords:

- **The "Main" keyword.** The focus keyword for the page - this generally has the most relevant intent and highest search volume. This keyword drives the main targeting of the page.
- **"Secondary" keywords.** The "long tail" keywords that support the "Main" keyword and give the page opportunity to rank for additional search queries.

Finding the "Main" keyword

Keyword research is essential when you onboard a new client, particularly if they work in a niche you have no experience in. Before you can get to work, you need an idea of what keywords you're going to target through the campaign.

Bear in mind, keyword research can be a bit dry. You're going to deal with long lists of search terms, narrow down the keywords you want to use, discard those with little value, and so on.

The good news is we already laid some groundwork for understanding your client's industry during the discovery process. Now, we need to narrow things down even further. Here are some questions to get you started:

- What keywords have you tried using in the past?
- Who's your target audience?
- Who are your primary competitors?
- What regions do your products/services target?

You can get a lot of this information yourself just by visiting your client's website. However, it's always interesting to find out if your client's ideas match what is actually going on with their business.

It's all too common to deal with customers that have been going about targeting the wrong keywords, either because they choose options that are too competitive or they don't have enough search traffic.

The keyword research process may be dry, but it gives you the data you need to make smart decisions.

Now, there are a lot of tools you can use to identify keywords. Most of them will throw hundreds of options at you. One of the tools we most commonly use is Google Search Console.

If you have access to Search Console, you can hop over to the Performance tab and look for the QUERIES section. Search Console will show you the top queries driving traffic to your website, including clicks and impression data.

What your main keywords are should be evident – they're the ones getting you the majority of your clicks. In some cases, we find that clients have never looked at this data and they have no idea what keywords are driving the majority of their traffic. In other words, they've been driving blind.

If you don't have access to Search Console, we can also recommend using Google Keyword Planner, Google Ads, and SEMrush. Which tool you use doesn't matter all that much since you'll end up with basically the same data.

Case study: Selecting the "Main keyword" for home pages

MoonClerk is an online payment platform that helps businesses accept payments, specifically recurring payments (such as gyms and personal trainers).

Our keyword research file turned up 2 "Main" keywords for the home page: *moonclerk* and *recurring billing software*.

There's a lot of debate in the SEO community about home page keyword targeting - should it be brand focused or keyword driven?

My answer is both.

A home page has incredible ranking power, you should always aim to combine your brand with your main keyword.

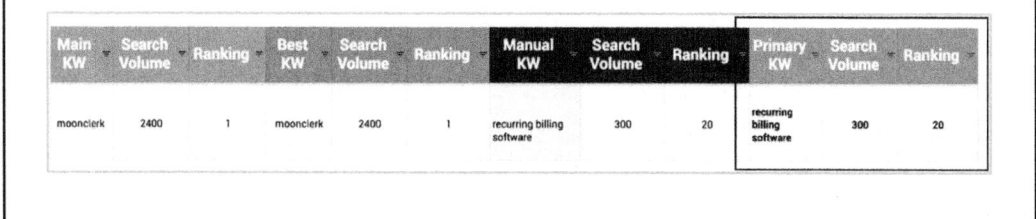

Main KW	Search Volume	Ranking	Best KW	Search Volume	Ranking	Manual KW	Search Volume	Ranking	Primary KW	Search Volume	Ranking
moonclerk	2400	1	moonclerk	2400	1	recurring billing software	300	20	recurring billing software	300	20

Finding the "Secondary" keywords

There's some amazing keyword research tools out there, but none better than Google. If you type your keyword into Google, you get 2 awesome keyword sources:

1. A list of the websites ranking for your Main keyword

2. A list of related searches

We can use both of these to mine Secondary keywords.

Stealing from the websites ranking for your Main keyword

Search Google for your Main keyword. Take the 1st URL that appears (organic listings, not ads) and enter it into Ahrefs (or SEMrush). The tool will report all the additional keywords and search volume that page is ranking for.

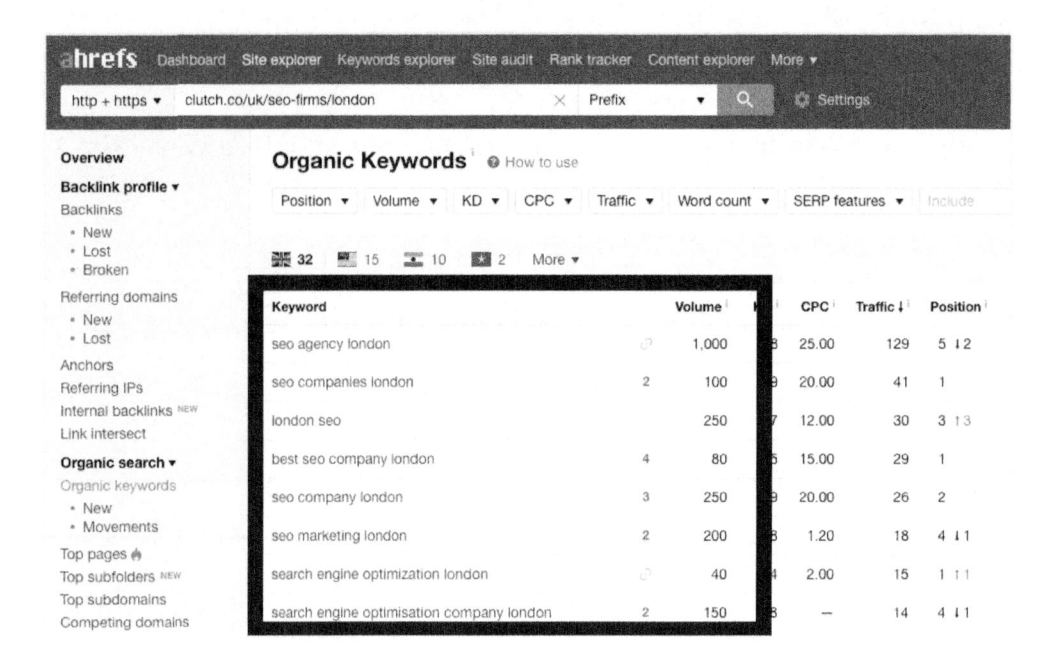

Rinse and repeat with organic results 1 - 4 and gather these keywords as the seedlings for your Secondary keywords.

Using Google related searches

Search Google for your Main keyword. Scroll to the bottom of the page and you will see Google's related searches. These tell us what **people are also looking for** when searching for your Main keyword. These always serve as some of the best Secondary keywords.

If you install the Keywords Everywhere Chrome browser plugin, you will also see the associated search volumes in the related searches.

Picking Secondary keywords

Do NOT mistake Secondary with synonyms or semantic keywords.

A synonym keyword would be the Main keyword, just stated in a different order like "Billing software that's recurring". These have no value to us here.

According to SEMrush[41], semantically related keywords are simply words or phrases that are related to each other conceptually.

For a keyword like "search volume," some semantically related keywords could be:

- keyword research
- paid search
- online marketing

For a keyword like "cook asparagus," some semantically related keywords could be:

- vegetable peeler
- lemon juice
- baking sheet

---

[41] https://www.semrush.com/kb/593-semantically-related-keywords

Semantic keywords are valuable, but not here - we're simply trying to find keywords that support the Main keyword, contextually.

In other words, what are the additional keywords we need to add to tell Google this page is truly about the Main keyword? Let's look at some examples.

Main keyword = Miami SEO agency

Secondary keywords =

- SEO consultants in Miami
- Results focused SEO agencies
- SEO agency pricing
- Reputable SEO firms in Miami

And another example...

Main keyword = criminal court process in Denver

Secondary keywords =

- Denver criminal court
- Colorado rules of criminal procedures
- How to prepare for a criminal court appearance
- Order of events in a criminal trial
- Recent criminal defence wins in Colorado

It's easy to picture how those secondary keywords could become H2 headers within your pages. They can help support the Main keyword and provide context. That means your content becomes both more informative and it gets more love from search engines – what's not to like?

Understanding Secondary keywords is the perfect segway into mapping keyword intent.

Mapping keyword intent

"Intent" refers to what the searcher is really looking for when using keywords.

Intent is critical because it represents the user's state of mind and it gives you insight into what type of content you want to rank for with that query. In the example above, for example, we assigned the "criminal court process" keyword to the "Discover" funnel stage.

Why? It's a broad search that doesn't indicate any intent to convert. At that stage, the user is still taking in information. Now take a look at stage two – it's more specific, which means the user already has an idea of what they want and now they're entering the consideration stage of the funnel.

That example shows you a few of the journey stages we like to use. In full, we like to map intent based on 5 journey stages that make up a keyword tunnel:

1. **Customer.** Keywords that your current customer based is looking for - this is generally support based or usage queries (i.e. how to use "product" or service).

2. **Consider.** Already aware of the options and looking to convert.

- These are pre purchase queries (best, reviews, top) and specific events ex. *"men engagement rings"*, *"Rolex watches reviews"*, *"top places to live in Florida"*.

- Keywords with clear purchase intent (cheap, buy, for sale) ex. *"cheap gold watches"*, *"coffee mugs buy in bulk"*, *"protein powder wholesale"*. These keywords also include local services, main services and branded search ex. *"carpet cleaner in New York"*, *"app design company"*, *"quest bars"*.

- These keywords will always map to product pages, category pages or the homepage.

3. **Discover**. Coming across your product or service offerings for the first time.

    - Inquisitive keywords (who, what, where, how) ex. *"where are Rolex watches made"*. These keywords usually map to expert guides type of content.

4. **Awareness**. In the market for a solution, but have no idea who you are or what you sell.

    - Very broad keywords ex. *"gold watches" "deserted islands"*, *"blue couches"*. These keywords can map to either product pages or content pages.

5. **Attention**. Very high level searches, topically related, but not purchase intent related.

    - Think viral topics ex. *"fanciest watch designs"*, *"things to do on a deserted island"*. These keywords will usually map to listicle type articles or infographics.

The goal is to scrape as much of the SERPs as possible, even for the high level attention based keywords that don't drive conversions. The more free, organic exposure we can get your brand, the better.

Analyzing Top 3 SERP Results

This part is optional, but highly suggested - especially if you're doing SEO for clients.

We analyze the top 3 search results ranking for each of the "Main" keywords. That enables us to know if our page has a legitimate shot of ranking for that keyword by comparison. If not, we determine the proper way ahead to capture that traffic. For each "Main" keyword we:

1. **Scrape the top 3 results in Google.** We manually pull the first 3 results in Google for a specific keyword using Ahrefs.

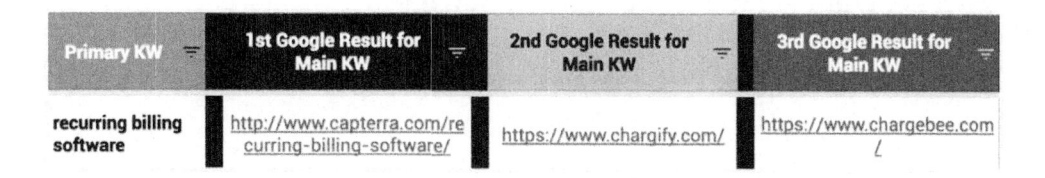

Primary KW	1st Google Result for Main KW	2nd Google Result for Main KW	3rd Google Result for Main KW
recurring billing software	http://www.capterra.com/recurring-billing-software/	https://www.chargify.com/	https://www.chargebee.com/

2. **Check DA and PA.** We check the Domain Authority and Page Authority of the top results. We use this data at the end of the analysis to formulate an accurate and realistic scenario of the opportunity that each page has to rank for the targeted keyword.

3. **Check the number of links pointing to each of those results.** We look for the amount of dofollow referring domains in the live index of the page. This helps us understand how many links the top results have,

The SEO Blueprint

and gives us a better idea of how much work it would take to compete with it.

4. **Check the "link velocity" of each result.** This tells us how many links that page is generating on a monthly basis.

Primary KW	1st Google Result for Main KW	RD to 1st Result (DOFOLLOW)	RD Velocity (Monthly)	PA of 1st Result	DA of 1st Result
recurring billing software	http://www.capterra.com/recurring-billing-software/	0	0	35	74

5. **Assess the "content type" of each result.** We need to understand if Google is ranking blog posts, product pages, Amazon listings, YouTube videos, etc for your main keywords. This helps us understand what Google wants to show for your keywords.

Crosswalk Data Against Your Site's Metrics

Having the data for our competitors, we can crosswalk that information against your site's metrics:

1. Current **ranking** for that keyword.
2. Current number of **referring domains** to that keyword's page.
3. Client's **domain** authority.
4. Client's **page** authority.

We have an in-house formula that helps us calculate an opportunity score for each keyword and page. These are the variables the formula includes:

1. **DA Average**: Domain Authority average across top 3 results.

2. **PA Average:** Page Authority average across top 3 results.

3. **Link Average:** Referring domain average across top 3 results.

We're not going to share the formula since that's proprietary (sorry!) but we *can* tell you the kind of metrics we get from it. In any case, once you have the competitor data we mentioned before, determining an opportunity value won't take much work.

Based on those variables and the client's site metrics we develop the following **Opportunity Scores metrics:**

1. **DA Opportunity Score**: this formula has the ability to compare *DA Average* against client current *DA* and return opportunity scores between 100 (highest opportunity to rank) and 0 (lowest opportunity).

2. **PA Opportunity Score:** comparison of *PA Average* against client current *PA* and return opportunity scores between 100 (highest opportunity to rank) and 0 (lowest opportunity).

Having these two Opportunity Scores we can calculate our final **Ranking Opportunity Score**, which takes into consideration our main data points: **DAOS, PAOS,** and current **ranking**. Scores between 100 (highest opportunity to rank) and 0 (lowest opportunity).

These scores help us to prioritize the next steps in the process:

1. How many links to build to that page.

2. How often to build links to that page.

3. The necessary "on-page corrections to make.

> Ok, take a deep breath - I know this is confusing to read, but I told you before we automated this whole file for you. All you have to do is find the keywords and enter the data, the rest will take care of itself.

2.4 - Putting Together a List of "Target Pages"

Here's a problem that plagues most SEO specialists. Modern websites tend to be too big to track every page and keyword using all the data we've talked about so far.

The smart move isn't to do away with SEO, but to build a list of high-opportunity target pages. That enables us to hyperfocus on the pages and keywords that are likely to return the best results.

This is a simple process that rolls up the data collected to this point from our Website Quality Audit and keyword analysis (of existing pages). We use it to prioritize the most important pages on a website based on opportunity.

Let's run through an example file:

- **Priority** - we calculate this based on the opportunity of a page. Generally speaking, we like to focus on "low hanging" fruit pages, ones that are already ranking for the "main KW" between positions 6 and 20. We also look at the number of links the top 3 pages have to understand the level of effort required.

- **Section** - depending on the scope / budget of a client, we can't optimize all pages at once. We segment pages into sections depending on the length and scope of a campaign.

- **Type** - pulled from the Website Quality Audit.

- **URL** - the target page.

- **Main KW** - pulled from the keyword analysis covered in the previous chapter.

Priority	Section	Type	URL	Main KW
1	Section 1	Resource Page	http://www.9001simplified.com/is	iso 9001 implementation steps
2	Section 1	Product Page	http://www.9001simplified.com/is	iso 9001 documentation templat
3	Section 1	Product Page	http://www.9001simplified.com/is	iso 9001 templates
4	Section 1	Product Page	http://www.9001simplified.com/is	iso 9001 quality manual
5	Section 1	Product Page	http://www.9001simplified.com/w	getting iso certified
6	Section 1	Product Page	http://www.9001simplified.com/is	iso 9001 2015 forms
7	Section 1	Product Page	http://www.9001simplified.com/is	iso 9001 2015 checklist
8	Section 1	Lead Generation	http://www.9001simplified.com/cc	iso 9001 comparison
9	Section 1	Homepage	http://www.9001simplified.com/	ISO 9001 certification
10	Section 1	Product Page	http://www.9001simplified.com/is	iso 9001 2015 download
11	Section 1	Product Page	http://www.9001simplified.com/is	iso 9001 update 2015

- **Volume** - the number of monthly searches for the "main KW".

- **Ranking** - the current ranking of the "main KW". We use this to benchmark campaign progress. You can use any rank tracking software to get this data.

- **Journey** - pulled from the keyword analysis file, this helps understand the intent of the keyword.

Volume	Ranking	Journey
0-100	12	3. Discover
0-100	29	2. Consider
0-100	26	2. Consider
0-100	81	2. Consider
0-100	12	2. Consider
0-100	100	2. Consider
0-100	100	2. Consider
0-100	100	2. Consider
1000 - 3000	100	2. Consider
0-100	100	2. Consider
0-100	100	2. Consider

The file then digs into comparative link metrics to understand the links required to improve rankings. The first 2 columns are for the site we're working on:

- **RD**. The number of referring domains the target page (on our site) has.
- **DA**. The Domain Authority of our website.

The next columns are pulled from the keyword analysis file, that look at the link metrics of the top 3 results in Google for the "main KW".

- **Avg RD**. The average number of referring domains for the "main KW".
- **Avg DA**. The average Domain Authority for the "main KW".
- **Avg Monthly Velocity.** The average number of links the "main KW" pages receive per month.

Comparing our site metrics to the top 3 results in Google, we're able to put together a high level link building strategy for each of the target pages:

- **Suggested # RD.** By comparing how many referring domains our target page has to the top 3 results in Google, we're able to deduce a total number of links we should acquire for that page over the life of the campaign.

- **Suggested Authority.** By looking at the quality of the top 3 results in Google, we're able to understand the power of domains we need to target for link building.

- **Suggested Velocity.** This tells us how many links we should acquire to the target page each month. We don't want to build too many links too fast, it's unnatural. Instead, we use the data to emulate what the top pages are doing to create a natural pattern.

Our Site RD	Our Site DA	Top 3 Results Avg RD	Top 3 Results Avg DA	Top 3 Results Avg Monthly Velocity	Suggested # RD	Suggested Authority	Link Budget:10 Suggested Velocity
5	19	2	45	1	5	55	1
0	19	6	52	1	7	55	1
1	19	6	52	1	7	55	1
6	19	2	64	1	5	55	1
0	19	122	53	12	123	55	2
0	19	3	28	1	5	55	1
2	19	2	47	0	5	55	1
0	19	5	40	1	6	55	1
31	19	1018	56	90	1019	55	3
10	19	70	74	7	71	55	2
1	19	185	95	16	186	55	2

With this file completed, we have a high level execution plan for which pages to focus on. We now can shift our focus to improving the "on page" quality and promoting them through links and social engagement.

2.5 - On-Page SEO Audit

The nuts and bolts of SEO still apply - page titles, meta descriptions, keyword usage (etc) impact how search engines rank your website.

These aren't new concepts by any means. However, in our experience, not a lot of SEOs pay enough attention to optimizing on-page SEO. Instead, they want to focus on 'sexier' things, like link building, which they imagine will yield better short-term results.

That is a **huge** mistake to make. We've been able to get better rankings focusing solely on improving the on-page elements of websites, without adding a single link towards them. That's not to say that link building isn't important, but that's not the focus of this section.

For this section section we're going to analyze the way you're tackling on-page optimization for existing assets and look for ways you can improve that process.

Traditional "on page" elements

The scope of on-page optimization has grown rapidly in the past years. Optimizing titles and metas is not enough anymore. These days, proper on-page optimization requires to analyze the overall context of each page.

There are a lot of areas to consider during this process. To help keep things manageable, we developed a 3-step process that breaks down on-page analysis:

- **Step #1** - The on-page checklist
- **Step #2** - On-page body recommendations

- **Step #3** - Schema markups

Step #1 The On-page Checklist

The first thing we want to do is check traditional on-page elements. Those include page titles, meta data, headings, subheadings, structured data, and keyword usage. At this stage, we're just giving our content a close look to see what we need to optimize. In the next steps, we'll go over keyword optimization and adding schema markup (structured data) to your content.

To help speed up the analysis process, we built a partially automated checklist that crosswalks data from the *Website Quality Audit*, *Keyword Research* and *Target Pages* files, and triggers a "Pass/Fail" outcome for each item. This pass/fail categorization is generated by custom formulas that compare the current page technicalities with the industry standard best practices.

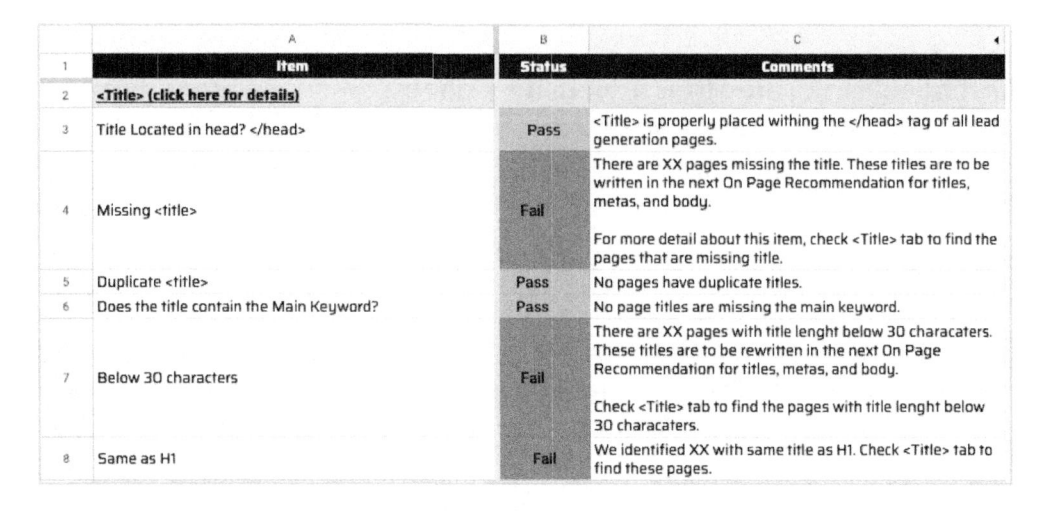

	A — Item	B — Status	C — Comments
2	\<Title\> (click here for details)		
3	Title Located in head? \</head\>	Pass	\<Title\> is properly placed withing the \</head\> tag of all lead generation pages.
4	Missing \<title\>	Fail	There are XX pages missing the title. These titles are to be written in the next On Page Recommendation for titles, metas, and body. For more detail about this item, check \<Title\> tab to find the pages that are missing title.
5	Duplicate \<title\>	Pass	No pages have duplicate titles.
6	Does the title contain the Main Keyword?	Pass	No page titles are missing the main keyword.
7	Below 30 characters	Fail	There are XX pages with title lenght below 30 characaters. These titles are to be rewritten in the next On Page Recommendation for titles, metas, and body. Check \<Title\> tab to find the pages with title lenght below 30 characaters.
8	Same as H1	Fail	We identified XX with same title as H1. Check \<Title\> tab to find these pages.

You don't have to build a similar checklist, but it comes in handy if you need to analyze a large number of pages. As usual, a simple Google Sheets document will suffice.

> **Visit www.theblueprint.website to check out a free version of our On Page SEO Checklist.**

The checklist into 4 sections. Each section includes notes on what parts of each page are already optimized and which ones need more work.

Again, this is simply a checklist to uncover how much effort will go into optimizing the on page of a website. This checklist is also a tremendous deliverable for clients because it alerts them of how much work is needed to improve the on page performance of their website.

Section 1 - Title Tags

These are the clickable headlines Google shows for a given result. They should contain your main keyword, convince users to click on it, and be under 55 characters. Title tags are HUGE on page ranking factors.

Our checklist verifies that a website's pages:

- <title> tags are placed within the </head> tag in the HTML.
- Has any missing or duplicated titles across pages.
- Is using the main keyword in the title.
- Are not using "Long title tags" over 70 pixels and/or short titles below 30 characters.
- Are not using the same page title and h1 on pages.

2 - Meta Description Tags

These are short page descriptions that should summarize the page content in 156 characters. They tell the user what content they can expect to find when they click on the result. Search engines display these under the title tag. While meta tags are not a ranking factor (like page titles), they do influence click behavior in the SERPs.

Our checklist verifies that a website's pages:

- <meta> tags are placed within the </head> tag in the HTML.
- Are not missing or using duplicate meta descriptions across pages.
- Are not using meta descriptions with over 156 and/or below 70 characters.

3 - Page Headings

Aka <h1> tags, are generally found at the top of the page and display the page heading (may be different from the title tag). They tell Google about important content on the page. This is a good place to work on secondary keywords different from the main keyword in the title tag.

Our checklist verifies that a website's pages:

- Contain source code to verify that H1 tags are being used as a complement to the page's title.
- Are not using H1 duplicated and reused across pages.
- Contain source code to verify that the site is using H2 - H6s tags properly in key landing pages (i.e. in proper order, using keywords,

breaking up content logically, etc). These tags are used throughout the page to reinforce the semantics (meaning) of the content.

4 - Structured data

A snippet of code that instructs search engines what your page is about. These markups come in different forms (local business, video, etc) and should be used based on your website and content type. This code makes it easier for Googlebot to get to the meat of what your page is about (I'll show you how these look in action in a minute).

We optimize structured data markups by:

- Putting the each page type (identified in the WQA) page into Google's Structured Data Testing Tool, and checking what type of structure data makrupts (i.e. schema) the website is currently using and if it shows any errors.

- Using Google Tag Manager we check if the markups were setup using JSON LD.

- Using Google Search Console we verify if the client is using Rich Cards and AMP pages setup properly.

Having your own checklist gives you a full breakdown of what actions you need to take for each page. As we mentioned before, these are the nuts and bolts of on-page SEO. However, proper on-page optimization these days also requires more in-depth analysis, which is what we'll focus on in the next section.

Step #2: On-page Body Recommendations

With the checklist done, we have a better overall picture of the website's on-page needs. However, this is just the tip of the iceberg, what we do next is what really tells us how big the challenge is.

What we like to do is go through each page and **manually** analyze its content. That covers titles, metas, headers, keyword density, word count, semantic keywords, images, internal links, etc. Your goal is to look for ways to improve the way you use all those elements, while keeping things natural.

Manually reviewing content also gives us an opportunity to compare its quality against our top competitors. Your content pages might be 'perfectly' optimized for SEO, but if your competitors have better writers or provide a more enjoyable experience, that's going to affect rankings. Without a manual review, you might miss those differences in quality.

I'm not going to lie – it's a ton of work. However, if you want to overtake the top results for a competitive keyword, you need to be willing to roll up your sleeves. To simplify the process, we broke things down into three parts.

1. Focus on the most important pages

As usual, we like to focus our efforts into the pages that are bringing in the most traffic and/or conversions to your website. At this stage, we compile a list of URLs and pull key data from each of those pages, including:

- URLs
- Main keyword
- Word count

- Page type
- Title
- Meta description
- Current H1

All of this data was already pulled during the WQA - we simply have to migrate this into a new document.

> NOTE: If you are following our process, the "most important pages" have already been identified. In the WQA, we assigned URL Actions to important pages that needed keyword research. We migrated those URLs into the keyword research template and discovered the proper targeting for those pages. Now, we're simply putting those keywords into action by performing on-page SEO. We're doing on-page for the same set of URLs we did keyword research for.

It shouldn't come as a shock that we like to use a sheet to compile all that information. Our document looks something like this, but feel free to adapt it to any format you want:

Before we sit down to take a look at each page and see what we can optimize, we like to take a look at what the competition is doing. That way, we can ensure we're doing everything better.

2. Compare your content against pages that outrank it

This is by far the most important section when it comes to on-page analysis. Here's where we find what the ranking websites are doing, that **we aren't,** in terms of content, structure, and keywords.

After this section, you should have a clear idea of what you need to **add**, **remove,** or **modify** for each page.

Here's a quick breakdown of how our process goes:

1. **Google the main keyword on incognito mode.** This allows us to make a transparent search and get unbiased results.

2. **Pay attention to the top ranking sites.** During this step, you want to exclude ads and highly authoritative websites such as Wikipedia, Amazon, and major media portals. We want to make a head to head comparison with websites we might actually be able to outrank.

3. **Choose at least 3 related sites to compare with.** Once you know what sites you want to analyze, go in and take a look. You want to check out what they're doing in terms of titles, images, the types of URLs they're using, what their linking strategy is, and whether the sites themselves load fast.

For a successful page content analysis, it's important you focus on websites of a similar nature. If you're doing a campaign for an online store, it doesn't make sense to compare it against a blog. Apples to apples and oranges to oranges, so to speak.

You can figure out quite quickly how on top of their game your competitors are by how they structure their pages. The quality of the content is a big factor, of course, but one of the things I notice first are the titles and headings.

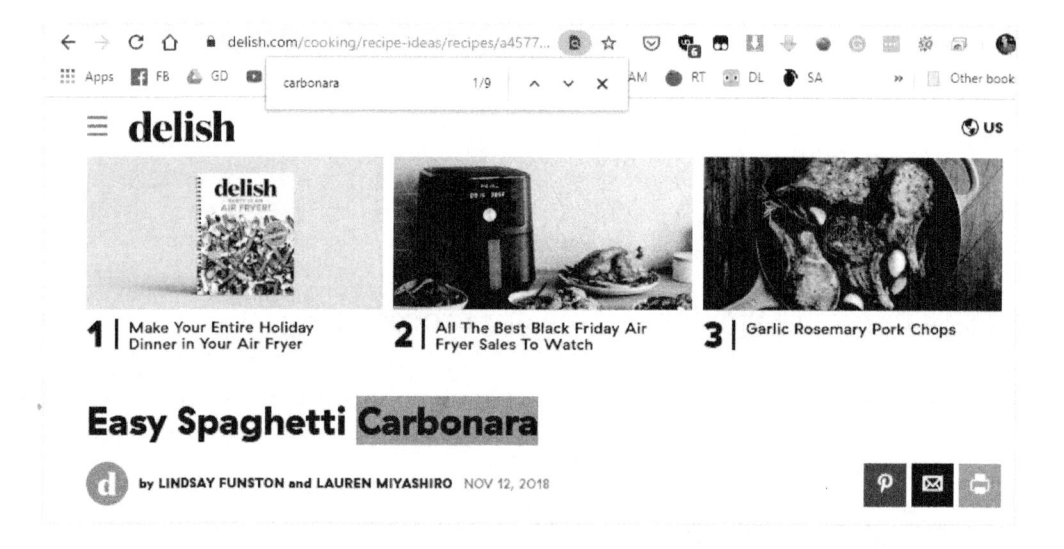

If your competitors aren't using SEO-optimized titles or they've over-optimizing, then it's a good sign they might know what they're doing. That's where the next step comes in, where we cover the basics of on-page optimization.

I cannot overstate the importance of keeping detailed notes at this stage. There are too many factors to account for, so you need something that'll help you track them all (hint: our favorite tool starts with an *s* and ends in *preadsheet*).

3. On-page optimization

All that research into your competitors needs to be translated into action. Earlier on, we showed you the spreadsheet we use to keep track of the URLs, keywords, titles, meta descriptions, and more for your top pages.

Your goal now, is to return to that spreadsheet and compare your top pages with the notes you took concerning your competitors. There's always room for improvement when it comes to on-page SEO, and these are the elements you'll want to work on:

- **Page titles:** As a rule of thumb, your pages' titles need to be informative and interesting enough for people to want to click on them. Whenever possible, you want to use your main keyword within the title and incorporate numbers (people love numbers in titles). See what your competitors are doing and come up with even catchier titles.

- **Headers:** Subheadings are critical for Google to understand what your content is about. You want to try and include both your main and secondary keywords within your headings, but within reason. If you just jam keywords in, you risk over-optimization. My advice is, use subheadings to break down your content into logical increments and keep an eye out for keyword-placement opportunities.

- **Meta descriptions:** Although Google sometimes allows up to 220 characters, you should keep your meta descriptions within the 160-character range. You want to make the best use of that space, so your meta descriptions need to both cover what your pages' content is and why users should be interested. If you can also include your main keyword inside, that's a bonus.

- **Image use and alt-text:** Images do a lot more work than just looking pretty. Proper image use within your pages can increase engagement, make for a better user experience, and help with SEO. Ideally, you should be adding alt-text to every single image on your website, explaining what it is. That alt-text gives Google context about those images, and it's something a lot of people overlook due to laziness.

- **Page URLs:** Your pages' URLs should be easy to understand and provide information about the content that users will see. If they're just long strings of numbers, it can cost you clicks as users might not want to click on them.

- **Internal Links:** As you know, links are one of the pillars of SEO. Every page provides you with opportunities to link to more of your content, helping users spend more time on your website. Including links to external, but relevant content can also help with engagement. You don't want to include links every couple of words, but whenever it makes sense to do so, don't be shy about it.

We can break down all on-page SEO elements into three categories. There's content, HTML, and architecture. A lot of people think that SEO is all about the content, but HTML elements, such as headings, meta descriptions, and alt-text are critical for search engines.

Even little changes in your page titles and meta descriptions can drastically increase your client's clickthrough rates, so it's important you go over everything with a fine comb.

Finally, it's also important that you take a look at your page structure. Websites should be enjoyable to use and it should be easy to find the information you need. If your competitors are providing a better experience when it comes to design and usability, then you need to rethink your page structure.

4. Schema Markup

Schema markup or structured data are snippets of code you add to your pages, which give Google information about what type of content it's dealing with. I'm a big fan of schema markup because it dramatically improves the way your content shows up on the SERPs. Here's an example of some recipe pages that use structured data:

> **Best Spaghetti Carbonara Recipe - How to Make Pasta ...**
> https://www.delish.com › cooking › recipe-ideas › recipes › easy-carbonara-...
> Nov 12, 2018 - ★★★★☆ Rating: 4.7 - 12 reviews - 20 min
> When you're craving a comfort food, nothing will cure you like creamy **spaghetti carbonara**. Here's ...
>
> **Italian carbonara | Jamie Oliver pasta & risotto recipes**
> https://www.jamieoliver.com › gennaro-s-classic-spaghetti-carbonara ▾
> 10 min - 860 cal
> A spaghetti **carbonara recipe** is a failsafe classic. This Italian carbonara uses the traditional guanciale and pecorino cheese for a real taste of Italy.

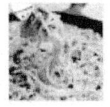

Those results are what we call 'rich snippets', because they include more information than your traditional results. If you look closely, you can spot calorie information and recipe cook time. Now compare that with traditional search results:

> In a rush: Spaghetti carbonara | Recipes | John and Lisa's ...
> https://www.itv.com › john-and-lisas-weekend-kitchen › in-a-rush-spaghett... ▾
> Jul 21, 2019 - This spaghetti **carbonara recipe** is a firm favourite with John's children, and a delicious mid-week meal to whip-up when you're in a hurry.

Which result looks more appealing to you? The answer is obvious, hence why using structured data can improve click-through rates dramatically. Plus, it enables you to include key information **without** using up your meta description characters.

Those examples focus only on recipes (because I'm hungry). However, there are hundreds of types of schemas you can use depending on what type of content you're dealing with. Some types of content you'll easily recognize include:

1. **Events:** This type of schema markup enables you to include location information, prices, and dates.

2. **Products:** This is one of our favorites, for obvious reasons. With product schema, you can include images, price, and even stock information.

3. **Place:** If you've ever looked up a restaurant or hotel online, you'll have seen this type of schema in action. It enables you to include ratings, pricing information, location, and more.

You can read more about every type of schema you can use at the following link:

Schema.org

For most websites, you'll usually focus on one type of schema or two at the most. For example, if you run an online store, you'll rely heavily on product markup. Here's a quick example of how the schema for a book page might look like:

```
<div itemscope itemtype="https://schema.org/Book">

<span itemprop="name"> Inbound Marketing and SEO: Insights from the Moz Blog</span>

<span itemprop="author">Rand Fishkin</span>

</div>
```

Adding schema markup to your website is relatively simple, but it can be time consuming depending on how many pages you're working with. If it's a low number, you can do so manually by editing each page's HTML file.

As for how to generate that data, Google enables you to use a free tool called Structured Data Markup Helper. With it, you can choose what type of schema you want to generate and for which URL:

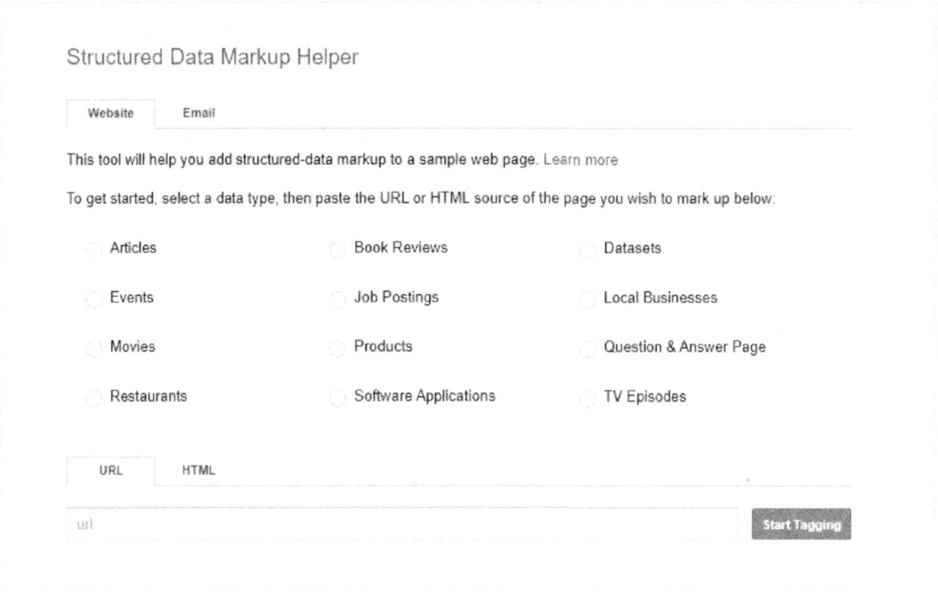
Structured Data Markup Helper
Website
Email
This tool will help you add structured-data markup to a sample web page. Learn more
To get started, select a data type, then paste the URL or HTML source of the page you wish to mark up below:
Articles
Book Reviews
Datasets
Events
Job Postings
Local Businesses
Movies
Products
Question & Answer Page
Restaurants
Software Applications
TV Episodes
URL
HTML
url
Start Tagging

Once you enter an URL, the helper will ask you to highlight or select the elements you want to include in your rich snippets and let you choose how to tag them:

31 Marketing KPIs to Use In Your Campaigns
Analytics
Name
Author
Date published
Image
Article section
Article body
URL
Publisher
Aggregate rating

Once you're ready, you can click the *Generate HTML* button to the right and Google will give you an HTML snippet you can add to your website.

If you use WordPress, this whole process becomes much simpler. You have access to plugins that enable you to add markup to any of your posts and pages while you're working on them, which saves you the trouble of having to edit HTML files manually. For this job, we like the Schema - All In One Schema Rich Snippets plugin.

Once the plugin is active, you can set a type of content for each of your posts and pages, and use the plugin to add schema markup to it without leaving the editor:

Regardless of what method you're using to add schema to your website, at some point, you might want to make sure the code is working as intended. The fastest way to do this is to use Google's Structured Data Testing Tool. With this service, you can enter any URL you like and Google will check if it uses structured data and if so, show you what its rich snippet looks like:

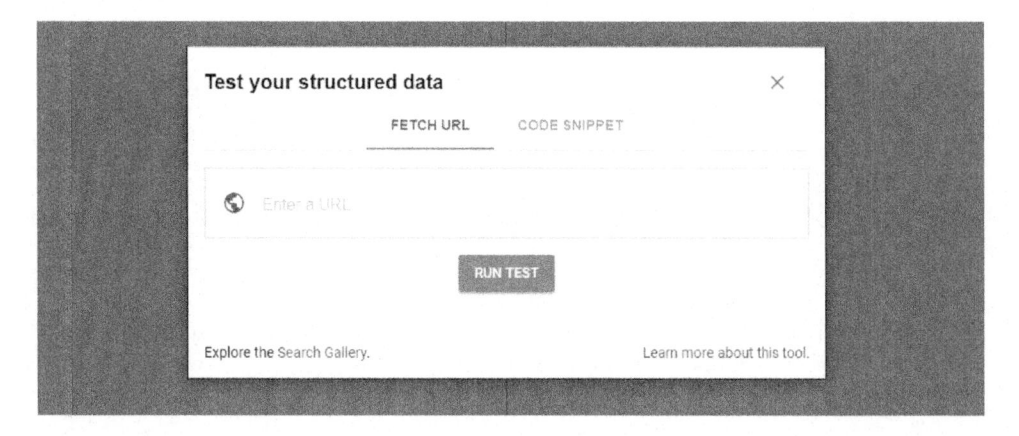

If you're working with a website that already uses structured data markup, you'll want to bookmark this tool to make sure your client implemented the code the right way. Otherwise, you won't get to enjoy all the benefits of rich snippets.

PHASE 3

The Building Process

Now that we've given your website an SEO makeover, it's time to start creating new assets. That means doing keyword research for content we haven't targeted yet, checking where we can compete with other websites and creating a new content calendar.

Building new SEO assets (i.e. content) is an ongoing process. If you want to keep bringing in more traffic, you need to play the long game, and that's what we're going to focus on in this phase:

- **3.1 - Auditing Your Existing Content.** So far, our audit process focused entirely on technical SEO factors. Now it's time to take a look at the content itself and gauge its quality in terms of how engaging it is.

- **3.2 - Filling In Your "Keyword Gaps".** In Phase 2, we discussed finding keywords for the existing pages on your site. Now, we can turn our attention to finding keyword "gaps". We do so with a "keyword gap analysis" that scrapes your competitors and finds opportunities for growth.

- **3.3 - Coming Up With New Topic Ideas.** Taking the keywords we just found and blowing them out into topics for content and new page generation. At this stage, you're probably already targeting most keywords that indicate "pre purchase intent" so you need to dig deeper.

For example, what do people search for *before* they're ready to make a purchase from you?

- **3.4 - Building a Content Calendar**. A content calendar ensures the timely and consistent creation of content for your website.

- **3.5 - Create or Update? An Introduction to Creating and Updating Great Content (By Julia McCoy).** With a calendar in place, it's time to work on your content. That means either developing new posts from scratch or updating existing ones.

3.1 - Auditing Your Existing Content

Our goal here is to make sure you're getting the most out of the content you've already created. That means ensuring the right pages are getting attention from search engines, improving the focus of your content, improving conversions, and ensuring your website remains relevant.

Start with data from The Website Quality Audit

In Section 2.1 we talked about The Website Quality Audit, a report that aggregates data from including Screaming Frog, SEMrush, Google Search Console, and Google Analytics. You may also recall we tagged blog posts and resource guides with a URL Action ("9. Update Content") to be assessed later - now's the time to dive deeper.

When we initially ran the WQA, we were looking at "bottom funnel" pages, the ones that hold the most conversion value to that website (product page, service page, etc). This time we will be focusing on "top funnel" pages, aka content.

The WQA already has all the data we need to run an advanced content audit - we just need to filter for the right pages and we're good.

Assigning new "URL Actions" to each content URL

We assigned "URL Actions" in the WQA - we need to do that again as content needs to be treated differently than the other pages on your website.

For each content page on the websites we work on, we like to assign them one of 6 possible actions. Those are:

1. **Leave as is.** For content pages that are less than 6 months old, we recommend you leave them as is. You probably don't have enough data yet to decide what to do, so hold your horses until the next audit rolls around. For any older content that *is* getting decent traffic (anything above 100 visits per year), you can also let it be.

2. **301 redirect.** Posts that don't get any noteworthy traffic or conversions are basically taking up space, so go ahead and redirect those URLs towards other pages with more value.

3. **Archive.** Some pages might not be all that relevant when it comes to SEO, but your audience might like them. For this type of content, we like to block Google from indexing it so it doesn't take up any of your crawl budget and your audience stays happy.

4. **Refresh.** If you see any content that's beginning to slide in the keyword rankings or losing traffic, you might want to make some small changes to it. Those include tweaking the title, meta description, subheadings, and media files. For your most valuable content pages, refreshers are in order every once in a while.

5. **Rewrite.** Sometimes, you have content that you know is targeting valuable keywords, but it's either not performing as well as you want or sliding too fast down the rankings. If you think a refresh won't be enough to save it, then it's time for a full rewrite.

6. **Merge.** Ideally, you don't want multiple content pages targeting the same topics or you risk cannibalizing your own traffic. The best course of action here is to consolidate both posts into a more in-depth page and set up a 301 redirect from one of the old URLs to the other one.

7. **Target with links.** Some pages can have amazing content and target the right keywords, but they may not be getting the results you want. In these cases, you want to focus on targeting that content with links. This involves what we call the 'pillar/cluster' system, which we'll cover in a minute.

Deciding what action to take for each URL is relatively simple, but it involves manual overview. You need to review each link and its content to determine what action to take. The only content you can exclude from this manual process are those posts less than 6 months old.

Once you've run a full content audit, you can start looking into page and keyword opportunities you haven't explored yet. Before that, though, we want to introduce you to what we call the topic clusters structure, which is key to our optimization process.

Consolidating your content into "pillars" and "clusters"

Managing a website's content is similar to managing a supermarket. We need a system to organize content into pillars (aka food, beverage, condiments, etc) and clusters (aka brands). We need to keep inventory on content so we know exactly what we've created and how it fits into our content strategy.

We like to divide content into two categories, which are:

1. **Pillars (aka Hubs):** Large topics that are core to the business operations. These topics must easily map back to your product / service functionality, audience or industry.

2. **Clusters:** The topics that support the hub and explore all possible options for traffic and engagement.

To make this easier to visualize, you can think of pillars as physical silos on your website (think blog categories) and clusters as the individual topics / blog posts that support them.

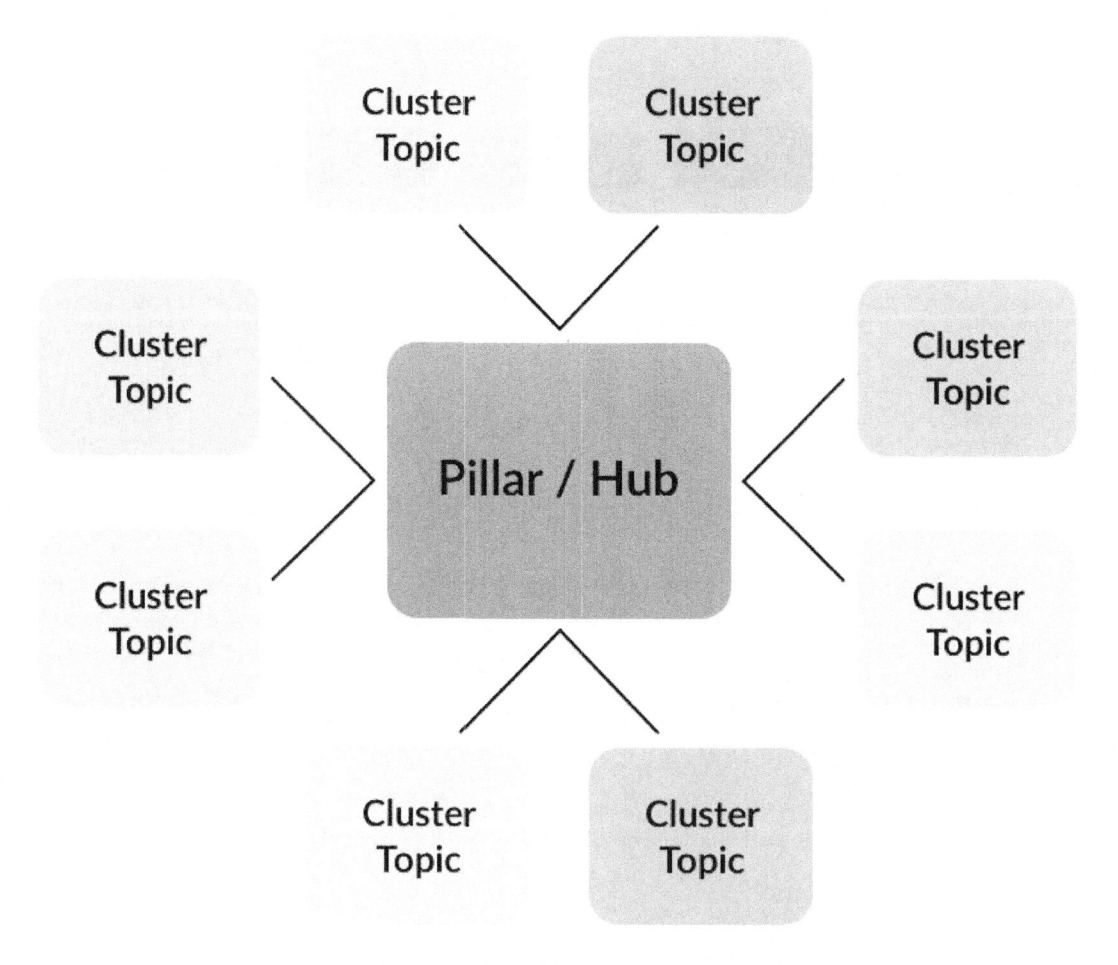

```
       Cluster        Cluster
       Topic          Topic

Cluster                          Cluster
Topic                            Topic
                 Pillar / Hub
Cluster                          Cluster
Topic                            Topic

       Cluster        Cluster
       Topic          Topic
```

The pillar/cluster system enables you to rank for more competitive keywords by building more in-depth pages than your competitors. It also improves the user journey by developing more natural links between pages.

The pillar/cluster system isn't just a catchy SEO term, it's a system you can use to build more in-depth content than your competitors.

Imagine, for example, you're working on a website for a local coffee shop. Once you know what your pillars are, you can begin to develop clusters of content around them. For location-based content, you might cover what to do in a local area, interview talented brewers, seek partnerships with local businesses, and much more.

```
                    Coffee Vendor
          ┌──────────────┼──────────────┐
        Coffee         Brewing        Locations
```

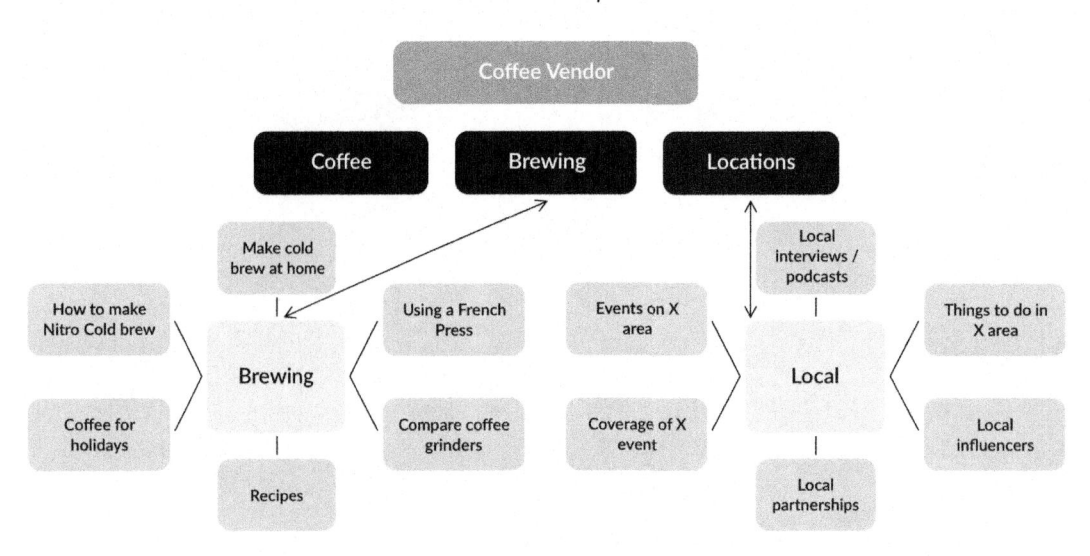

```
                Make cold                          Local
                brew at home                       interviews /
                                                   podcasts
  How to make                  Using a French   Events on X              Things to do in
  Nitro Cold brew              Press            area                     X area
                   Brewing                              Local
  Coffee for                   Compare coffee   Coverage of X            Local
  holidays                     grinders         event                    influencers
                   Recipes                              Local
                                                        partnerships
```

I'm a big fan of the cluster/pillar system because it provides a quick reality check when we're brainstorming content ideas. If we come up with an angle we want to tackle for content, but it doesn't map to any of our client's pillars, then perhaps it's not a good fit for them.

As a whole, the pillar/cluster system enables us to improve our client's websites on two fronts:

1. Building the website around its pillars provides a better user experience. It enables visitors to find the content they need faster and it becomes easier for your clients to stay organized.

2. Google loves topic clusters as they tend to provide more in-depth content.

Naturally, your client's pillars need to map directly to the services and products they provide. If they don't, then you end up focusing on content that doesn't provide a direct economic benefit to your clients.

If you didn't skip the content audit, then you should have a pretty good idea of what your client's pillars and clusters are. Having that information at hand will enable you to identify content 'gaps'. That is to say, potential clusters you haven't explored yet.

3.2 - Keyword Research and Gap Analysis

A minute ago, we talked about content gaps, which is to say, topics and keywords you're not targeting yet. Ideally, you want to rank for as many keywords as your competitors do and to show up on top of them in the SERPs.

To do this, you need to know what keywords they're targeting that you aren't – that's the gap you need to close. Analyzing each page by hand would take an eternity, so we have a system in place that simplifies the whole thing.

What we do is set up a file that contains both our client's keywords and those from their competitors. Then we crosswalk that data to find the gaps.

At this stage, you should already have a list of your client keywords, so let's focus on finding your competitor's. Our favorite tool for the job is the Ahrefs Site Explorer. Go ahead and run a search for your client's domain, then click under Organic Research and select the Top Competing Domains option.

That will give you a list of websites that are in direct competition with your client's for the same keywords. Take a minute now to identify the ones you think are more relevant.

Once you're locked into your targets, you'll want to generate new Ahrefs reports for each one of them. The data we care about is located under the Organic Keywords tab. Here, Ahrefs will give you a list of all the keywords they're ranking for, which you can (and should) export as a .csv file:

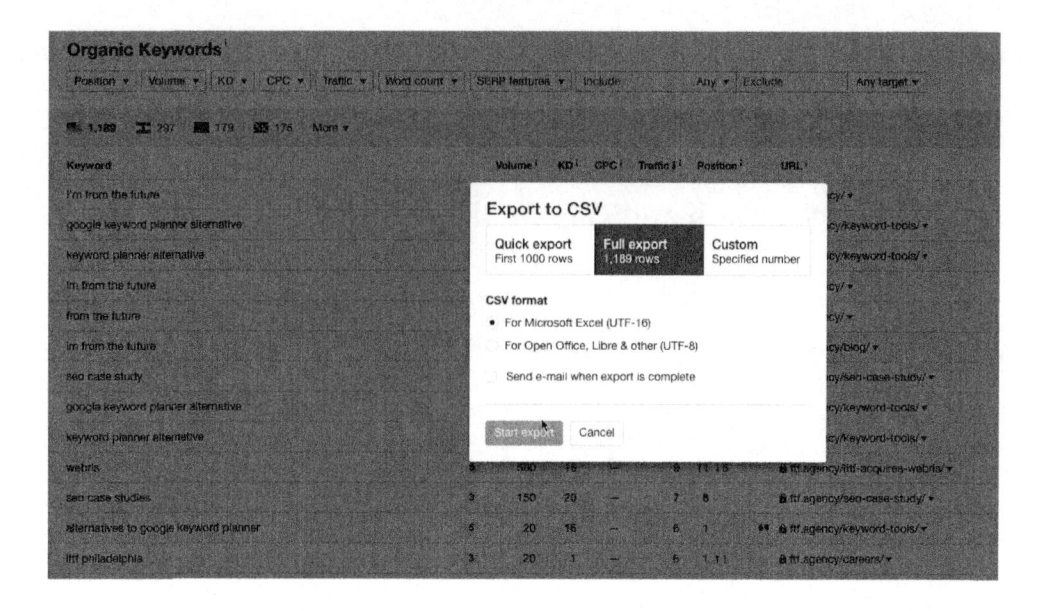

By the end of this process, you should have multiple spreadsheets containing all your competitor's keywords. What you want to do is compile all those keywords into a single file, so you can compare them with your client's.

That's a lot of data to sift through, though, so to make your life easier, we've put together a template you can use to compile and crosswalk that data using Google Spreadsheets.

> **Visit www.theblueprint.website to get access to our Keyword Gap Analysis.**

If you're using that template, you'll notice there are tabs for individual competitors. Go ahead and paste their keyword data inside, including position, volume, URL, and difficulty – all information that Ahrefs gives you. There's also a separate tab for your client's keywords, which you should already have:

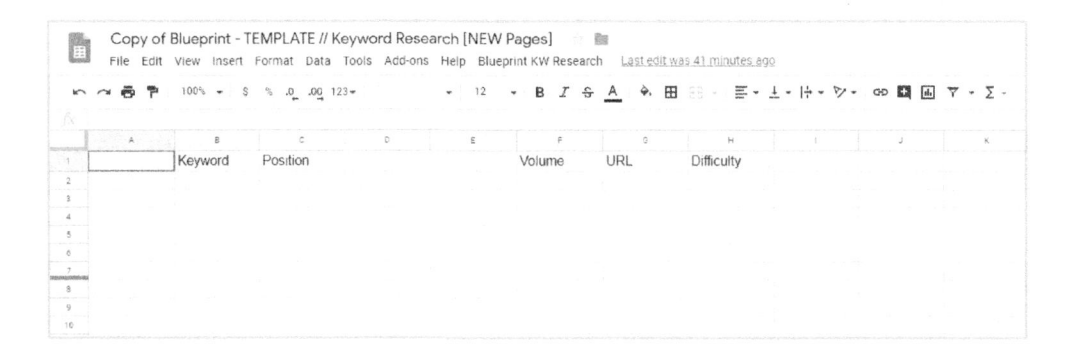

The template includes a script that will automatically crosswalk all that information and spit out a list of keywords your client isn't targeting yet, which you can locate under the MASTER tab. To run that script, hit the Blueprint KW Research button at the top of the page.

Here's what you should be looking at now:

That's a full list of all your client's missing keywords, including difficulty scores, what your competitors' best ranking is, and a ton more data.

Using that template will save you a lot of time, but there's work to be done. Not all the keywords within your client's gap will be worth the effort to target. It's your job to manually sort through that list and discard the keywords you don't think are valuable enough.

For the keywords you have left, you'll want to categorize them into existing clusters and pillars, as well as assign a priority level. The higher the search volume and the lower the difficulty, the more you should prioritize those keywords.

3.3 - Coming Up With New Topic Ideas

Right now, you have a goldmine of data on keywords your competitors are using. Those are raw materials, which we need to transform into full topic ideas.

As mentioned before, you want to discard anything that's obviously of no use to your client. For example, branded searches are a no-brainer, as are misspelled keywords. Once you narrow down the keywords that have real value, the easiest way to come up with content ideas is to look up what other websites are doing.

Let's say, for example, one of the keywords that's missing from your website is "best running shoes". A quick search reveals the top results for that keyword all dominate with "best of" product lists.

```
www.t3.com › features › best-running-shoes
Best running shoes 2020: rule the road with road running ...
Best running shoes: the best trainers from Nike, Adidas, Asics, Mizuno, Hoka and more. Shoes
built to smash your PB.
Best trail running shoes · Best women's running shoes · Best running headphones

runrepeat.com › ranking › rankings-of-running-shoes
30+ Best Running Shoes (Buyer's Guide) | RunRepeat
★★★★☆ Rating: 4.7 - 4,100 votes
All 2157 running shoes ranked by the best – based on reviews from 8720 experts & 1131352
runners. The ultimate list. Updated February 2020!

www.cnet.com › news › best-running-shoes
9 of the best running shoes for 2020 - CNET
When the day comes to replace your trusty running shoes, it can be hard to ignore the signs.
Your feet are sore and your heels have fresh blisters, the shoe's ...
```

The obvious solution, in this case, would be to put together a list that's longer, more thorough, and more engaging. Right there, you went from a keyword that you pulled from a list to a real idea you can run by your client for approval.

What we like to do, as usual, is put together all those brand new ideas into a spreadsheet. It's not enough to know what keyword you want to target and with what type of content, though, we like to dig a little deeper.

Topic	Main KW	Pillar	Cluster	SERP Intent	Page Type	Content Tactic	New or Rewrite?
How to Deal With Bad Online Reviews	Bad Online Reviews	SEO	ORM	Focused	Blog Post	Expert Guide	New
How to Start a Podcast	how to build a podcast			Focused	Blog Post	Expert Guide	New
How to Start a Podcast	how to build a podcast			Focused	Instagram Post	Graphic	New

For every content idea we consider, we like to come up with a potential title and classify it into our existing pillars/clusters. At this stage, you also want to specify what type of content you're dealing with (i.e. expert guides, roundups, infographics, etc.) and the type of page you want to put together. We focus a lot on blogs, but you'll also have to deal with product pages, guides, and even social media posts, in some cases.

You'll also notice we include something I like to call "SERP Intent" in our list of potential topics. In a nutshell, SERP intent is a method we put together to create content based on Google (you guessed it) user intent.

If we return to that running shoes example, you can see that most of the top results are buying guides for the best running shoes. The SERPs are telling us the intent behind a "best of" search is not to see a single product page, but instead a roundup style guide listing out multiple shoes for a searcher to browse. Trying to rank a product page for a search like this will never work, we need to work within the constructs of what Google is telling us is a good result type.

Running a search for a different topic, such as "how to get rid of pimples", reveals a similar result. Most pages are focused on fast or overnight solutions, which only one result going in-depth about the causes of acne and how to fight it:

```
www.seventeen.com › beauty › makeup-skincare › how-to-get-rid-of-...
How to Get Rid of Pimples Overnight – 8 Tips to Get Rid of ...
Sep 19, 2019 - We talked to dermatologists Dr. Robin Evans and Dr. Whitney Bowe to get their
top tips on how to get rid of pimples overnight. This list is ...

www.goodhousekeeping.com › beauty › anti-aging › how-to-quickly...
How to Get Rid of Pimples Fast — Quick Ways to Eliminate ...
Jun 14, 2019 - Here's how to get rid of that pimple as quickly as possible with these tried-and-
true at-home acne fighting methods, topical treatments, acne ...

www.medicinenet.com › acne › article
How to Get Rid of Acne (Pimples) Causes, Symptoms & Home ...
Blackhead & Cystic Acne Causes Symptoms Treatment of Acne Scars How to Get Rid of Acne
Hormonal Acne Diet Treatment for Acne Scars Skin Regimen.

www.verywellhealth.com › ... › Skin Health › Acne › Treatment
How to Get Rid of Pimples Fast - Verywell Health
When you need to get rid of that big pimple fast, try these tips to help banish the breakout and
speed healing.
```

In this case, the SERP intent tells you to focus on how-to content for getting rid of pimples in the least amount of time.

As a rule of thumb, if the SERP intent is highly focused, you want to follow the trend. However, if you see mixed results, then you can be creative about the type of content you produce.

Here's the issue, though – even if you're very aggressive about weeding out keywords that have little potential, chances are you will still end up with a massive list of potential topic ideas.

Tackling those ideas at random might work in the long term, but that's no way to run a campaign. What you want to do is prioritize the ideas and keywords with the most potential, and that can bring in the most revenue for your client, as we talked about in the last section. That order will tell you where to add that content within your calendar, which brings us to the next step.

3.4 - Building a Content Calendar

Let's recap what we've put together so far during the building process:

1. We've taken a look at existing content to see which pages have the most potential.

2. We've done keyword research and gap analysis, to figure out where to focus our efforts in.

3. We've used that information to come up with in-depth content ideas.

What we have is a lot of data and now it's time to put it to action. The way we do that is through a content calendar.

The idea of a content calendar might sound rudimentary, but content is at the heart of every SEO campaign. For 90% of our clients, we focus on blog posts, because they produce the most traffic. However, as we learned during the last section, SERP intent sometimes points towards a different direction.

In practice, that means you may have to deal with page types beyond blogs and put together a framework that enables you to manage all those content types.

In our experience, you can break down content and page types into different categories. Most of them are self-explanatory and we can divide those content types into 5 categories (which we'll break down even further in the next chapter):

1. **Blogs, whitepapers, and resource guides.** Here we have basic and in-depth blog posts as well as whitepapers. With this type of content, your goal is to put together something better than anything else the competition is doing. To do that, it's helpful to have basic outlines and a word count range to aim for at the content calendar stage.

2. **Multimedia content.** This includes infographics, videos, and podcasts. There's often less competition when it comes to in-depth media content, which can make it a great source of traffic if you have the resources to produce it (we'll go over this in a minute).

3. **Social media content.** We're going to talk a lot more about social media content later on, but suffice it to say, it can be a huge source of traffic. Social media posts need to be frequent though, which means you need a calendar and possibly automation tools to manage everything.

4. **Landing pages.** The goal of landing pages is to lead users directly to conversions. Usually, the copy tends to be much more direct and to the point, and they require a different approach than regular blog pages. Landing pages are usually found on local or B2B websites (think service pages).

5. **E-commerce pages.** These include product categories, pages, and more - basically any page that accepts a transaction. Your goal is to provide

more details, better images, and keep everything up-to-date, to beat competing online stores.

This level of detail is essential at the content calendar stage because the type of pages you deal with will determine how often you need to publish new content.

Take blogs, for example – if you're aggressive about growth and you're focused on a long-term strategy, daily or weekly updates are the way to go (depending on how fast you can produce well-researched pages). Social media posts operate at a higher frequency, because most people check social media multiple times per day.

On the other end of the spectrum, you have content such as product pages. Generally speaking, you don't need to update product pages all that often. You publish the page as soon as the product is available and that's it.

In practice, most campaigns boil down to a few page types, which will vary depending on the client and niche you're targeting. However, the sheer number of tasks that involves requires you to have a framework, which in this case, is a content calendar.

Building the content calendar and scheduling pages

Once we have our content ideas ready and we know what kind of pages we want to focus on, it's time for client approval. The way we like to approach this is we submit a list of potential content ideas, including the primary keyword we're targeting and their traffic potential.

When we submit a content idea for approval, it's because we're confident that it can be beneficial for the client's campaign. We know there's an interest for it, thanks to our keyword research, and that it can translate to economic benefit for our clients.

Although you might understand the value of every idea you pitch, you're probably going to find some pushback on a few topics. That's only natural, and while frustrating, it saves you from issues where you schedule content the client isn't happy with (back to that service layer!).

The whole process becomes much simpler when you have final say on the campaign you're working with. That means you can skip directly to the calendar creation, where we once more, turn to the faithful spreadsheet to do our good work.

Client	Status	Topic	Type	Outline (Link)	Start Date 9/23/2019 Draft Due	Draft Completed? (Link)	Images Added?	Planned Go Live Date
WEBRIS	1. Ready for Outline	How to Deal With Bad Online Reviews	Blog Post	VIEW	10/5/2019	No	No	10/9/2019
WEBRIS	1. Ready for Outline	How to Start a Podcast	Blog Post		10/17/2019	No	No	10/21/2019
WEBRIS	1. Ready for Outline	XX Best CRM for Small Businesses - 2019	Blog Post		10/17/2019	No	No	10/21/2019
WEBRIS	1. Ready for Outline	XX LinkedIn Marketing Strategies for 2019	Blog Post		10/29/2019	No	No	11/2/2019
WEBRIS	1. Ready for Outline	XX Best Marketing Podcasts (Updated in 2019)	Blog Post		10/29/2019	No	No	11/2/2019
WEBRIS	1. Ready for Outline	XX FREE Ways to Get More Instagram Followers in 2019	Blog Post		11/10/2019	No	No	11/14/2019
WEBRIS	1. Ready for Outline	XX BEST Facebook Advertising Tips for 3x ROAS (2020)	Blog Post	VIEW	11/10/2019	No	No	11/14/2019
WEBRIS	1. Ready for Outline				11/22/2019	No	No	11/26/2019
WEBRIS	1. Ready for Outline				11/22/2019	No	No	11/26/2019

The calendar we use is fairly simple, at least from a technical standpoint. It covers what stage the content is currently at, what the topic and titles are, what type of page we're dealing with, due dates for drafts, and when we're planning on going live.

On top of that, we like to have outlines in some cases, depending on the complexity of the topic we're dealing with. Outlines help you and the writers stay on the same page about the keywords (both primary and secondary) you want to hit and what aspects they need to cover.

How often to schedule content mainly depends on two factors:

1. How fast you can produce it

2. How long the client needs to go over the content to approve it

By 'produce', we don't mean write. As an SEO agency, it's not your job to write content, which is a trap a lot of people fall into. Unless you have experience as a writer or an in-house team, it's much more efficient to use a third-party to provide that service.

In our experience, agencies that provide writing services for SEO clients often end up focusing more on the 'writing' aspect instead of running effective campaigns. One of the reasons we're successful is because we know what our strengths are. By focusing on big-picture SEO and having a framework to manage every small task, we can deliver more consistent results.

One problem you'll often run into is clients expect you to take care of the writing. What we do, when needed, is lean on a content-creation partner we can trust (shoutout to Express Writers!), so they focus on the writing and we can lean on our team to do the SEO.

Naturally, you want to use writers that have at least a notion of basic SEO practices, so you don't need to micromanage every aspect of their work. By contracting out writing work with a reputable partner, you can go back to your clients and tell them "This is how long it usually takes to write a well-researched piece that's X words long". Pending approval, that gives you a timeframe you can set on your content calendar.

Ideally, both you and your client will have access to this spreadsheet. That way, you both can reference it at any time to get a quick overview of what content you're working on and where your campaign is headed.

So far, we've talked a lot about producing new content, though. Sometimes, that won't be necessary and instead, you'll want to schedule updates.

3.5 - Create or Update? An Introduction to Creating and Updating Great Content (By Julia McCoy)

Content creation is a process not many people master. It's unfortunate because when you DO master it, you start earning a return on investment (ROI) on auto-pilot. It's true. How do I know? I am a perfect example of this in action.

My writing agency, Express Writers, has thrived online due in large part to our content marketing prowess. The content we create brings in 99% of our leads. That has amounted to millions of dollars in sales, thousands of clients, and 100,000 – 200,000 visitors coming in monthly to our website.

Needless to say, I know content creation. That's why I'm here to guide you through a can't-fail process for coming up with profitable content ideas, writing content that ranks, and extra steps for both pre-publishing and post-publishing that will shoot you past the competition.

Let's start where every great content piece begins – the ideation phase.

Ideation

Out of all the content creation stages, ideation is perhaps the most important part. The ideas you come up with will eventually turn into your content assets – the pieces bringing you rankings, traffic, leads, and engagement. But – and this is a big "but" – without solid, profitable ideas behind your content, none of those things will happen.

Every single great content piece starts with an equally great idea. However, expecting to come up with that idea out of thin air is like playing the lottery. You might win if you're lucky, but more often than not, you'll lose.

Instead, it's important to get strategic with your ideation phase. You're counting on your content to work hard for your brand, so you must lay the foundation with solid, data-backed ideas. These are the ones you can confidently point to and explain WHY they will succeed once they're published. To come up with these idea heroes, you need a workflow that includes:

1. **Research**. Research is the key to finding great target keywords and discovering proven content topics to back your content pieces. Doing initial content idea research means better chances for engagement and rankings later.

2. **Smart tools**. The right tools help you find profitable, data-backed keywords and topics in unlikely places.

3. **Your content goals**. Keeping your content goals firmly in mind helps you ideate content that moves your brand forward.

This is how you get productive and strategic with ideation. Let's get into how it all comes together so you'll never struggle to generate content ideas and topics again:

Map Your Content Ideas to Content Goals (The 3-Bucket Topic Strategy)

Before you go any further, you need to have your content goals laid out. What do you hope to achieve with content marketing? Narrow it down to 2-4 major goal buckets to hit.

Why start with goals? Because every content piece you publish should strive to advance your brand toward at least ONE of them. If your content doesn't help you move forward or earn ROI, it's not worth your time to create. Starting with your goals *before* you ideate is how you stay on track.

To help map your content ideas to goals, I created a concept called the **3-Bucket Topic Strategy**. Basically, I imagine my 3 major content goals as "buckets" into which all of my content topics need to fit. Every piece of content I create needs to serve at least one of these goals:

- **SEO rankings**. The content has the potential to rank for profitable, long-tail keywords in Google.

- **Sales and connections**. The content is engaging, informative, entertaining, and/or educational and encourages backlinking and reader action.

- **Brand awareness**. The content is highly shareable, or tells a compelling story, and helps build a name for my brand online.

If a content topic idea won't fit into one of these goal areas, I scrap it, even if the idea sounds amazing at a surface level. If a topic won't help you reach your goals or earn ROI, it's not worth it.

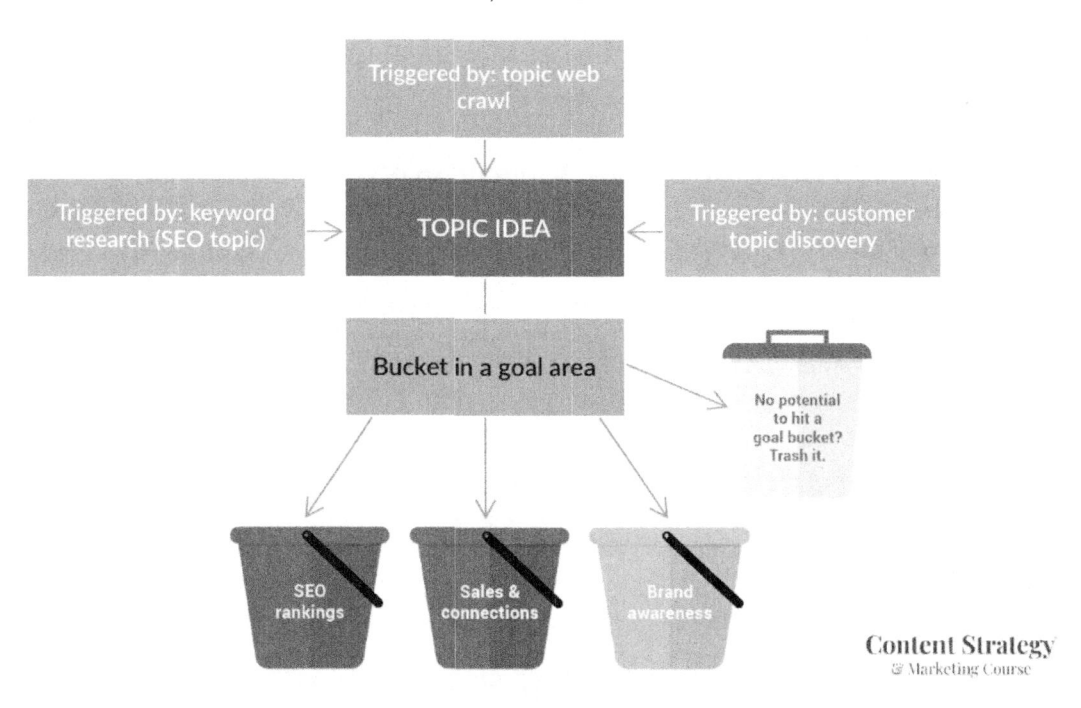

```
                  ┌─────────────────────┐
                  │ Triggered by: topic web │
                  │       crawl           │
                  └──────────┬──────────┘
                             ↓
┌───────────────────┐  ┌──────────────┐  ┌─────────────────────┐
│ Triggered by: keyword │→│  TOPIC IDEA  │←│ Triggered by: customer│
│ research (SEO topic)│  │              │  │   topic discovery    │
└───────────────────┘  └──────┬───────┘  └─────────────────────┘
                              │
                   ┌──────────┴──────────┐
                   │ Bucket in a goal area│──→ No potential
                   └──────────┬──────────┘    to hit a
                              │                goal bucket?
                              │                Trash it.
           ┌──────────────────┼──────────────────┐
           ↓                  ↓                  ↓
         SEO             Sales &              Brand
       rankings         connections         awareness
```

Content Strategy
& Marketing Course

Now, your content goal buckets might look slightly different from mine. You might want to include "more traffic" as one of your goals, or "customer retention," "conversions," or "lead generation." Remember, these are your personal brand goals – the ones that are most relevant to what you need from content marketing.

Use Broad, Industry Head Terms (Seed Keywords) to Begin

Once you have your content goals laid out in front of you, it's time to start ideating. An ideal place to begin is with broad head terms, or seed keywords, from your particular industry. Once you have a few of these in hand, you can further drill down to find the best content topics for your content marketing.

For example, if your industry is health & wellness, you can probably reel off a shortlist of head terms without any help. (E.g., "gut health," "paleo diet," or "low-sugar desserts"). If, on the other hand, your mind has gone as blank as a sheet of printer paper, turn to some trusty tools.

- **Google autocomplete**. Think of the broadest possible industry term. Enter it into the Google search bar, and Google will automatically offer you related long-tail options. Write these down to explore later.

```
G    gut health
Q    gut health - Google Search
Q    gut health diet
Q    gut healthy foods
Q    gut health probiotics
Q    gut health detox
Q    gut health and depression
```

- **KeywordTool.io**. This tool dives deep into Google's autocomplete feature. Enter a broad keyword into the search bar, and it will return *hundreds* of related terms. Write down 10-20 to start with. (Don't worry about search volume at this stage.)

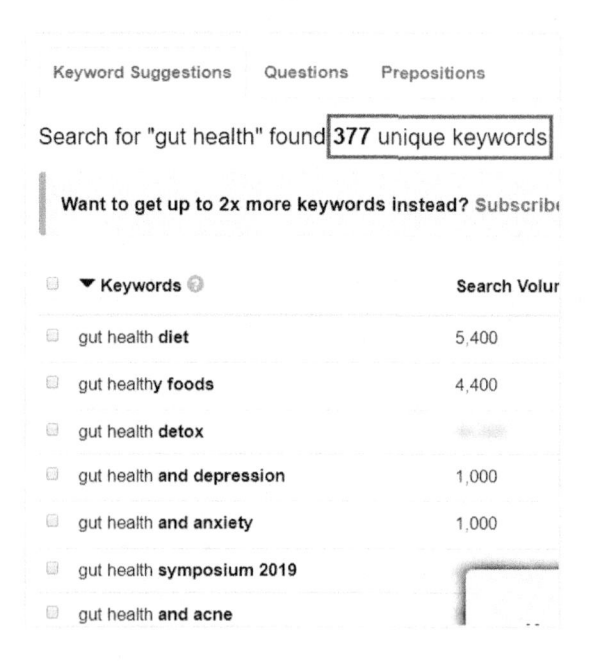

Keywords	Search Volume
gut health diet	5,400
gut healthy foods	4,400
gut health detox	
gut health and depression	1,000
gut health and anxiety	1,000
gut health symposium 2019	
gut health and acne	

Generate Content Topics from Profitable Long-Tail Keywords

By now, you should have a big list of long-tail keywords relevant to your industry. From these, you can generate content topics by the dozens. Start with one long-tail keyword that looks promising. Then do some deeper digging by entering it into the keyword research tool of your choice (I always recommend SEMrush or KWFinder).

In your keyword tool, you want to look at a few major metrics:

- **KD (or keyword difficulty).** This is a measure of how difficult it will be to rank for that particular keyword in Google right now. Generally, if you're starting from zero with content, you want to find keywords with a low difficulty score (40 or below). The more established and known you are online, the easier it is to rank for higher-difficulty keywords.

- **Search volume.** This is an estimate of how many people are searching for that keyword during a given month. Keywords with a high search volume and low KD are every content creator's dream – however, you won't always find that unicorn. *Remember*: Search volume data may vary wildly from tool to tool and is always just an estimate, so take these numbers with a grain of salt. Even if a keyword has an *incredibly* low search volume (I'm talking 5 or below), it could bring in an **extremely** qualified lead – someone who might buy immediately after reading your awesome content! (Moral of the story: Don't discount a keyword just because the search volume seems low.)

Once you start searching keywords, write down every possibility you find. Look for low difficulty keywords, first and foremost. Include all synonyms, related terms, and alternatives you discover. From this list, you will choose ONE keyword to use to generate content topic ideas.

For example, under my search for "gut health" I found the long-tail keyword "restore gut health." It has a KD of 21 and a search volume of 2,925, according to KWFinder data. From this one keyword, I'll come up with 5-10 possible content topics.

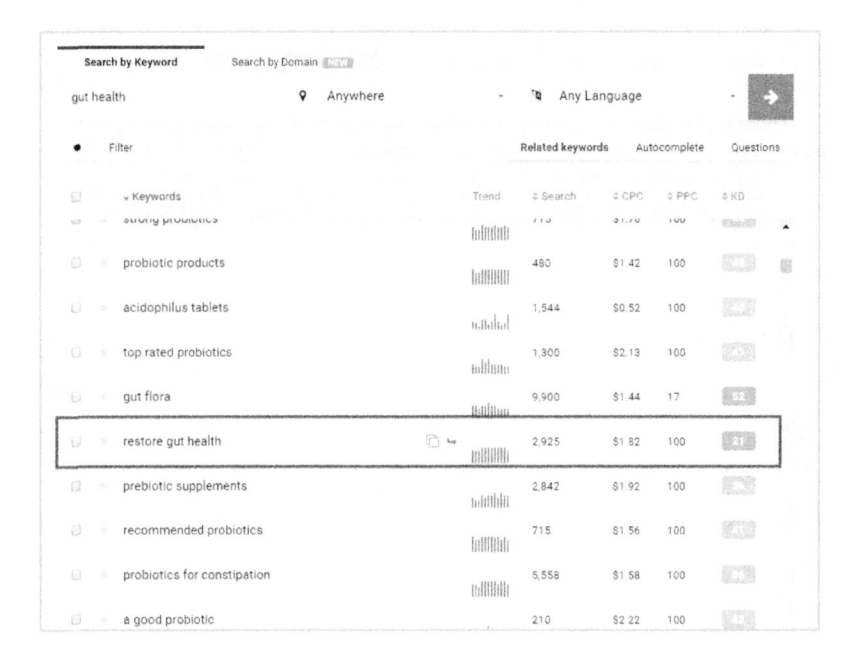

Keywords	Trend	Search	CPC	PPC	KD
strong probiotics		715	$1.70	100	
probiotic products		480	$1.42	100	
acidophilus tablets		1,544	$0.52	100	
top rated probiotics		1,300	$2.13	100	
gut flora		9,900	$1.44	17	
restore gut health		2,925	$1.82	100	21
prebiotic supplements		2,842	$1.92	100	
recommended probiotics		715	$1.56	100	
probiotics for constipation		5,558	$1.58	100	
a good probiotic		210	$2.22	100	

The important thing here is to just get the ideas down on paper. Don't judge whether they're good or bad yet; just get them recorded so you can evaluate them later against your goal buckets. Here's my list of potential ideas:

- *How to Restore Gut Health: 5 Habits to Start Today*
- *Restoring Gut Health: 10 Foods to Add to Your Daily Diet*
- *Why Should You Restore Gut Health? Here's What a Dietician Says*
- *Want to Restore Gut Health? Here's What NOT to Do*
- *Restoring Gut Health, Explained*

If your mind is totally blank when attempting to ideate topics from a long-tail keyword, don't worry – there are tools for that, too. In particular, using HubSpot's Blog Topic Generator is a good way to get your brain gears turning. You could also check out the content that's already ranking for that keyword in Google to find topic inspiration. (More on that in the next section.)

Look at What the Competition is Doing, Then Do Better

One of the best ways to find profitable content topics is to check out the competition on Google. What kind of content is Google prioritizing for the keyword? What's resonating with readers? The top 3-5 results for each long-tail keyword will give you a good idea.

While you're doing content reconnaissance in the search results, look for trends and commonalities. Once you find a promising topic, determine how you can rework that same topic to make it better, fresher, more accurate, or more researched. Figure out how to put your unique spin on the topic – approach it from a different angle or perspective. Do NOT, by any means, outright copy what you find in the search results. Instead, you're looking for inspiration **only**. Think of the search results solely as a jumping-off point, and you'll be good.

Gather Your Best Content Topics

By this point, you should have lists of profitable long-tail keywords tied to relevant content topics. It's time to run these past your content goal buckets to see if they fit. (If they don't, say bye-bye. No ROI, no regrets.) For example, let's look at one of the topics I came up with in section 3: *How to Restore Gut Health: 5 Habits to Start Today.*

I want this topic to help me either 1.) build SEO rankings, 2.) generate sales & connections, or 3.) build brand awareness. For starters, since I'm targeting an industry keyword with a high possibility of ranking according to the keyword data I researched, this topic will absolutely slot into my #1 goal bucket. Since this topic also is educational, I'll be showcasing my expertise and know-how in the content, too. Score one for another goal bucket (#3 brand awareness)!

I've hit at least one goal with this topic, so I have the green light to move to the next content creation stage: Writing.

During the writing stage of content creation, you have a few big decisions to make. This section will cover all of them, as well as provide an overview of potential content types to add to your publishing wheelhouse. We'll also go over the nitty-gritty of how to write and structure content that ranks. Let's go!

1. 7 types of online content and how to choose the best formats of focus for your brand

There are seven major types of online content. That said, you don't have to create content for every format (nor should you want to – unless you *like* getting in over your head). Instead, it's best to choose a few major content formats your brand can excel in creating. Because face it: You don't have the resources or the time to create *everything*. If you focus on just a few, instead, you'll be able to make your resources and investment really count.

When you consider content formats, think about:

- Your time and money investment, plus resources and your overall content budget

- The creative team at your disposal (writers, editors, graphic designer, web designer, video/audio producer, etc.) OR who you're willing to hire to help

- Your expertise and comfort with different mediums (Are you better at writing than speaking? Or are your thoughts more coherent/better expressed when spoken?)

- The formats that will lend themselves well to your brand voice, and the ones that won't

Now that those considerations are out of the way, let's dig into content types and formats.

Blogs and articles

Blogs and articles are the most familiar types of content for most people. These two terms are used interchangeably, but in general, blogs are less formal while articles tend to be fact-driven and objective in scope. That said, many articles are opinion pieces, and many blogs are researched down to the last punctuation mark. For now, we'll assume these terms mean the same thing: They both refer to pieces of content posted on a content platform intended to inform, educate, guide, or entertain the target audience.

Web pages

Web pages are the building blocks of websites. A website is nothing more than a collection of web pages all located on the same root domain (i.e. "https://example-domain.com/webpage"). As such, web pages contain the most general content on your site. They include information about your business and employees, contact information, descriptions of your services, and product pages.

Infographics

Infographics are a powerful form of visual media. They combine images, words, and design in a way that explains a particular topic (or tells a story) to your reader. The resulting image is easy to save, share, and promote across the web, especially on social media.

Ebooks and whitepapers

Some of the lengthiest content formats include ebooks and whitepapers. Ebooks are pretty self-explanatory. Shorter ebooks on a specific topic can be anywhere from 3 – 50 pages in length and usually are presented in PDF format. Traditional book-length works in electronic format are hundreds of pages long. A good representation would be the books you'd normally find in the Kindle store.

Whitepapers are long articles businesses publish to present specific solutions to industry problems. Whitepapers always include extensive research and data to back up points.

Videos

Video content is exactly what you think it is – head to YouTube and it's all over the place. As we forge ahead into the 2020s, more and more marketers are (rightly) putting an emphasis on creating videos. However, this medium isn't for everyone, and the really well-produced videos can get expensive, fast.

Podcasts

Podcasts have seen a spike in popularity over the last few years, but it's easy to see why. These audio-recorded series and episodes include fabulous storytelling, interviews, reports, and conversations that are easily accessible and listenable on-the-go. This is becoming a go-to content format for many marketers because you can record podcast episodes with relatively inexpensive equipment.

Webinars & presentations

Learning online is going strong, with more and more people investing in continuing training, education, or both in all kinds of industries. Today, live webinars are a fun way to learn and interact with experts and other students. They include a mix of audio, video, and image components (such as slides) presented on a single topic.

2. Writing and structuring successful SEO content
Use keywords naturally, in the right places

Keyword stuffing is *so* 2005, I think we can all agree. This is when you use your keyword in excess in an attempt to rank, like this:

This keyword is my keyword. I use this keyword a lot to rank for this keyword. This keyword is a good keyword. Keyword keyword keyword keyword.

It's pretty laughable, right? Don't worry – search engines are WAY too smart to fall for this anymore. In fact, search engines today are relying more on semantic search and contextual relevance to determine the keywords for which your content will rank. **Semantic search** looks at the underlying meaning of the user's search terms – what are they looking for, exactly, when they use those keywords? What's their search intent?

That means using keywords naturally, with variations and synonyms, will do a lot more for your rankings versus rigidly ensuring you have used your keyword X number of times in the content. Let's put it this way: Search engines are NOT counting instances of keywords in your content. You don't need to, either.

Instead, what matters more is **keyword placement**. Placing your keywords strategically inside your content, along with using them naturally, gives search engines valuable clues. You're saying, "HEY. This is my focus keyword and topic! Rank me for these terms!" So, where are these strategic placements?

When to use the focus keyword in SEO content writing:

- Once in the main header (also called the headline, title, or H1), preferably near the beginning of the sentence/phrase

- Once in the first paragraph

- Once in at least one of the subheaders (also called subheads, or H2s)

- Once in the concluding subheader/H2

- Multiple times in the body copy, naturally, with variations as needed for better sentence flow

- Once in the meta title and description, preferably near the beginning of both

When to use related keywords and synonyms in SEO content writing:

- At least once each in the body copy, naturally, with variations as needed for better sentence flow
- Once each in a few subheaders and sub-subheaders (H2s and H3s)
- If it makes sense, choose one to use in the meta title or description

How to write keyword variations:

Let's say you find a great keyword to use in your content, but it's worded strangely, like "gut health women" or "gut health probiotics." In this scenario, using the keyword verbatim in headers and sentences will sound unnatural and forced, which is NOT what you want.

In all cases, remember you're writing for a human audience. You need to make sure your language is understandable and smooth for a better reading experience, *even if that means changing up the keyword slightly*. No worries, though. Search engines will still understand which keyword you're targeting, and rank you accordingly.

For example, if I'm trying to rank for "gut health women," I need to employ keyword variations to smooth out the text when I use it in my content. To that end, "gut health **for** women," "women's gut health," and "women **and** gut health" are ALL acceptable alternatives that search engines will still recognize, regardless of word order or prepositions inserted. More importantly, your content won't sound robotic or stilted, which gives your readers a better experience.

Format for readability and clarity

Poorly-formatted content is a recipe for disaster. Without clear, readable formatting, readers will more than likely pass over your efforts. They just don't have time to squint and strain their eyes to read long, overwhelming text blocks, messy paragraphs, and inconsistent headings.

Implementing clarity and readability in your content doesn't mean dumbing down your writing or message, either. Instead, it's about presenting the information in the manner that's easiest to read, digest, and understand. It's about getting your ideas across without any roadblocks to comprehension. Here's how:

- **Embrace white space**. White space around your text gives the words room to breathe, which is easier on the eyes reading electronic screens.

- **Write shorter paragraphs**. The online reader's attention span is notoriously short, probably because there are too many options for content and not enough time to consume it all. (According to a widely publicized Microsoft study[42], the average American has an attention span of 8 seconds!) Writing shorter paragraphs is a common online writing technique to keep your reader's eyes moving down the page (this is often called "bucket brigades").

- **Every time you switch to a different angle of your topic, use a new subheader**. Subheaders are helpful for readers who are scanning a page for specific information. They also alert your reader a new topic is forthcoming and break up large chunks of text for better readability.

---

[42] https://time.com/3858309/attention-spans-goldfish/

- **Structure subheaders logically**. Just including subheaders isn't enough for stellar content writing. Along with that, make sure they're structured logically. For instance, if you're writing a guide with steps, order your subheaders in the right sequence. If you're exploring a specific subject, include subheaders in a way that helps explain and break it down clearly as the reader moves down the page.

- **Use transition sentences**. Transition sentences are simply guiding sentences that let your reader know you're moving on to another section or subtopic of your content piece. As your content moves from one idea to another, transition sentences help smooth the way. They ease readers into your next point or subtopic so they feel expertly guided, not haphazardly yanked around. A wonderful guide to using transition sentences is this resource[43] from The College of Saint Rose Writing Center.

- **For long lists of related items, use bullet points**. Bullet points are another way to break up long text blocks and make your content easier to read and skim. Use them whenever you find yourself creating long lists of items or points that are better off neatly organized into bullets.

Edit and revise

Finally, remember the best writing is honed and edited. Nobody produces their finest content in the first draft. Instead, use the first draft to get your ideas down on paper. Then, get back into the trenches and edit, revise, and rework.

- Trim and clean up sentences.

---

[43] https://www.strose.edu/wp-content/uploads/2015/10/Transition-Sentences-Handout-2012B.pdf

- Fix grammar and spelling mistakes.

- Tweak your keyword usage and make sure it sounds natural.

- Make sure all your focus and related keywords are placed strategically.

- Include more research where needed.

- Make sure your points are arranged in the most logical order for clarity and readability.

- Hand off the content to another person (preferably someone with editing experience) who will do another pass-through and polish it until it shines.

Once your content piece is researched, written, and polished, you can move on to the pre-publishing stage.

Pre-Publishing

So, your content is edited and ready to go. But, wait! Not so fast. You still have some important work to do.

Search engine optimization is a critical piece of the puzzle. Good news: If you followed my content writing tips, then half the work is already done. What I'm outlining below are the final steps to push your content into "mega-optimized" territory. Don't skip these final SEO stages, and you'll make the path to ROI inevitable for every piece of content you put out into the world.

Optimize your content in WordPress for social sharing and Google search results

If you're using WordPress to manage your content and blog, there are a TON of steps you can do each time you publish a blog to make it even more SEO-ready. The step-by-step I personally use for every one of my blogs is right here.

(Note: Even if you don't use WordPress for content management and publishing, the general principles here can be applied to any other platform.)

Proofread and edit

I'm repeating this essential step here because... well... it's THAT necessary. Errors, formatting problems, keyword misplacement, and shabby writing can all trip up your content's success. Readers will spot anything amiss from a mile away and wonder about your quality standards. Search engines won't rank inaccurate content riddled with errors, either.

Edit. Proofread. Polish. You'll be glad you did. And, to make it easier, I recommend a tool like Grammarly for Chrome. It checks your content right inside the WordPress platform for spelling and grammar mistakes.

Add relevant images in-text

Written content performs 1,000,000x better if you include relevant images inside the text to complement points, illustrate concepts, and explain ideas. (Blogs and articles with images get 94% more views than their text-only counterparts! (Jeff Bullas, 2019) Of course, it's important to do this in the SEO-friendly way.

- **Make sure images are inserted and spaced correctly in the content.** An image with wonky alignment or spacing will throw off the design and readability of the rest of your page. Place images consistently (for instance, on their own line and centered) for the best look.

- **Use images at original size.** You want all images to be clear and crisp, not blurry and distorted.

- **Add alternate text (A.K.A. "alt text") to EVERY image.** Alt text is a little snippet of code that describes the content of your images for search engines. Additionally, screen readers use alt text to describe images to people with impaired sight, which provides context and a richer on-page experience for everyone.

    o **How to add alt text to an image in WordPress**: Insert the image where you want it placed in the content, then click it. A toolbar will pop up. Click the "edit" icon (the pencil) to bring up the image details editor, where you can add descriptive alt text.

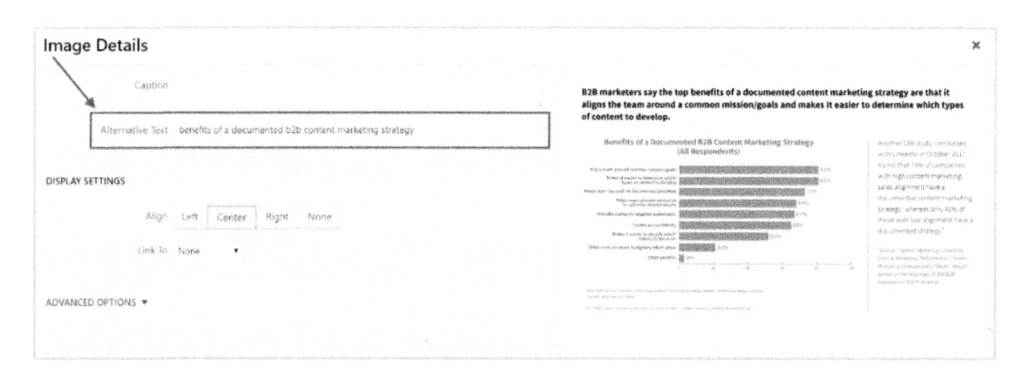

Tweak your blog formatting for SEO and readability

As we've discussed, readability is major for online content. If your text isn't readable, readers won't stay on the page for long. Thus, you want to make it as organized, seamless, and clear as possible. A few major points to follow:

- **Be consistent with formatting**. For an overall cleaner look, keep your formatting consistent all the way down the page.

    o Make sure images all have the same spacing around them.

    o Use the same style of bullet points for all bulleted lists.

    o If you start using a numbered sequence for your H3s, do this for ALL of them.

- **Tweak the spacing**. Add more line breaks between chunky-looking paragraphs and remove double-spacing after periods.

- **Code the H1, H2s, H3s, etc. correctly**. In WordPress, there's a drop-down menu in the text editor that lets you assign headings so they're properly coded in the published blog.

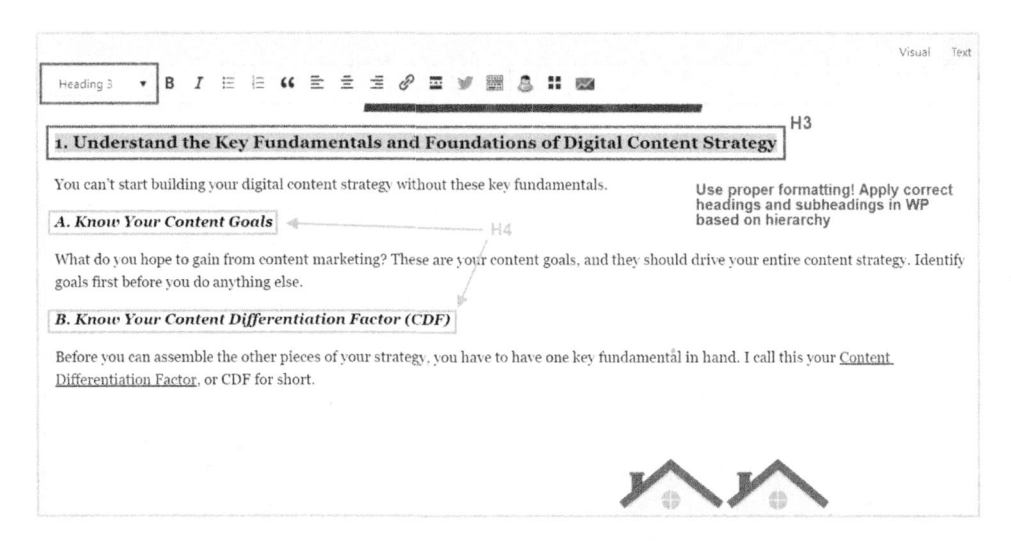

Add super-easy, one-click social sharing codes

If you have an active social media presence on a particular platform, make sharing your content to that feed super-simple for users. Include one-click social sharing codes right inside your content!

For example, for my blog posts, I use a WordPress plugin (Better Click to Tweet) that inserts "Click to Tweet" snippets inside the content.

The plugin adds a little bird icon in my WordPress toolbar. All I have to do is click it to pull up a generator that lets me format my Click to Tweet:

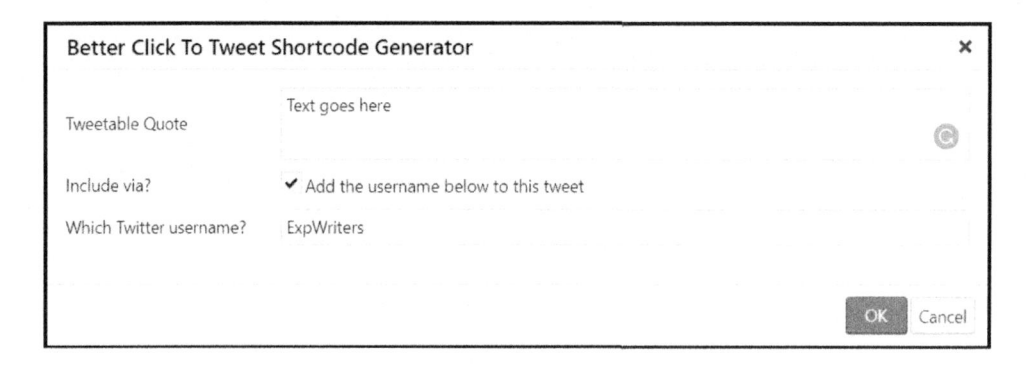

Don't go overboard with this, however. 1-3 in one blog post is plenty.

Double-check your links (both internal and outbound)

Always, always double-check your links are working and point to the right destinations. This includes both internal links (ones pointing to other pages on your site) and outbound links (links pointing to other domains).

- **To edit links in WordPress**: Click the link in question. A toolbar will pop up. Click the "edit" button to edit the URL.

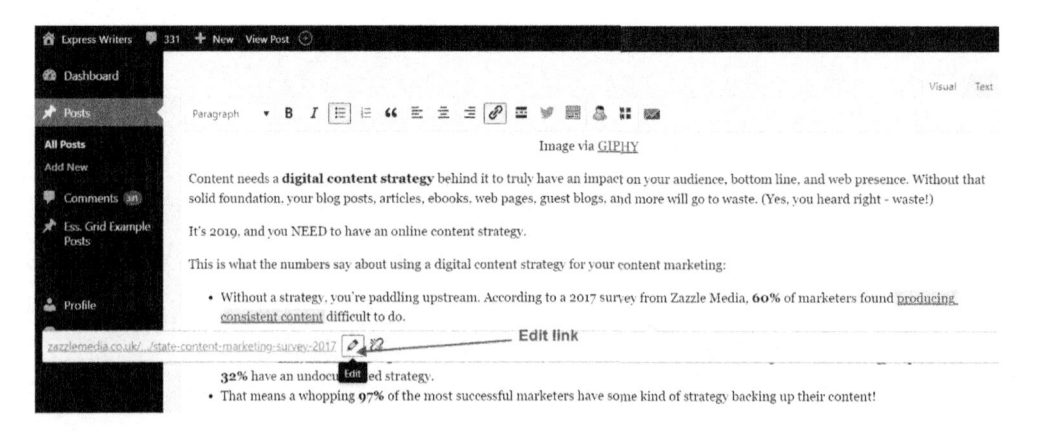

- **To access link options**: Click the "edit" button, then the gear icon.

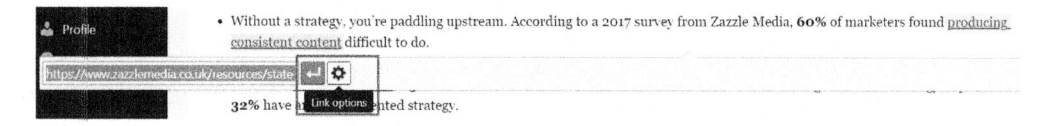

Craft a relevant CTA (call-to-action)

The call-to-action, or CTA, is one of the most important pieces to optimize in your content. This little bit of text tells the reader what to do after they have read your piece. If you built trust and authority along the way (which is inevitable if you offered readers valuable information), the CTA helps you leverage those feelings of goodwill in the reader. They like you (they really like you), so encourage them to take the next step!

- **Use punchy, visceral language**. Be descriptive. Catch their eye with language that jumps off the page. (Don't be afraid to pull out a thesaurus for this.)

- **Include benefits**. Tell readers *why* they should take the next step and why it will benefit them.

- **Include a command**. Now is not the time to beat around the bush. Tell the reader exactly what to do next with a command, i.e. "download our free guide," "sign up for our list," "subscribe today."

- **Keep it short and sweet**. You don't need a paragraph for a CTA. 1-2 short lines will do.

- **Link to the next step the reader can take**. Remember to include a link that will enable the reader to carry out the action you want. For instance, link your CTA to a page where the reader can sign up for your email list.

- **Always include at least one CTA at the end of the content.** You ALWAYS need at least one CTA in every piece of content. Without the CTA, you have no way to capture your readers' growing interest and trust in your brand after they finish taking in the information you've offered.

Add an optimized meta title and description

Don't skip optimizing your meta title and description for your content. Your meta title shows up in search results, and Google may use your description in the listing, too. To add a meta title and description to a blog post in WordPress, use an SEO plug-in like Yoast SEO[44].

- Once installed, scroll to the bottom of your post in the WordPress editor to access the Yoast SEO tool.

- Under "Snippet Preview," select "Edit snippet."

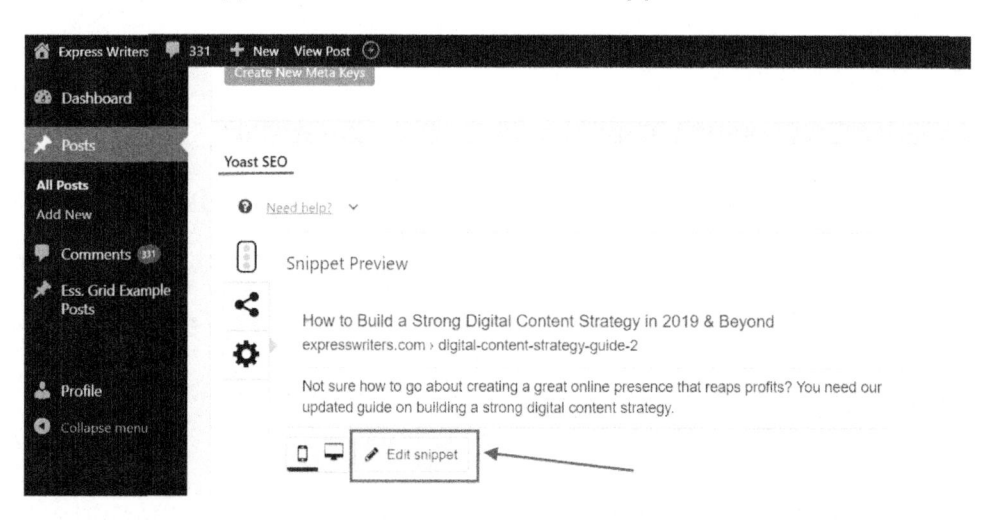

- Enter your meta title (it should include the focus keyword and remain under 60 characters in length for SEO)

---

[44] https://yoast.com/wordpress/plugins/seo/

- Enter your meta description. Make sure it's under 158 characters, includes the focus keyword, and summarizes the topic of your blog post accurately.

- You'll notice Yoast rates your meta title and description using a color-coded bar. Red means you have some work to do, yellow means you're close, and green means you're good to go. Length, as well as your use of keywords, will affect your rating.

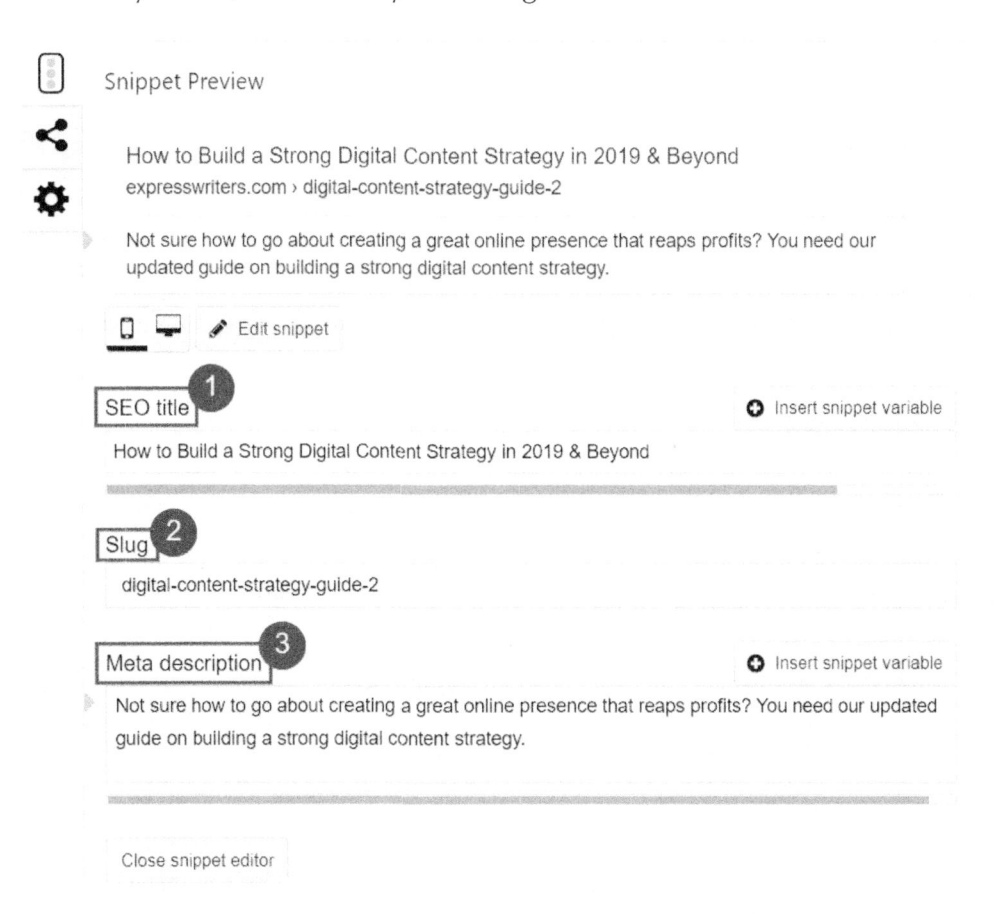

Snippet Preview

How to Build a Strong Digital Content Strategy in 2019 & Beyond
expresswriters.com › digital-content-strategy-guide-2

Not sure how to go about creating a great online presence that reaps profits? You need our updated guide on building a strong digital content strategy.

Edit snippet

1 SEO title — Insert snippet variable
How to Build a Strong Digital Content Strategy in 2019 & Beyond

2 Slug
digital-content-strategy-guide-2

3 Meta description — Insert snippet variable
Not sure how to go about creating a great online presence that reaps profits? You need our updated guide on building a strong digital content strategy.

Close snippet editor

  - *Note*: Take the Yoast SEO color rating with a grain of salt. I have created meta titles and descriptions that were in the yellow and yet did *amazingly* well in the search engine results. **Remember**: A tool isn't always 100% accurate. If your metas read well, keep to length requirements, and include your keyword, don't worry about the color rating too much.

Optimize for social sharing

Finally, optimize your content for social sharing on Facebook and Twitter. This ensures your post link looks good no matter where it's shared or who shares it. (This feature is only available with the Yoast plug-in for WordPress.)

- Click the "Social" icon under the Yoast SEO options.

- Skip the title and description fields. The tool will pull from the main meta fields you already filled out for this part.

- Upload the Facebook and/or Twitter images you want to appear when people share your content. (Remember to add alt text to these images. You can do this by clicking the image in your WordPress image library.)

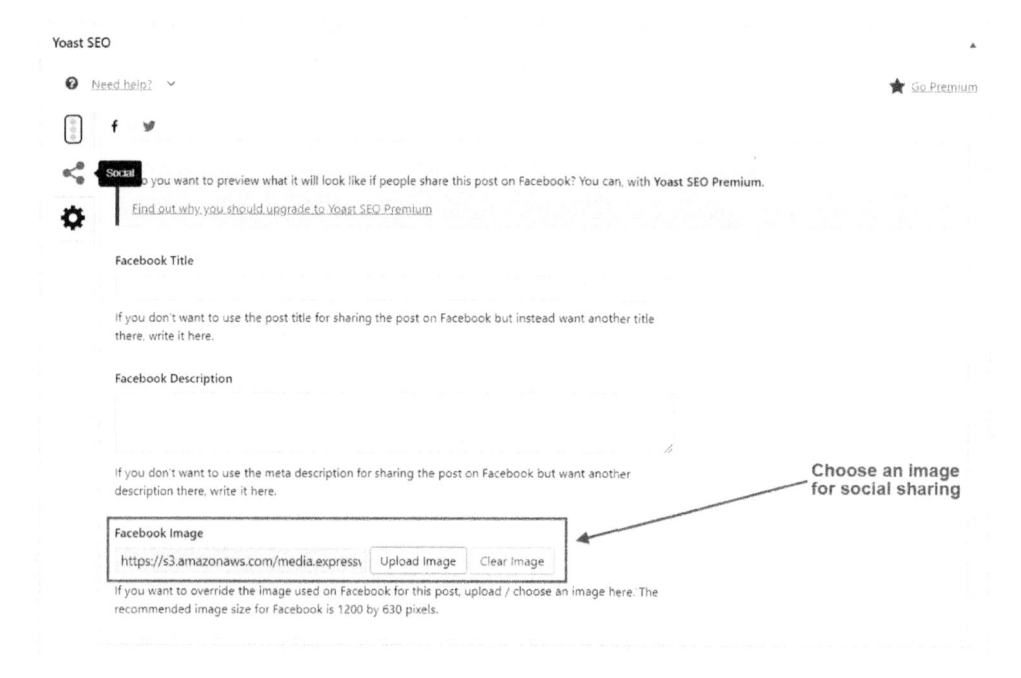

Once you have all the pre-publishing steps completed, your content is SEO-ready. It's time to hit "publish" and promote that baby! Don't get too ready to move on, though – we're not quite done with this content, yet. Once you have some content pieces out in the world, you need to move on to post-publishing best-practices.

Post-Publishing

Older content – those pieces you published one week ago, one month ago, one year ago, etc. – all need care and attention after the fact. Why? Because content can't survive on its own without a little intervention. It needs your help to get read, stay up-to-date, and remain on the search engine radar. That's why, in this section, we're diving into the concept of content maintenance. In particular, we'll discuss why this is the one major post-publishing activity you need to do A.S.A.P. (For the nitty-gritty HOW component, continue to the next chapter.)

Why content maintenance matters after publishing (Turn old content into "money content")

To explain the importance of content maintenance and updates for your brand's content ROI, I'm going to reference a case study I did a few years ago. This study looks at two different content pieces on my roster: One I published years ago but updated recently, and one I published recently.

The old post's original publish date was back in 2013. By 2017, that post was ranking in the #3 spot for the target keyword in Google. The only problem: The content was outdated and the writing was poor. Any traffic I received from the post's Google ranking would **not** lead to results (leads, conversions). So, I updated it:

- I added new, updated images.

- I updated the copy with better writing.

- I crafted a fresh, more compelling CTA.

- I updated the meta title and description.

That same week, I published a new blog post targeting a different profitable keyword. This one hit all the checkmarks for my content quality standards and SEO out of the gate. The question is, **which content piece do you think was worth more money to me that month?**

If you guessed the old, updated post, congratulations – you're correct. Why was it worth more? A few reasons:

- It was already ranking well because it had longevity on its side. My newer content piece would take a full month to climb the search engine ladder to the first page of results.

- Older content has more weight with search engines. I leveraged the old post's age and upped its value in other ways.

- A qualified lead found the older post through a Google search, read it through to the end, then contacted us to ask more questions. That week, the lead ordered the type of content the post covered (press releases for movies)!

To sum up, your older content matters, but only if you give it care and attention. Unless these pieces include timeless information (A.K.A. "evergreen" content), your posts will need updating at some point in the future. This ensures all that hard work you put into creating your content assets won't go to waste. Instead, you'll keep on earning that ROI long after the initial publish date.

PHASE 4

The Promotion Process

It's not enough to put keywords on a website and hope it ranks. If you want a slice of that sweet organic traffic, you need to promote your website. That means getting valuable engagement signals that shows Google our websites are "popular" and therefore worthy of receiving traffic.

This phase focuses on how to generate those signals through outreach and manual promotion tactics.

- **4.1 - Link Building 101 (And Beyond).** "Links" are one of the top ranking factors in Google's algorithm. Link building refers to the process of getting links to a page on your website. Building links is one of the many tactics used in search engine optimization (SEO), as links are a signal to Google that your site is a resource worthy of citation.

- **4.2 - The Current (And Future) State of Links.** Link building is very different now from what it was a few years ago. The types of links you should prioritize have changed and understanding why is key to your website's growth.

- **4.5 - Influencers, Social Media, and Links.** There's no denying the rise and impact of social media on our culture. Even though "links" from social media don't count towards ranking your website, these platforms are where your audience spends most of their time online. For that reason, we need to establish a presence here - the best way to do so is using "influencers" to help promote our brand

4.1 - Link Building 101 (And Beyond)

A "link" or "backlink" refers to when another website "links" to yours. Generally speaking, a link is used as attribution - similar to a footnote in a research paper.

For example, let's say you have a website that sells organic dog food and the Huffington Post writes an article about the "best organic products for dogs" and includes your website in the article. Generally speaking, they will place a "link" in that article that refers visitors to your website.

Google *essentially* counts "links" as a vote of popularity for your website - they are widely agreed upon to be a top ranking factor with search engines.

However, "links" come in different shapes and forms - not all of them are created equal.

DOFOLLOW vs NO FOLLOW links

As soon as SEO professionals realized links were a major ranking factor, we began to spam the crap out of them.

To fight back, Google released guidance for websites to add a piece of HTML to outbound links that would tell search engines not to "follow" that links, i.e. not to count it towards SEO rankings (Search Console Help, 2019).

This HTML is known as NOFOLLOW - if a website sets a link to "NOFOLLOW", it does not pass SEO equity to the linked website.

A lot of major publishers now use NOFOLLOW links as a standard practice to beat back people who want to abuse their websites as link sources (INC, Forbes, etc).

All links from social networks are set to NOFOLLOW - so before you get any ideas, links from social networks have no [direct] impact on SEO rankings (i.e. Facebook, Twitter, etc).

While there are some benefits to NOFOLLOWED links, generally speaking, seeking them out is a waste of resources when it comes to SEO.

The "type" of link impacts the equity it passes on

For example, the Huffington Post example is what we call a "contextual" or "editorial" link. These types of links to pass the most "ranking equity", as the linking website wants to refer traffic to your website. An editorial link will pass much more SEO equity than a link from the comments section of a website.

The "placement" of link impacts equity passed as well

The Huffington Post example is what we would call a "contextual" or "editorial" link. These types of links sit within the body text of a page are also known to pass a high amount of "ranking equity", as the linking website wants to refer traffic to your website.

Links in Content > Links Outside Content

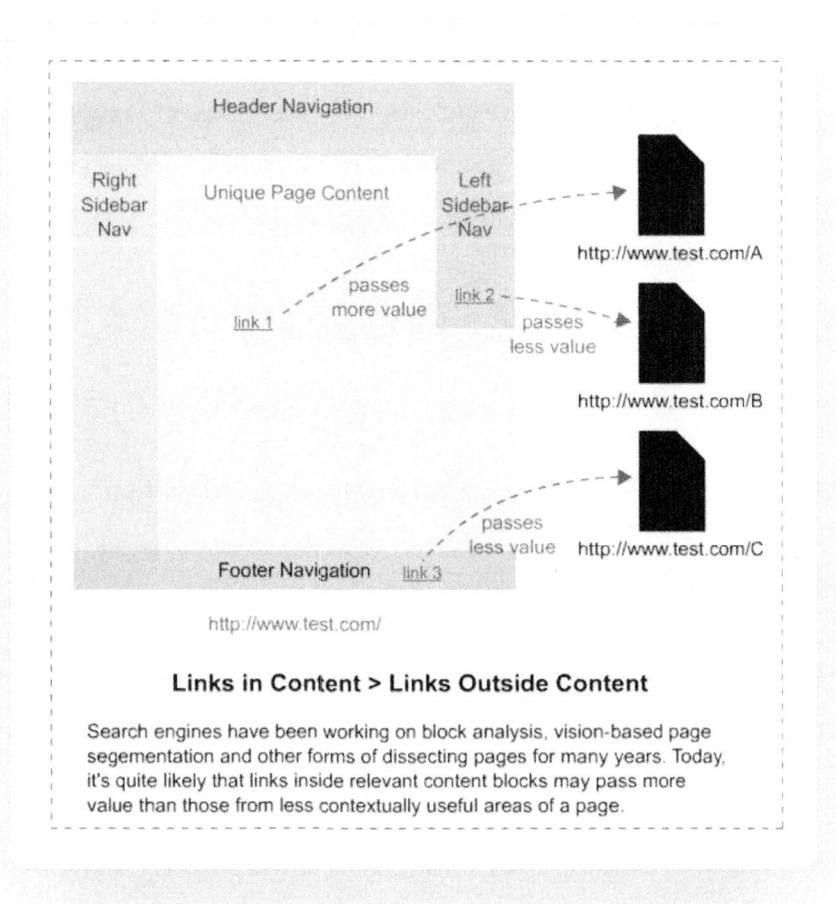

Search engines have been working on block analysis, vision-based page segmentation and other forms of dissecting pages for many years. Today, it's quite likely that links inside relevant content blocks may pass more value than those from less contextually useful areas of a page.

The "quality" of the website linking to yours is critical

If you're getting links from low quality websites, you're running the risk of getting penalized by Google. When engaging in link building, it's critical that you only aim to land on websites that are relevant, real (aka not link farms) and authoritative.

4.2 - The Current State of Links

Google launched the "Penguin" algorithm update in 2012 to fight back against "link spam". The algorithm detected when websites were engaging in low quality link building and penalized them by removing them from Google's index altogether.

Up to that point, SEO was easy. All you had to do was:

1. Put the keyword you want to rank for in the title and body text
2. Purchase links from vendors and point them to that page

When this algorithm launched, it devastated millions of businesses who relied on organic traffic to stay alive. Many of these website owners were innocent – they just hired the wrong SEO company to manage their sites.

Google caught a lot of flack for this, especially because it took them so long to roll out the Penguin update that re-indexed sites who cleaned up their link profile.

They've made significant adjustments to the algorithm, [I believe] most notably on *ignoring* links, as opposed to *penalizing* for them.

In a recent Google Webmasters Hangout, John Mueller said this (Search Engine Roundtable, 2017):

*"So that's kind of a two-pronged approach that we take there. On the one hand manually we try to take action where we think it's necessary on the other hand **algorithmically we try to ignore things that we can kind of isolate.**"*

In other words, if a website is giving away signs of brokering links, the algorithm will not give any weight to the value of outbound links.

This was a brilliant move for Google, as no longer have to devastate business owners, those websites will just not get increased rankings from shitty SEO.

Moreover, Google is sticking it to SEOs, HARD.

Without a penalty, you're thinking/hoping/expecting those links to work. When they don't, you're not only wasting resources trying to look for other causes of "why" those pages aren't ranking, but you wasted resources on acquiring those links.

Analyzing the impact of building over 20,000 links

We build a lot of links for clients, over 20,000 in the last 36 months. Each of these links is meticulously tracked in a spreadsheet that includes:

- Link origin (the URL from where the link is coming from)
- Date of link's placement
- Link destination (the URL on the client site where the link is pointing)
- Anchor text of the link
- Domain Authority of the link's origin
- SEMrush traffic stats of the link's origin domain
- Cost of the link (content writing, advertising fee, etc)

The SEO Blueprint

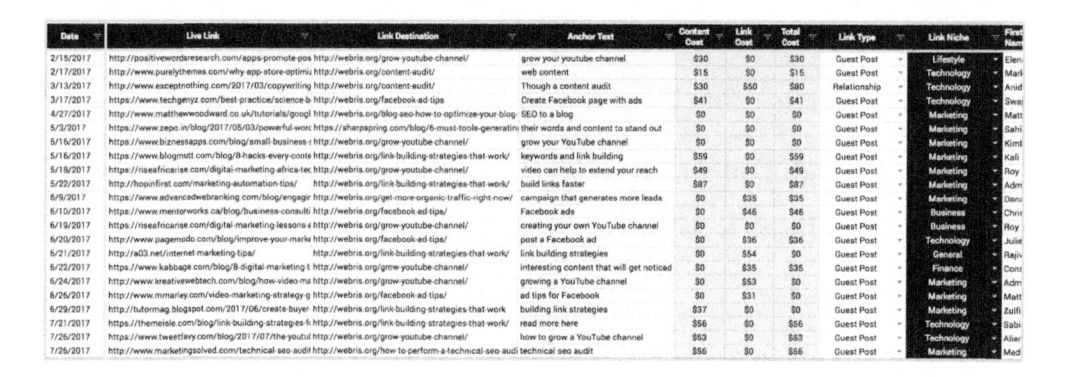

We took our spreadsheet and cross walked it with additional data to understand the impact of those links:

- Organic traffic data (from Google Analytics) of every page that's received a link over the last 2 years

- Keyword ranking data (from SEMrush) of every page that's received a link over the last 2 years

At first, *our findings were unclear* - we couldn't draw any specific conclusions that the links we were building had an impact on traffic. Sometimes they *did*, sometimes they *didn't*.

Much like the other case studies on this subject, we were focusing on purely topical elements:

- Number of "FOLLOWED" links a page has

- Link velocity (i.e. how often a page is receiving links)

- Anchor text ratio of a page

- "Quality" of links a page has (generally using Domain Authority or Citation Flow as the gauge of quality)

While there's nothing wrong with that, it's analyzing the impact using principles from an algorithm that penalizes, not *ignores*.

John Mueller said it himself, "algorithmically we try to ignore things that we can kind of isolate".

A change in focus was needed, so we looked at the data from the scope of if Google "ignoring" certain links as opposed to others. This required us to open up every backlink and visit its source. It took a while, to put it lightly, but we had to try and understand potential patterns the algorithm was picking up on.

It didn't take long for us to see that Google has gotten incredibly adept and picking up patterns and ignoring our links.

Our internal data overwhelmingly supports the notion that Google is "ignoring links" as opposed to penalizing them. That means there's a new set of quality metrics you need to live by when it comes to finding link opportunities. Here are some red flags to look out for:

- If a site has an "advertise" page that solicits "sponsored" blog content.
- If a site has a "write for us" page and is clearly relying on "guest posts" as the main source of content. If none of the author images have pictures or a REAL bio, then it's pretty easy to detect.
- Websites that have no supporting pages (i.e. no about page, FAQ, etc).
- Websites that have no purpose other than publishing content and have random categories and hierarchy (i.e. posts about fitness, parenting, finance and other random shit that doesn't go together).
- Blog posts with thin, poorly written content (500 words or less).

- Blog posts with no media, images, etc.
- Blog posts that ONLY link out to 1 or 2 places, neither of which are relevant or authoritative.

It sounds pretty logical when you lay out all the information like that, but you'd be surprised at how many links get ignored *because* of that criteria.

4.3 - Scalable Link Strategies That Work

My **biggest** pet peeve about the SEO community is the inability to understand anything outside of search engines. The worst culprits when it comes to that phenomenon are bloggers.

It's true that blogging is one of the best tactics when it comes to SEO. However, it's important to understand there's a whole world beyond search engines.

While Google does drive the majority of traffic for a lot of industries, it doesn't make sense to ignore all the other sources of users available for you and your clients. I'm talking about social media, guest posting, press releases, and more.

All those approaches fall under the category of link building. That is to say, direct links from other pages and social media, that completely bypass search engines and their results pages. The best part is, as you know by now, link building synergizes with SEO. Google sees links from other sources as bits of 'vouches' from third parties. The logic is, the more people link to your website, the better its content must be.

Link building not only complements SEO, it's a critical aspect of a holistic campaign. That means it's essential you understand what approaches work and which ones don't when it comes to link building.

Resource Pages

The idea behind a resource page is simple. You put together a list of tools and services that are important for a specific audience. Think about it as a link roundup, but on steroids. The key differences between both types of pages are:

1. Link roundups become outdated fast, as they tend to focus on recently published content.

2. Resource pages are built to be evergreen, which means they require frequent updates.

Take hosting, for example. If you look up hosting comparisons, you'll notice most of the top content focuses on helping you find the best providers. For results to remain relevant, they need constant updates. WordPress, for example, curates a shortlist of hosting providers they recommend:

That's a very rudimentary example of a resources page, but it works. If you look up "wordpress hosting recommendations", that boring resources page is the first result. Needless to say, that's a very popular web search.

From a link building standpoint, resource pages are a goldmine. The most popular results tend to be highly credible. If you can get a link from a resources page, it often becomes easier to find your way to others. From then on, it's a cascading effect.

It's important to understand, though. Not every type of link building opportunity works for every industry. If you're working in an industry that offers highly-targeted products and services, resource pages can be a great fit. Otherwise, you're better off focusing on other link building strategies that map more closely with your audience.

Your goal then, is to find "resource page opportunities. Our method for this process is downright simple – we use Google. Even a simple search using an operator such as **inurl:resources "seo"** is likely to bring up several link building opportunities:

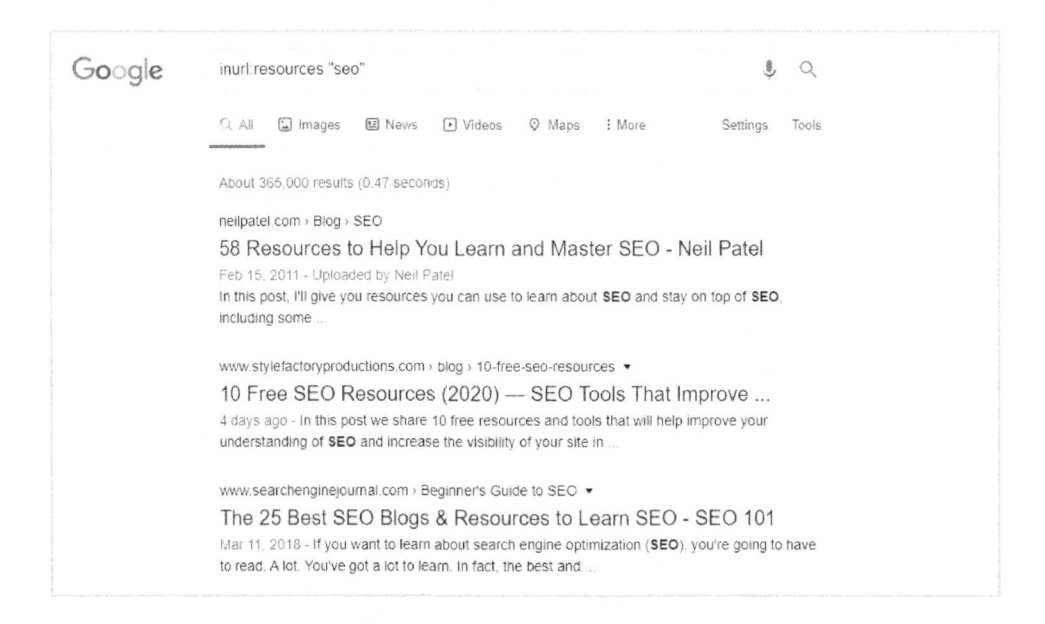

Ideally, you want to find pages that get regular updates, which you can easily check using Google. Check out the website and see if they have any contact information or any other way you can reach them. We handle all of this via email, so we can pitch several pages at once.

At this stage, the smart move is to put together a spreadsheet containing link building opportunities and contact information. After we've talked about other strategies, I'll walk you through our outreach process.

Guest Posting

It's impossible to talk about link building without diving into guest posting. As far as I'm concerned, guest posting is still the easiest way to build links to your client's websites. It's not an exaggeration to say I built my (very successful) agency on the back of guest posting.

You probably know how guest posting works, in a nutshell. You identify the blog you want to target, you pitch them an idea, and if they decide to go with it, you get to include a link to your website, and they get a full post. It's a win-win scenario, in more ways than one, including:

It can net you significant traffic depending on the popularity of the website you target.

Beyond traffic, it also gives you brand exposure and a lot of people take it as a tacit signal they can trust you. It enables you to build relationships with other key players in your industry.

That last benefit can be particularly powerful. Convincing websites to approve your guest posts can be tricky at first. If you're trying to build links for a client no one knows, you're going to get a lot of negative responses and worse yet, no response at all.

Here's the thing, though: once someone says yes to you, they're much more likely to keep saying yes down the line. That means the more outreach you do and the more websites associate your work with high quality, the easier it becomes to find guest posting placements. That only goes as long as the content is relevant to their audience, of course.

If you're ready to get to work, the first thing you'll need to do is identify guest posting opportunities. Thanks to Google, that's fairly simple. Your best bet is to focus on websites that openly call for guests posts, which you can find using operators such as "write for us" or "guest posting opportunities":

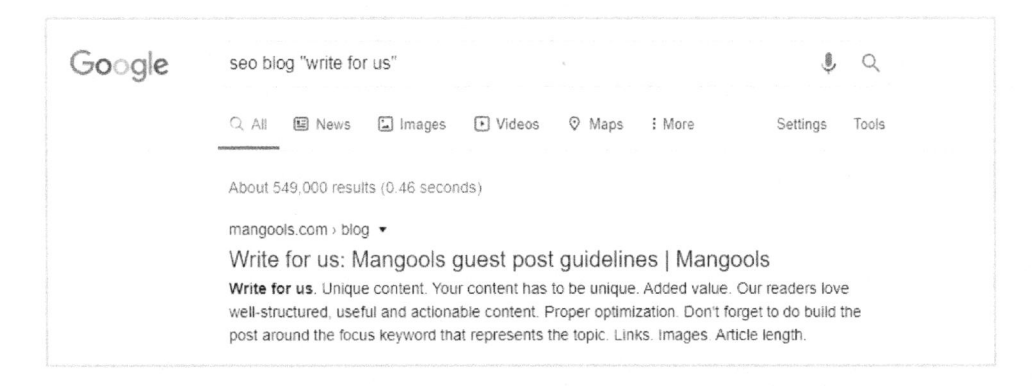

> **Google** seo blog "write for us"
>
> About 549,000 results (0.46 seconds)
>
> mangools.com › blog
> **Write for us: Mangools guest post guidelines | Mangools**
> **Write for us.** Unique content. Your content has to be unique. Added value. Our readers love well-structured, useful and actionable content. Proper optimization. Don't forget to do build the post around the focus keyword that represents the topic. Links. Images. Article length.

Usually, websites that explicitly accept guest posts will outline how the process works. It's your job to read those requirements, as you're much more likely to get your pitch ignored if you don't.

The downside to guest posting is that usually, you have to tailor your pitch for each blog. That means it takes time to do link building at scale since you can't submit the same pitch you do to everyone else. One way to identify websites that are worth your time is to submit an exploratory email and see if you get any responses:

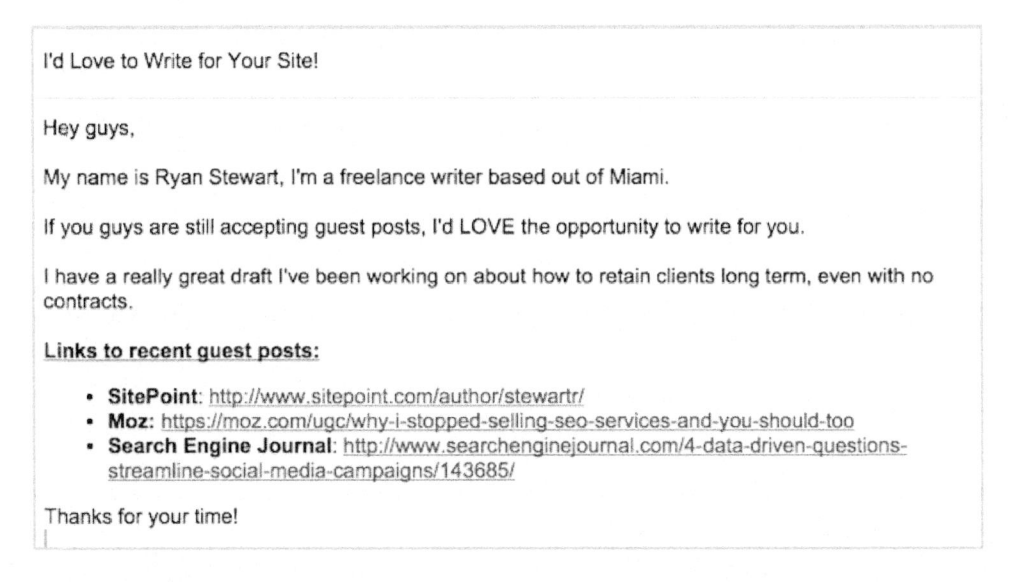

> I'd Love to Write for Your Site!
>
> Hey guys,
>
> My name is Ryan Stewart, I'm a freelance writer based out of Miami.
>
> If you guys are still accepting guest posts, I'd LOVE the opportunity to write for you.
>
> I have a really great draft I've been working on about how to retain clients long term, even with no contracts.
>
> **Links to recent guest posts:**
> - **SitePoint**: http://www.sitepoint.com/author/stewartr/
> - **Moz**: https://moz.com/ugc/why-i-stopped-selling-seo-services-and-you-should-too
> - **Search Engine Journal**: http://www.searchenginejournal.com/4-data-driven-questions-streamline-social-media-campaigns/143685/
>
> Thanks for your time!

I always like to include links to some of my best content, so right off the bat, they know I'm serious about guest posting. If I get a response, then we can sit down and talk about post ideas. That way, I save time over having to brainstorm for dozens of websites only not to hear back from them.

Sponsored Posts

Sponsored posts fall into a gray area when it comes to link building. As the name implies, you're paying a website in exchange for publishing a post. Sometimes, that'll involve a positive review of your products or services, whereas in other cases, you're essentially paying for a link.

In the past few years, it's become more and more common for some websites to ask for payment in exchange for "guest posting". As far as I'm concerned, if you're paying for it, it's not longer a guest post, it's sponsored content.

The benefits of sponsored content are evident. In many cases, money opens doors to websites that might not look at you twice otherwise. To put it another way, if you're going to pay for links, you might as well get your money's worth.

The challenge, in this case, is to find sponsored post opportunities that are "native" or fit in with the rest of the site. You do not want posts that get tagged as sponsored or paid placement since users are much more likely to ignore those. In a nutshell, here's what you want to *avoid* when you pay for links:

1. Low-cost marketplaces such as Fiverr.

2. Private blog networks, PBNs, and pretty much anyone that openly advertises they're selling links.

The way we like to approach sponsored posts is as advertisement opportunities. We look for real websites and blogs, with native audiences that can actually benefit from the products or services we want to promote. We're looking for posting opportunities and not traditional ads, such as banners. However, the way we find them is by looking for websites that are open to advertising of all kinds: email blasts, banner ads, influencer placements, etc.

As usual, once you've identified multiple opportunities, you want to reach out. In this case, I like to approach the conversation by asking about advertising in general and check if they're open to native opportunities.

> Interested in Advertising on [SITE]
>
> Hey [Insert Name],
>
> We're interested in advertising on media sites and blogs, like Boston.com.
>
> Are you able to let me know the different advertising options you offer?
>
> We're specifically interested native advertising, similar to a guest post.
>
> Thanks for your time.
>
> --
> **Ryan Stewart, MBA**
> Twitter | LinkedIn

If the answer is yes, you're off to the races. Then comes the really tricky part, which is figuring out how much that post is worth to your client.

Unlinked Mentions

Imagine if every time you mentioned a product or a service online, you had to publish an accompanying link to it. If that were the case, I'd personally have to pay a lot of fines. It's not because I don't appreciate the products I recommend either, it's just that sometimes, we all forget to include those links.

In practice, that means there's probably a ton of unlinked mentions for your clients, on blogs, post comments, and all sorts of pages. Doing a little outreach to convince the original authors to add a link is simple and often, you're met with very little resistance. After all, the hardest part of link building is often convincing people to vouch for you in the first place. If they're already doing so, adding the link becomes simple.

Here's the problem, though – finding unlinked mentions worth your time can be a hassle. For every mention where it may be worth reaching out for a link, there may be a dozen that aren't worth your time.

The best way to tackle this problem is using automation. For example, you can set up a Google Alert that tells you every time someone mentions you or your clients:

To avoid spamming my own inbox, I set the alert to notify me about new findings once a week. Then I can set a little time aside to check out which ones are worth pursuing and if I can find contact information for those.

If my team or I can find an opportunity that ticks both boxes, then we'll send an outreach email:

> Hey [NAME], Just Wanted to Say Thanks!
>
> Hey [NAME],
>
> A friend of mine just sent me a link to your article (http://blog.wordsyouwant.com/2015/12/01/what-does-seo-mean-today/) after he noticed you mentioned my name and brand (WEBRIS).
>
> First off, thank you! I really appreciate it.
>
> Second, I noticed you didn't include a link to my site - would you mind including one for attribution purposes?
>
> I'm working incredibly hard to build a business and earn a living, a link from your site would go a long way to help me out.
>
> Thank you!
>
> --
> **Ryan Stewart, MBA**
> Twitter | LinkedIn

As far as link building goes, unlinked mentions are one of the most scalable methods you can employ. If you find your client is getting mentions constantly, that can translate to an influx of new links very quickly – all you have to do is reach out.

Landing Press Links

If you run a popular website, you will have people knocking on your door 24/7 trying to get you to link to them. That gets old fast and while direct outreach does work for me and my agency, sometimes, you need to think outside the box to get those links.

One 'hack' I use to get links from publications such as Thought Catalog, Huffington Post, and Forbes is I pay for them. The real trick lies in knowing who to contact, which makes this link building technique fall into a gray area.

In major publications such as those I mentioned above, you have two kinds of writers:

1. In-house staff

2. Contributing freelancers (who, in most cases, work for free)

Popular publications can get away with not paying freelancers because they know there's always people willing to work for free in exchange for a piece they can add to their portfolio. It sucks if you're a freelancer, which is where link building opportunities arise.

What we do is, we find those contributors, and then we work out a deal where we pay them in exchange for coverage.

Is it 100% ethical? Definitely not. However, as long as the posts you pay for are relevant for the website where they will get published, it's a win-win scenario for everyone involved. You get links from reputable websites, freelancers get paid for their work, and the publications get their free content.

To identify "press" opportunities, you want to look for any major publications that have "contributors" working for them. The way we like to approach this is, we put together lists of the keywords we want to target (we cover this in phase 3) and see if there are any publications we're interested in that are using them.

If we find an overlap and that content was written by a contributor, then we know there's an opening. We look for that contributor's contact information and we send them an outreach email. With a big enough budget (we usually offer around $150 per post) the results can be astounding.

This whole approach might seem too unethical, but it's far more efficient than spending thousands of dollars on a "PR" firm that often does precisely the same. I'm a results-focused guy, so if I see a way to get those results for WEBRIS' clients where everyone involved wins, I'm going to take it.

If you apply that same mindset to your campaigns, you're going to crush it.

Cold Blogger Outreach

We've already talked about guest posting and how it's one of the most powerful link building techniques you can use. Sometimes, though, you'll want to reach out to blogs that don't have guest posting opportunities asking for links. That's what we call "cold blogger outreach".

There's millions of blogs online, each representing an opportunity to get new links to your clients' websites. You will, of course, want to focus on blogs within your same niche, but even so, there's still a mind numbing number of opportunities available to you.

Here's the problem, though – direct link outreach, which is where you blatantly ask someone to link back to you, has a minuscule success rate. Why, after all, should I take the time to read your email and give you something valuable in exchange for nothing?

Your success rate when it comes to cold blogger outreach depends on the value you can offer. For example, one of my favorite tactics involves reaching out to writers that consistently blog about the same theme and let them know when I publish a post they might be interested in.

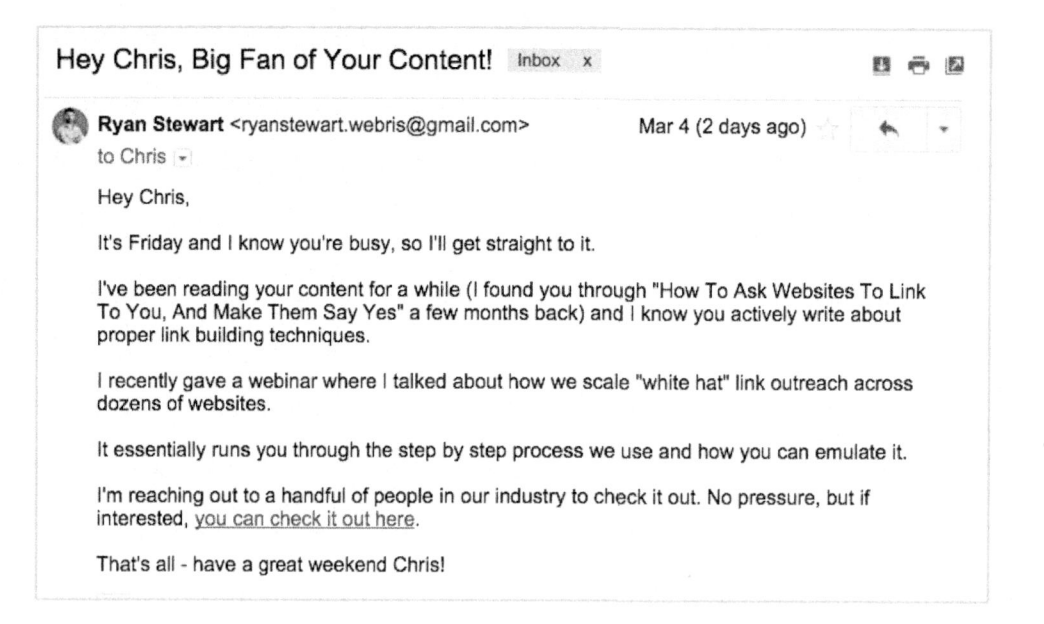

> **Hey Chris, Big Fan of Your Content!** Inbox x
>
> **Ryan Stewart** <ryanstewart.webris@gmail.com> Mar 4 (2 days ago)
> to Chris
>
> Hey Chris,
>
> It's Friday and I know you're busy, so I'll get straight to it.
>
> I've been reading your content for a while (I found you through "How To Ask Websites To Link To You, And Make Them Say Yes" a few months back) and I know you actively write about proper link building techniques.
>
> I recently gave a webinar where I talked about how we scale "white hat" link outreach across dozens of websites.
>
> It essentially runs you through the step by step process we use and how you can emulate it.
>
> I'm reaching out to a handful of people in our industry to check it out. No pressure, but if interested, you can check it out here.
>
> That's all - have a great weekend Chris!

I call this process "seeding" because I never outright ask for a link. What I do is plant the seed so they might reference that content or some of my other posts in the future. In many cases, just reaching out without asking for anything in return can be the start of a fruitful collaboration. Blogging is, after all, a lonely job.

Another tactic I like to use is to offer promotional exchanges. If you have a healthy following on your blog or social media accounts, you can go ahead and tell other bloggers "I'll Tweet this if you Tweet this". That way, everyone benefits from the exchange.

The Outreach Process

Every single approach we've covered so far shares one thing in common – they require outreach. You have to establish contact with the right person and pitch them convincingly. The more links you want, the more work that outreach takes.

Some people will tell you that you can just sit back and wait for links to come organically. If you publish amazing, in-depth content, that will happen. However, just waiting for links to fall from the sky is no way to run an SEO campaign. If you want results, you have to hit the streets.

For us, "hitting the streets" means putting together a link building process we can scale. As usual, it all begins with a spreadsheet:

Website	Social Profile	Followers	Location	First Name	Email
http://www.miamifoodporn.com/	https://www.instagram.com/miami_foodporn/?hl=	58.3k	US	Nathalie	info@miamifoodporn.com
http://www.hungrypost.com/	https://www.instagram.com/thehungrypost/?hl=e	59.7k	US	Jose	info@hungrypost.com
http://www.miamitimes.us/	https://www.instagram.com/miamitimes/	112k	US	Daniel	Info@MiamiTimes.us
http://www.eatitmiami.com/	https://twitter.com/eatitmiami	954	US	Colin	colinohiggins@gmail.com
https://www.myfab5.com	https://www.instagram.com/bestfoodmiami/	50.7k	US	guys	mia@myfab5.com
http://www.chatchow.com/	https://www.instagram.com/chatchowtv/?hl=en	23.5k	US	Gio	gio@chatchow.com
http://www.thefood-e.com/	https://www.instagram.com/thefoode/	9,701	US	guys	thefood.e@gmail.com
http://www.fatgirlhedonist.com/	https://www.instagram.com/fatgirlhedonist/	64.3k	US	Cari	FatgirlHedonist@gmail.com
http://www.kd-interiordesign.com/	https://www.pinterest.com/kddesignzinc/	25k	US	Kathy	kathy@kd-interiordesign.com
http://marksikes.com/	https://www.instagram.com/markdsikes/	68.7k	US	Mark	mark@markdsikes.com
http://www.parkerkennedyliving.com/	https://www.pinterest.com/parkerkennedy/	19.9k	US	Parker	parker@parkerkennedyliving.com
http://everythingcurvyandchic.com/	https://www.instagram.com/everythingcurvyandc	200k	US	Chanté	everythingcurvyandchic@gmail.com
https://jrazzcollection.com/	https://www.instagram.com/jrazzcollection/	3,869	US	guys	jrazzcollection@gmail.com
http://www.eddieotero.com/	https://www.instagram.com/eddieotero/	113k	US	Eddie	hello@eddieotero.com
http://www.cultofreal.com/	https://www.instagram.com/cultofreal/	159k	US	Nina	info@cultofreal.com
http://dianadazzling.com/	https://www.instagram.com/dianadazzling/	105k	US	Diana	contact@dianadazzling.com
http://www.bysarahbarlondo.com/	https://www.instagram.com/sarahbarlondo/	66.1k	US	Sarah	sarah@bysarahbarlondo.com
http://www.thefreesoulchic.com/	https://www.instagram.com/thefreesoulchic/	5,444	US	Alejandra	thefreesoulchic@gmail.com

When it comes to social media, for example, our offshore team constantly looks for accounts in our client's niches, which we can contact. They put together all that information in a list we can reference later.

The same approach works for pretty much every type of outreach. Before you get in touch with anyone you need their name, website, and email. You will also want to ascertain how valuable each opportunity is. For example, is their website one of your top competitors? Are they ranking for keywords you want to target?

The more valuable the link building opportunity, the higher on your list of priorities they should be. Once you have all that contact information, you want to use a tool that enables you to send outreach emails en masse.

We use Pitchbox (https://pitchbox.com/) for outreach. It's expensive, but by far the best email outreach solution on the planet (tell them I sent you).

Below is a screenshot from the outreach template we use to bring influencers on board. It's important that you use different templates depending on what type of opportunity you're pursuing, so keep that mind.

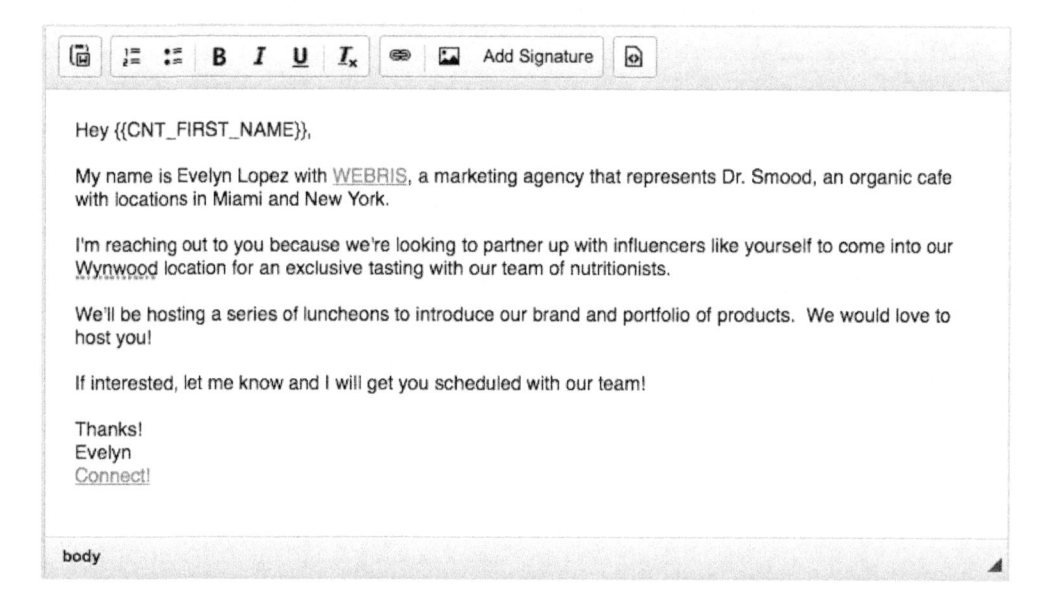

```
Hey {{CNT_FIRST_NAME}},

My name is Evelyn Lopez with WEBRIS, a marketing agency that represents Dr. Smood, an organic cafe with locations in Miami and New York.

I'm reaching out to you because we're looking to partner up with influencers like yourself to come into our Wynwood location for an exclusive tasting with our team of nutritionists.

We'll be hosting a series of luncheons to introduce our brand and portfolio of products. We would love to host you!

If interested, let me know and I will get you scheduled with our team!

Thanks!
Evelyn
Connect!
```

For high-value opportunities, you might want to set the time aside to send fully personalized emails. When it comes to cold blog outreach, for example, I may take the time to mention which of their posts are my favorite and how long I've been following them. Small details such as those that can have a huge difference in your success rate.

Finally, it's critical you understand that link building outreach is a numbers game. You don't want to get inside your head trying to get links from a specific site or two. Ideally, you'll identify dozens or hundreds of opportunities, construct outreach emails accordingly, track your success rate, and then repeat the process all over again.

Without a scalable process, you're no different from a guy sending cold emails from his basement.

PHASE 5

The Evaluation Process

Now that we've run through the entire SEO process, it's time to measure our results and adjust our campaigns accordingly. We do so by building reports to analyze data and feed our insights back into the campaign to make sure it stays on track.

This phase focuses on how to evaluate the performance of your SEO campaign.

- **5.1 - Creating a web analytics measurement plan.** A very simple but powerful strategy to ensure you're measuring the right KPIs for your website.

- **5.2 - Evaluating your campaign's key performance indicators (KPIs).** A very simple but powerful strategy to ensure you're measuring the right KPIs for your website.

- **5.3 - Building your own SEO report (using my full template).** A very simple but powerful strategy to ensure you're measuring the right KPIs for your website.

- **5.4 - Why SEO is an ongoing process (and what your next steps should be).** A very simple but powerful strategy to ensure you're measuring the right KPIs for your website.

5.1 - Creating a Web Analytics Measurement Plan

If you want to be at the top of your SEO game, you need an understanding of analytics. You need to be able to look at complex datasets and understand how to break them down, as well as what each indicator tells you. The best way to do so is with an analytics measurement plan.

Building a measurement plan

Why you need a measurement plan:

- Defines your company's objectives; maps those objectives to goals, metrics and key performance indicators (KPIs)
- Defines what success looks like; gets buy in from top executives
- Assists in optimization and improvements

A measurement plan is part 1 in your overall analytics process. Without a proper measurement plan, everything else fails.

Step One: Document Business Objectives

We need to start from the very beginning - why do you have a website?

Some examples are:

- Sell my products
- Sell space for ad revenue
- Create a 1 to 1 relationship with my customers
- Provide a platform to use my software

Answering this question is the first step in getting a hold of your data. Once you have this defined you have an overarching objective that everything maps back to.

Every dollar that your business spends should drive towards achieving these objectives.

An example of a business objective could be:

"The purpose of our website is to increase total sales by allowing customers to buy our products online".

Step Two: Create Goals / Strategies

Goals are what drive success of a given business objective. It completes the following sentence:

In order to increase our online sales, we must ....

Goals should be all of the following:

- Actionable
- Measurable
- Understandable

When structuring goals, I always lead with a verb – this implies action. For example, here is how I completed the sentence…

In order to increase our online sales, we must ....

- [reach new customers through Google Search]
- [increase repeat purchases]

- [grow our email list]

All 3 of the above are measurable goals that drive towards the overall business objective. Easy. Simple. Clean.

Step Three: Choose Key Performance Indicators (KPIs)

KPIs are digital outcomes that help you gauge success against your goals. There's a lot of debate about picking KPIs – some argue metrics like visits, page views and time on site are "vanity metrics".

FALSE!

If you're BuzzFeed, those metrics are critical to your advertising model, aka how you generate revenue. What matters is picking KPIs that matter to your business. Dig deep into metrics that will help gauge the success of your goals.

For example, I chose the following KPIs for our goal "reach new customers through Google Search". Some KPIs to help gauge success are:

- Number of organic sessions and pageviews
- Bounce rate and time on site from organic search
- Goal completions from organic search

Step Four: Set Targets/Benchmarks

You got 2 million new sessions from your SEO campaign. That's amazing! Wait, that's amazing right?

Targets (or benchmarks) put your website's goals into perspective. They are a numeric value that force you to measure the success of your goals.

You should use your company's historical data to choose targets. If no such data exists, use industry benchmark data (a simple Google search will help you track down the data).

For example

- Goal = Number of organic sessions and pageviews. Target = 100,000/month

Step Five: Determine Reporting and Segments

We're going to talk about reporting in the coming section, but before we get there I wanted to share a graphic depiction of what our measurement plans look like at the agency.

	BUILD 1 TO 1 RELATIONSHIP WITH CUSTOMERS		
BUSINESS OBJECTIVE			
CAMPAIGN GOALS	SUCCESSFULLY REACH AUDIENCE (OUTLINED IN STRATEGY)	COLLECT INFORMATION VIA OPT IN FORM	IMPROVE CUSTOMER DATA/LEAD QUALITY (ONGOING GOAL)
KPIs TARGETS REPORTS SEGMENTS	KPI: 301 Hits & Conversion Rate Target: Hits > 20% Conversions > 2% Report:Custom Segment: None	KPI: Total opt ins Target: 2,000 Report:Goals Segment: Campaign, Traffic Sources, Visitor Type	KPI: Email CTR (ling term measurement) Target: >2% per send Report:ET Segment: None
	KPI: Ad Unit/Link CTR Target: Facebook >5% Display >1% Email >1% Text >5% Twitter >5% Search (Home) >2% Report:Ad server reports, BitJy Segment: None	KPI: LP Conversion rate Target: >2% Report:Goals Segment: Campaign, Traffic Sources	KPI: Database match Target: >2% Report:Manual Segment: None
	KPI: Form abandonment rate Target: >10% Report:Custom (Possibly heat/click map) Segment: Campaign, Traffic Sources	KPI: Level of submission (Prizes 1 -3) Target: Leval 1 Only >50%; Level 1 & 2 >40%; Level 1,2 & 3 >20% Report:Goals, Custom conversion Segment: Campaign, Traffic Sources, Visitor Type	KPI: Visitor loyalty Target: >50% return to site with in 30 days and consume 2 pages of content Report:Goals Segment: Email Traffic
	KPI: Cost per lead Target: >$15 Report:Ad server + AT Internet Segment: Campaign, Traffic Sources, Visitor Type		KPI: # of Social follows from LP Target: >1% Report:Goals Segment: Social follows

WEBRIS

You can clearly see how our goals, KPIs and business objectives align. This is a great tool for guiding internal conversations or giving clients peace of mind that you're striving to meet their business goals (not just traffic goals).

5.2 - Evaluating Your Campaign's Key Performance Indicators (KPIs)

We've covered so many processes so far, it's difficult to know how to measure the impact your efforts have had during the life of your campaign. The answer, of course, lies in the numbers.

Every campaign has a few KPIs that tell you almost everything you need to know *if* you know how to read them. Throughout this entire book, we've been helping you develop your first professional SEO campaign. Now let's go over how to measure your success.

In my experience, if you want to get a quick overview of your campaign's progress, you want to focus on the next KPIs, using the tools and methods we discussed in the last section:

- **Overall keyword counts.** This covers how many keywords your website is ranking for and in which positions. You want to focus, particularly, on rankings that fall within the 1-3 and 4-10 positions since those are the ones that will bring in the most traffic to your website.

- **Ranks for target landing pages and keywords.** One key aspect of our process, so far, has been to focus on target pages instead of spreading yourself too thin. At this stage, you want to measure if there have been changes in rankings for those top pages, as well as which keywords they're showing up for.

- **Rank changes for top keywords by volume and position.** Your top keywords are the ones that bring in the most traffic to your website. That means you want to make sure you're not slipping through the rankings for any of them, which could cause you to lose a significant part of your traffic.

It's important to remember, SEO is an ongoing process. You're never really done optimizing your website, because your competitors never are.

At any point, another page could knock one of your top traffic-earners off the top rankings, to give you an example. That's one of the many reasons why you want to monitor KPIs closely.

If you're working with a client, you're going to need to deliver all these KPIs in a format they can understand. We do that through our monthly SEO reports, which cover those metrics and *a lot* more. Let's talk reports.

5.3 - Building Your Own SEO Report (Using My Full Template)

One of the hardest parts of running an SEO agency is communicating the results of your efforts to clients. For many customers, the only metrics they understand are conversions and sales. If they hire you and they don't start seeing more sales, then they're going to think your services aren't worth it.

If you've made it this far, you know the massive undertaking that is SEO. A scalable SEO strategy goes well beyond the things you're usually taught, such as keyword research and on-page optimization.

To avoid any miscommunications, we decided to put together a comprehensive SEO report template that we could use for all our clients. It compiles data from multiple sources, including several we've talked about so far, including Search Console, Google Sheets, and Google Analytics.

If that sounds intimidating, it shouldn't, because you're **already** familiar with parts of this report. We went through some of the metrics it covers during phase one in "How to Analyze Your Website's Numbers".

Ultimately, our report comes down to numbers. If there's one universal language, it's numbers, and with our report, your clients will understand the scope of work that goes into an SEO campaign.

Even if you're not an agency and you're using this book to develop an SEO campaign for your own website, putting together a report that tracks all your metrics is incredibly useful. A periodic report will enable you to track your progress, see which areas you're flagging behind in, and keep track of what is still left to do.

How to build an SEO report

The reports we put together each month for our clients include 17 unique pages and they include hundreds of metrics altogether,

Putting together all that information by hand would be a huge drain on our time. The reports are so massive, we'd need to hire new workers just to put them together.

To automate the process as much as possible, we needed to find a tool that would enable us to:

1. Pull the data we want from multiple sources

2. Enable us to configure how it displays that information

3. Support data graphs to provide clients with a visual representation of progress

Since we rely heavily on Google products, we decided to use their Data Studio tool. As you may know, Data Studio is a tool that enables you to connect data (big surprise there!) and create visually appealing reports.

To give you an idea oh what a Data Studio report looks like, check out one of their templates for Search Console data:

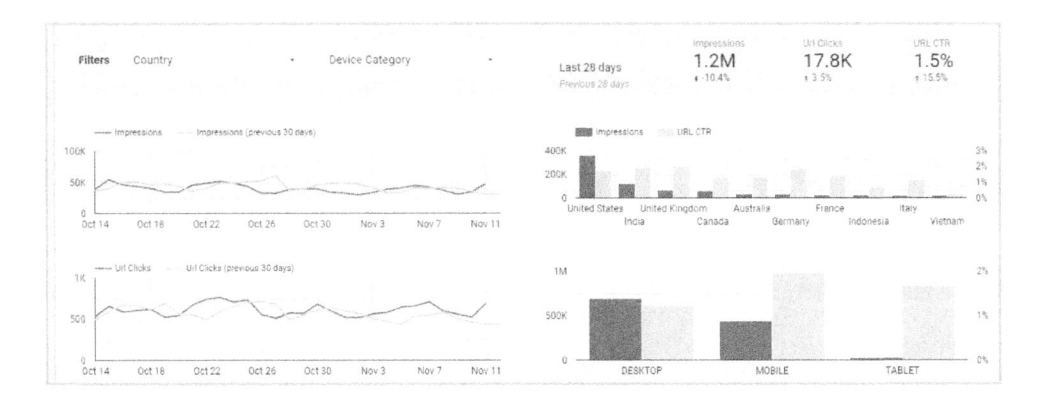

If there's one thing that should be evident by now is we're big data nerds, so Data Studio was the obvious choice.

More importantly, it enabled us to pull the metrics we wanted from almost all the tools we've used so far for our SEO campaign. When you create a new report, you get to choose from dozens of data sources to connect with:

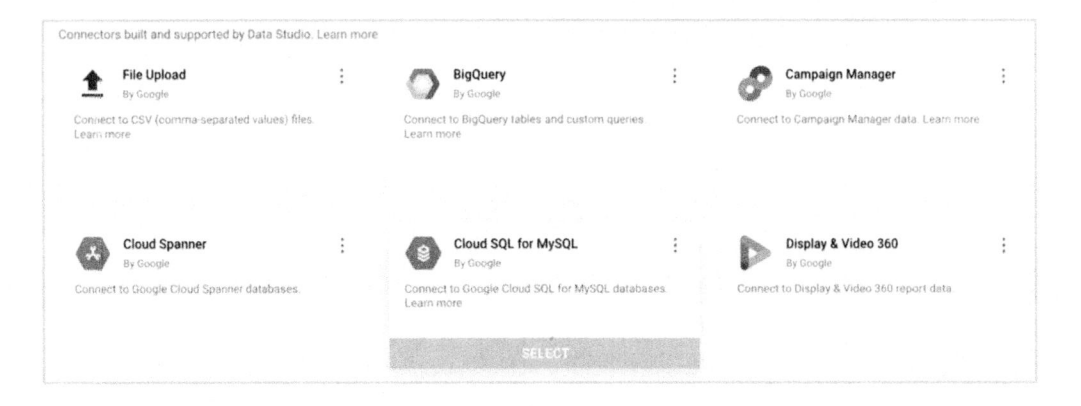

Four our SEO reports, we built a template that connects with three data sources:

1. **Google Sheets.** We use Google Sheets to track overall keyword count, changes in ranking for our top keywords (by volume and position), and ranks for target landing pages.

2. **Google Search Console.** For our report, we use **two** Search Console sources, one at the keyword level and another at the URL level.

3. **Google Analytics.** This is where the bulk of the data for our reports comes from, including more in-depth information, such as time-per-session, pages-per-session, bounce rate, goal conversions, and **much** more.

Putting together all the data points required to make our report work took a **long** time. Throughout the next sections, I'm going to break down the key parts of that report, so you can use them as a template to build your own.

> **Visit www.theblueprint.website to check out our Monthly SEO Report template.**

For a one time fee, we can also help you set up a full report (including all 17 pages we use) for any of your websites, using a copy of the template we use in Data Studio.

Monthly overview

The goal of a SEO report is to provide you with a comprehensive view of how well your strategy is working. However, sometimes clients just want a quick overview of your progress, which is why we like to open every report with a monthly overview.

Our monthly overview includes five elements:

1. **Introduction.** This is where you warm up clients before you dive into the numbers. There should be a quick paragraph or two covering your progress throughout the last month.

2. **Notable items.** For this section, we usually include a point-by-point list that covers areas where we made significant progress during the month.

3. **Tasks completed.** Any specific tasks you finished during the month go here.

4. **Open action items.** These are tasks that you're going to carry over to the next month and hopefully wrap them up by the time the next report is ready to go.

5. **Planned action items.** We've put together a lot of task calendars so far, so for this section, you want to make a list of all the action items you want to tackle next month.

Building reports on a monthly basis enables us to gather enough data that it has statistical relevance. Moreover, it gives us enough time to make real progress. Weekly reports would be overkill and no one would read 17 pages of daily reports.

This first page of your SEO report should be very easy to digest, so we rely heavily on lists. Here's what it might look like in action:

Introduction

Organic traffic increased significantly during the last month, which we can attribute to multiple keywords rising through the ranks sharply. We've also been focusing heavily on backlink outreach, which resulted in 5 new high-quality links to some of our top landing pages.

Notable items:

- Keyword rankings improved by 34%

- Organic traffic increased by 49%

- Obtained featured snippet for keyword "how to bake a cake"

Tasks completed:

- Finished sitemap overhaul

- Published new content targeting the following keywords:

    o How to bake a pie

    o How to make pie crust

    o Baking a blueberry pie

Open action items:

- Finish implementing AMP for our existing assets

Planned action items:

- Send an outreach email to our updated list of influencers

You're going to overwhelm clients plenty with the rest of your report, so let's keep things simple when it comes to your monthly overview.

How is your website performing?

The number one question on any client's minds when they open a report is "How is my website doing?" Your monthly overview should give them an idea of whether to expect good news or bad, but now it's time to dig into the data for real.

After the overview, we like to jump right into organic traffic data within the next page:

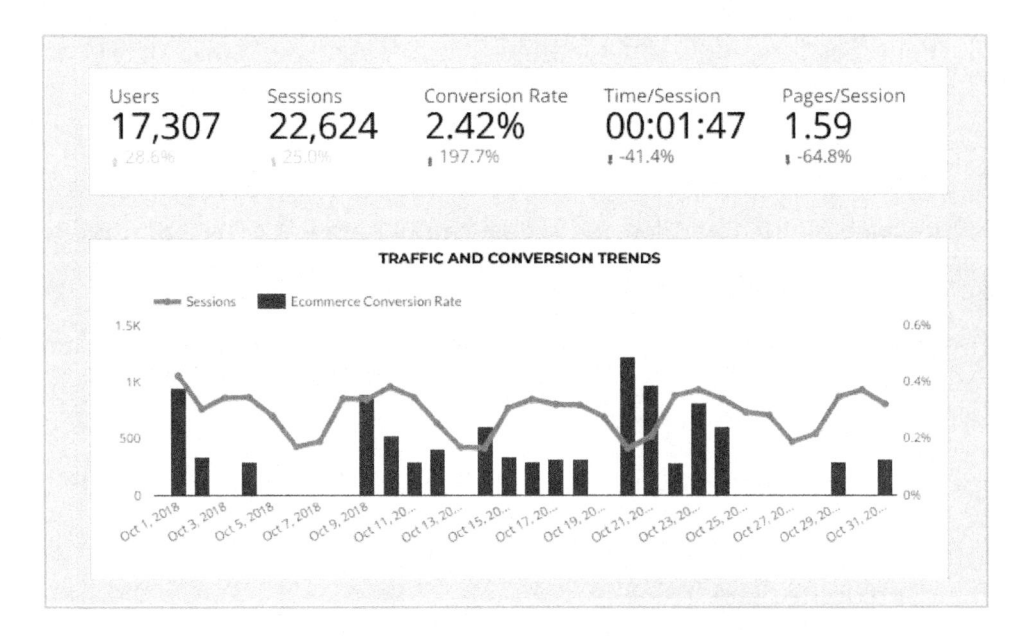

There's a lot to unwrap here, but if you've been paying attention, these metrics should be all too familiar by now. However, if you're using this report to show progress to clients, you need to be able to explain what each metric means, or simplify your own template to avoid miscommunication.

Here are the key metrics this section of the report covers:

1. **Users.** How many users visited your website altogether.

2. **Sessions.** The same users might visit your website multiple times, each of those visits is what we call a session.

3. **Conversion Rate.** We pull goal tracking information from Google Analytics to lead with one of the metrics that most customers hold dearest, conversions.

4. **Time/Session.** Naturally, you want visitors to spend as much time as possible on your website. A lot of the changes you make during the technical optimization process can improve this metric

5. **Page/Session.** How many pages visitors see per session. Technical optimizations and internal links can improve this metric.

Note each metric includes percentages right below. For us and our clients, those are as important as the raw numbers. As you might imagine, green represents progress whereas red means that metric dipped from last month.

This first page of the report closes with a list of traffic sources and what your top landing pages are. Each month, we recommend you compare both tables to see if any landing pages have dipped out of the list and what sources of traffic are doing better or worse.

How is organic traffic trending?

In an ideal world, your website's traffic would always trend upwards. If you laid out your visits or sessions on a month-by-month basis, you'd see a definite upward curve. Within this page of the report, we open with such a graph:

![Chart: HOW IS YOUR WEBSITE'S ORGANIC TRAFFIC TRENDING? - Data from Google Analytics. HOW YOUR ORGANIC TRAFFIC HAS PERFORMED - THIS YEAR COMPARED TO LAST YEAR. Values: 13,889, 13,291, 13,567, 13,076, 13,095, 12,323, 12,469, 12,164, 14,463, 12,588, 11,413, 14,010, across Jan 2018 – Nov 2018.]

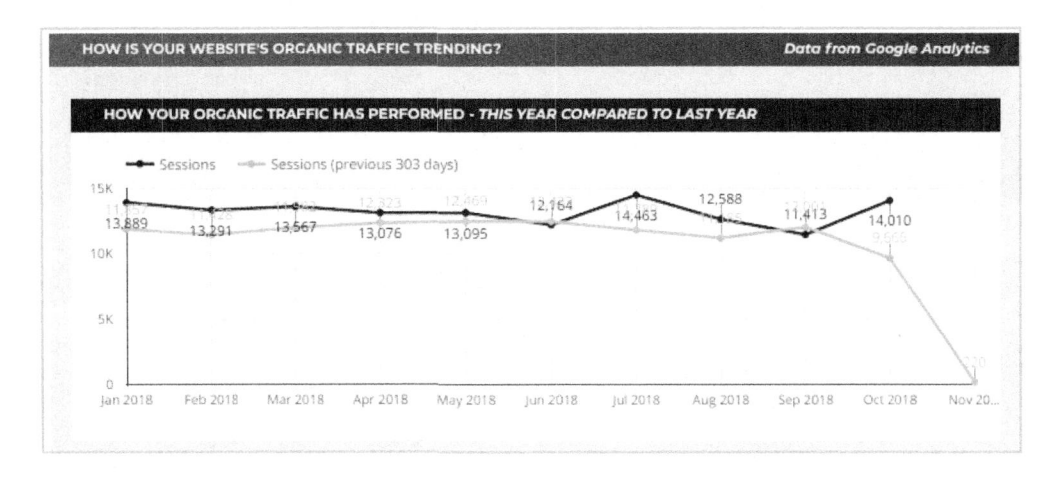

What we do is pull data from Google Analytics that shows how many visits you got on any given month over the past year. We also correlate that data with the same reports from the *previous* year, to give you an even better idea of your website's growth.

Beyond that, you also want to pay attention to daily traffic trends. For online stores, Sundays and Mondays tend to be the best days for sales, to give you an example. That may vary depending on what type of site you're working on, but the idea is – if you can understand your audience's patterns, you can time new content so it gets the most engagement.

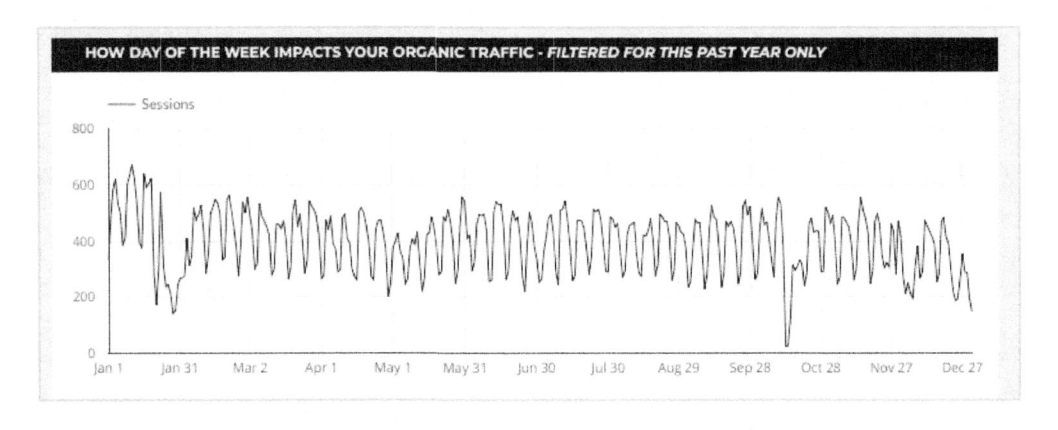

![Chart: HOW DAY OF THE WEEK IMPACTS YOUR ORGANIC TRAFFIC - FILTERED FOR THIS PAST YEAR ONLY. Sessions plotted from Jan 1 through Dec 27.]

Now let's move on graphs and charts for a little bit and go over one of my favorite pages from our monthly SEO report.

The SEO Blueprint

What are your top pages from organic search?

For this section, we break down what pages are bringing in the most traffic to your website, using a simple list.

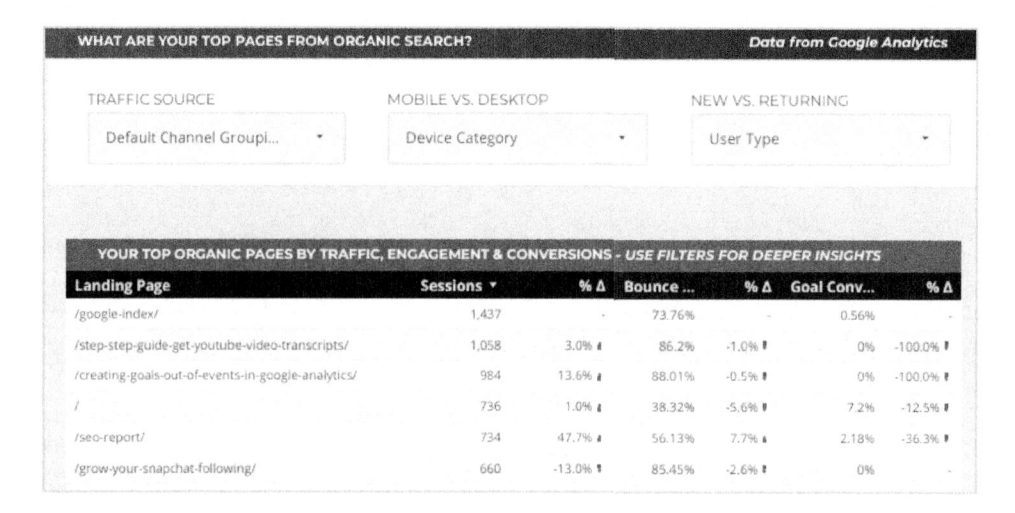

WHAT ARE YOUR TOP PAGES FROM ORGANIC SEARCH?				Data from Google Analytics	
TRAFFIC SOURCE: Default Channel Groupi...		MOBILE VS. DESKTOP: Device Category		NEW VS. RETURNING: User Type	
YOUR TOP ORGANIC PAGES BY TRAFFIC, ENGAGEMENT & CONVERSIONS - *USE FILTERS FOR DEEPER INSIGHTS*					
Landing Page	Sessions ▼	% Δ	Bounce...	% Δ	Goal Conv...	% Δ
/google-index/	1,437	-	73.76%	-	0.56%	-
/step-step-guide-get-youtube-video-transcripts/	1,058	3.0% ▲	86.2%	-1.0% ▼	0%	-100.0% ▼
/creating-goals-out-of-events-in-google-analytics/	984	13.6% ▲	88.01%	-0.5% ▼	0%	-100.0% ▼
/	736	1.0% ▲	38.32%	-5.6% ▼	7.2%	-12.5% ▼
/seo-report/	734	47.7% ▲	56.13%	7.7% ▲	2.18%	-36.3% ▼
/grow-your-snapchat-following/	660	-13.0% ▼	85.45%	-2.6% ▼	0%	-

Let's go over what each column tells us:

- **Landing Page.** This is the URL for each page on the list – simple stuff.

- **Sessions.** How many hits that URL got during the past month. To the right, you can see if traffic increased or decreased in comparison with the past month.

- **Bounce Rate.** Your bounce rate gives us an idea of how engaging each page is. The standard bounce rate across the industry is somewhere in between 20-30%. If you see any URLs with much higher percentages, you want to take note so you can optimize those pages.

- **Goal Conversions.** If any of these URLs has a conversion goal, here's where you track it.

As usual, we pull all that data from Google Analytics. In most cases, you'll see a lot of the same pages within this list, month after month. As we've talked about before, most websites have a few URLs that bring in a significant amount of their traffic.

Even so, if you've been working on new pillar content within the past few months, it *should* show up within this page of the report at some point, so that's something worth keeping an eye out for.

You also want to pay close attention to any pages that show significant declines in traffic from the last month. We can usually attribute such a decline to one of two things:

1. **Seasonal changes.** Some types of content do well only during specific seasons. For example, if you set up holiday sale pages, it's only natural that traffic plummets after those dates pass.

2. **Optimization issues.** In many cases, sudden drops in traffic can be explained by technical issues that can impact your SEO.

There is a *lot* of data to unpack here as Google Analytics will pull all your website's URLs for this report. For the sake of expediency – and for your sanity – I recommend you focus on the first page or two of URLs.

What keywords are you ranking for?

For this section, we focus on two things. First off, you get an overview of how much organic traffic you're getting from Google. You can break down this data by year, month, and the last 30 days:

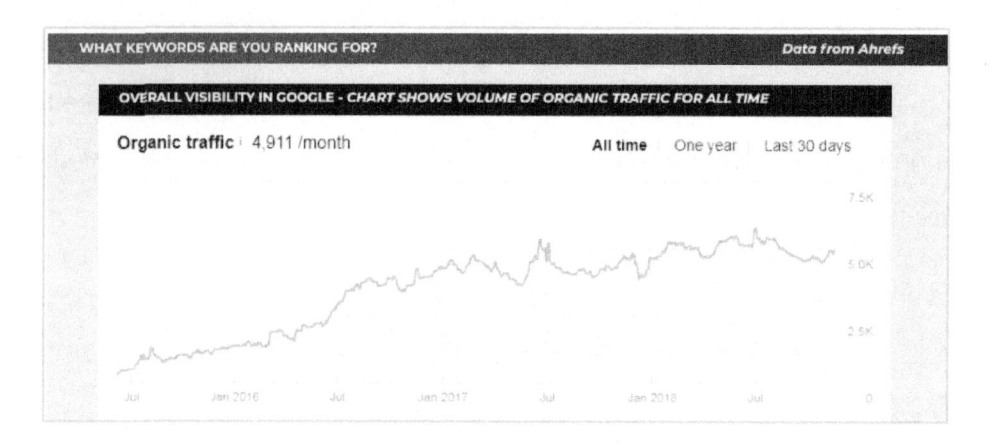

There's a direct correlation between how visible you are in search engines to how much traffic you're getting. That means the more keywords you're ranking for, the more visits you get. At least, that should be the case in theory.

By now, you understand that although you might rank for a lot of keywords, if you're not within the first results, you're not going to get a significant amount of traffic from them.

Right below, you can see how many keywords that example website is ranking for:

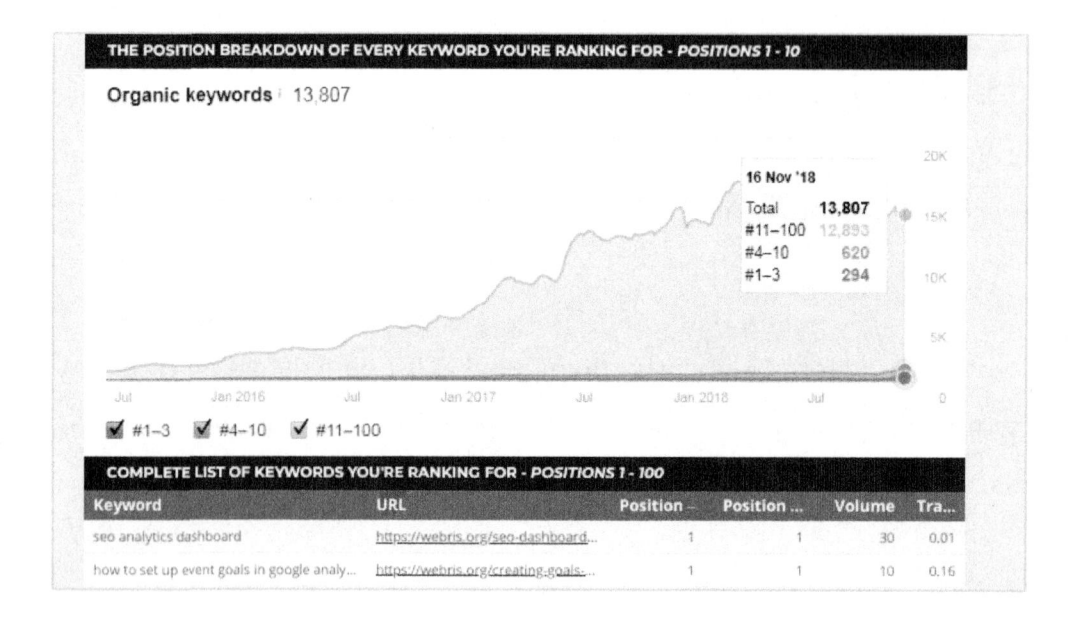

Almost 14,000 keywords is an impressive number. However, once you mouse over the graph, you can get a look at ranking distribution. In our experience, anything below ranks 1-10 will not bring in much attention to your website.

Your main takeaway from this section of the report should be the keywords that you're ranking for between positions 4-10. Those are keywords that may have the potential to break through to the top 3 and dramatically increase your organic traffic.

As I've mentioned before, it's much easier to optimise existing content to improve its ranking than to start from scratch. With this report, you can get a good look at all the optimization opportunities available to you.

If you scroll down a little further, you'll get details on each keyword and its corresponding URL, so you can take note and get to work on improving them.

What types of queries are you ranking for?

Near the start of the book, we talked about branded search. A branded search is when users look up your products directly. Google values this signal enormously because it implies that users know and trust your brand.

For this page of the report, we take a look at branded vs. non-branded clicks from the SERPs:

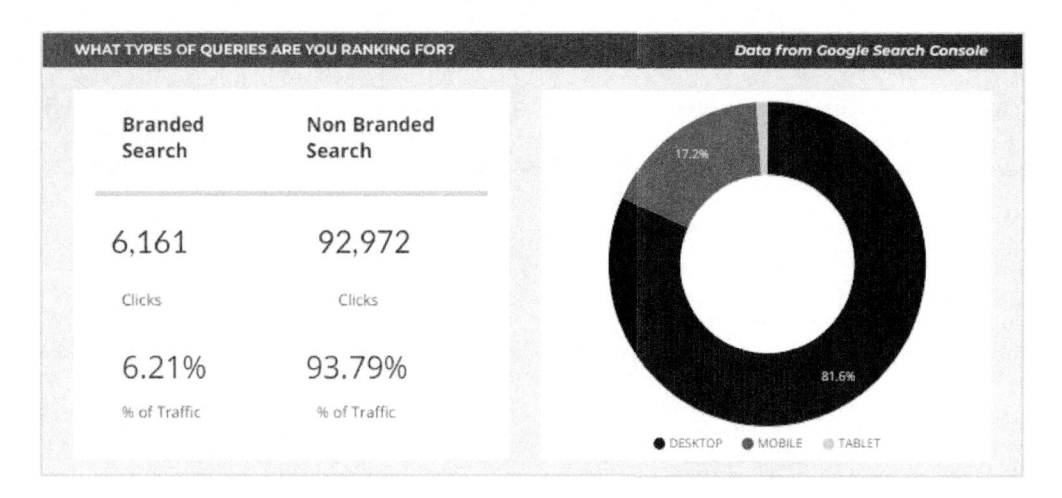

WHAT TYPES OF QUERIES ARE YOU RANKING FOR?		Data from Google Search Console
Branded Search	**Non Branded Search**	
6,161 Clicks	92,972 Clicks	17.2% / 81.6%
6.21% % of Traffic	93.79% % of Traffic	DESKTOP · MOBILE · TABLET

It's par for the course for branded searches to be lower than their counterparts unless you're working on SEO for a household-name brand. Even so, if you're getting a decent volume of traffic from branded searches, it means you're building visibility and trust, which are two key aspects of SEO.

Clicks tell you a lot about how well your pages are doing within Google. To get better clickthrough rates, you need to work on three key elements:

1. **Page titles.** Informative and catchy titles play a big role in whether a user decides to click on your pages or not.

2. **Meta descriptions.** Between your titles and meta descriptions, users need to have a clear idea of what each page offers them in terms of value.

3. **Schema markup.** We covered schema markup in detail during Phase 2, but in a nutshell, it's code that enables you to 'punch up' the way your pages show up in the SERPs.

The top 3 pages in the SERPs average a 10-30% clickthrough rate. By position 9, that number falls to below 2% (Smart Insights, 2018). That goes to show, once more, the importance of rankings when it comes to traffic.

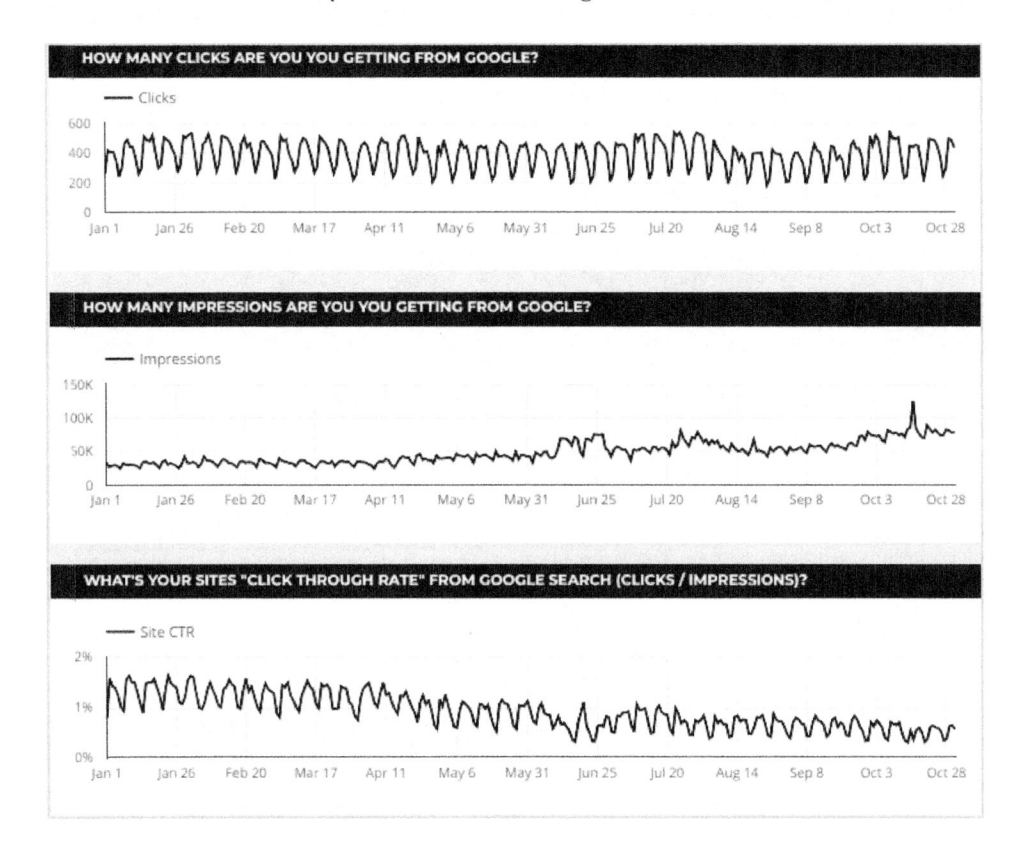

I'm reminding you of those figures, at this point, so you don't get disappointed once you get to the click through rate section of the report, which you can see above. Ideally, you want to see a few spikes on that graph, going over the 2% mark, but if you don't it's no reason to panic yet.

As long as you focus on keywords with decent search volume and you keep publishing new content, those small percentages add up. That's the magic of organic traffic – it's always scalable.

Exactly how much traffic are critical keywords driving?

Knowing what searches drive users to your website is key to figuring out what they want. That means the things they're looking for, questions they need answers to, the way they formulate queries, and more.

For this last page of the monthly SEO report, we use Google Analytics to pull a list of all the queries that drive traffic to your website through Google. Let me tell you right away, it's a goldmine.

THE EXACT KEYWORDS DRIVING TRAFFIC TO YOUR SITE

	Query	Clicks ▼	Impressions	CTR	Position
1.		57,592	1,676,717	3.43%	32.6
2.	webris	4,792	8,110	59.09%	1
3.	seo proposal	1,447	14,260	10.15%	3.54
4.	seo proposal template	528	4,523	11.67%	2.62
5.	youtube transcript	416	10,440	3.98%	5.8
6.	marketing kpis	393	14,535	2.7%	9.91
7.	youtube transcription	348	11,309	3.08%	6.87

I love looking through this list, in particular, because it shows me the way people think. By taking a look at the top queries, I can look for content gaps that might help me lead more traffic to the website I'm working on.

You can see our top result is "webris". That's a branded search, so it's not relevant to our case study, but if you look further down, you've got "seo proposal template" right there. It's a query that drives a decent amount of traffic, with a great clickthrough rate.

Right now, there are a few websites beating us in the SERPs for that precise keyword. What we could do is create a content pillar around that keyword, which should help us climb through the rankings.

Bear in mind, that's just an example. The point is, if you see any keywords where your position isn't as great as you'd like, but they're *still* getting you decent traffic with a great click through rate, those are prime opportunities for optimization.

5.4 - Why SEO is an Ongoing Process (And What Your Next Steps Should Be)

If there's one thing you should know after getting this far is SEO is never 'done'. Some of our campaigns last for months if not years, and there's always more work to do.

The problem is, no matter how great your SEO strategy is, you're not playing solitaire. Getting to the top of the SERPs can mean a lot of money for most businesses. That means someone will always be nipping at your heels.

You have an advantage, though – **no one** else in the field is as thorough as we are when it comes to SEO. The processes my agency uses, and which I've shared with you, should put you far ahead of your competitors. Once you're in the lead, your focus needs to be on staying there, and you can achieve that in two ways:

1. Making sure your content is always better and more up-to-date than anything else in the field.

2. Stay on top of the numbers from your campaign, so you know when you need to improve assets or build new ones.

Before we wind down, let's go over some critical steps to help you maintain content domination, so you don't slip down the SERPs.

Next steps...

SEO is an ever-evolving field. Our entire business depends on keeping up with best practices to get better rankings. The only way to do that is through constant analysis and a hunger for learning.

When I set out to write this book, my goal was to create the ultimate SEO blueprint. The kind of book you can pick up and reference whenever you have doubts about what the next steps of your campaign should be. Over time, my hope is you will take the processes I've laid out in this book and make them your own.

Most people tackle SEO as an afterthought. However, you and I understand the true importance of search engines. In less than two decades, search engines have already shifted the way we look for new information and services, and I have no doubt they will continue to do so in the future.

As the algorithms that power search engines continue to evolve, we need to do the same. You have to stay hungry, keep up with SEO news, publish more content, and optimize your content further. Your website might be number one in the rankings now, but there will *always* be others nipping at your heels.

If you want to know what your next steps should be, the answer is simple:

1. Keep improving the UX, technical structure and performance of revenue generating pages.

2. Keep publishing new, high-quality, engaging content that targets valuable keywords.

3. Keep building new links and don't forget to look beyond traditional methods to do so.

4. Keep evaluating your progress, to find out what your weakest areas are, and get to work on fixing them.

What we do is all about optimization and there is *always* more room for improvement. Your website might not be number 1 now, but imagine where it could be in a year, 2, or 5. If you know the rules when it comes to SEO, there's no telling how far you can go.

APPENDIX

Tools & Resources

Cheat Sheet: 20 Tools Mentioned In the SEO Blueprint

There's a massive number of tools you can use to simplify SEO work. The great news is, a lot of them are free, so you don't need to blow your budget to get cozy with search engines. Throughout the book, we've touched upon a number of services and software, so let's go through a brief recap for all of them:

1. **Google Search Console.** One of the **many** Google tools we use. With Search Console, you get access to a broad range of tools and reports related SEO and website performance.

2. **Google Docs and Sheets.** The world runs on freaking spreadsheets, even if a lot of people don't like them. WEBRIS wouldn't exist without spreadsheets and with Google, you can share your spreadsheets and collaborate with your team members. Oh, and Google Docs is also nice, I guess!

3. **Google Analytics.** By far the most thorough analytics tool in the market and it doesn't hurt that you can set it up for free on any website.

4. **Google Structured Data Testing Tool**. If you're using schema markup on your website, you want a tool that enables you to test its validity, and this is the one you should be checking out.

5. **Google Data Studio.** If you run a SEO campaign, you better not be afraid of numbers. I'm a big fan of them, but even I must admit that sometimes, I'd rather see a nice chart or graph. With Google Data Studio, you can pull data from almost any source you like and use it to put together some nice, user-friendly graphs.

6. **MozBar.** A browser plugin that provides you with SEO information for every website you visit, at a quick glance.

7. **SEMrush.** A collection of SEO tools you can use to analyze websites, whether they're your own or your competitors'.

8. **Screaming Frog and SiteBulb.** Two powerful website crawlers you can use during the audit process.

9. **Ahrefs.** An al-in-one SEO research tool you can use to analyze and monitor websites, as well as uncover what they're doing.

10. **Graylog, SEOluzer, and Loggly.** Three of the best tools you can use to set up and monitor website activity logs.

11. **All in One Schema and Rich Snippets.** Two powerful WordPress plugins you can use to set up stylish rich snippets, which can help increase your search engine clickthrough rates.

12. **Yoast SEO.** The best WordPress SEO plugin in the market. It gives you SEO and readability scores and it enables you to quickly add metadata to your pages.

13. **Keywords Everywhere.** A browser add-on that gives you real-time data on the keywords you use within search engines.

14. **KeywordTool.io.** This tool pulls data from Google Autocomplete to help you find keyword suggestions.

15. **HubSpot's Blog Ideas Generator.** If you're stuck coming up with new content ideas, HubSpot's Blog Ideas Generator can help give you muse a wake up call.

16. **Capture & Convert**. A free WordPress plugin that helps generate more leads on your website.

17. **Query Recipes**. Helps push your data to Google BigQuery for faster processing of large SEO datasets.

18. **DeepCrawl**. An alternative to ScreamingFrog that provides more data and visualizations for technical SEO analysis.

19. **Clearscope**. A tool to help optimize the "on page" performance of your content and pages.

20. **The Blueprint Training**. This entire book as a video training course, along with all the mentioned templates and tools.

Done-For-You: How To Hire WEBRIS to Scale & Automate

Running a successful SEO campaign takes a lot of time and effort. If you're a single person or part of a small team, there's no way around the fact that SEO work will take up a significant part of that manpower.

If you'd rather hire out for SEO, so you and your team can focus on other aspects of running your business, then reach out. You've come this far, so you're aware we know what we're doing when it comes to SEO.

webris.org

We not only offer world-class affordable marketing services, but we work with clients across a broad range of fields. Whether you're a small business or a large Fortune 500 company, we have the tools and know-how to help you scale.

DIY/Learn: Get Access to Ryan's Advanced SEO Training Membership

I'm a big fan of businesses and people that take the time to learn the ins-and-outs of SEO. If I weren't I wouldn't have written this book in the first place, so you better believe me.

During the past few years, I've been working to put together an online course that covers everything we've talked about in this book. If you'd rather learn by watching videos, then the web version of The SEO Blueprint should be right up your alley:

theblueprint.training

In exchange for a one-time fee, you get a lifetime membership to The SEO Blueprint. Since SEO never stops evolving, that means you're going to get a *lot* of updates. If you've made it this far, then I know you're a DIY kind of person, so let's keep learning together!

> **Visit www.theblueprint.website to get access to all the templates, tools and extras mentioned throughout the course of this book.**

Printed in Great Britain
by Amazon